D0919520

Restoration Theatre Production

Theatre Production Studies

General Editor
John Russell Brown
Associate of the National Theatre of Great Britain
and
Professor of Theatre Arts, State University of New York
at Stony Brook

Already published

Victorian Spectacular Theatre 1850–1910 Michael R. Booth
The Revolution in German Theatre 1900–1933 Michael Patterson
Elizabethan Popular Theatre Michael Hattaway
Shakespeare's Theatre Peter Thomson

Restoration Theatre Production

Jocelyn Powell

Routledge & Kegan Paul
London, Boston, Melbourne and Henley

PR
691
.P68

First published in 1984
by Routledge & Kegan Paul plc

14 Leicester Square, London WC2H 7PH, England

9 Park Street, Boston, Mass. 02108, USA

464 St Kilda Road, Melbourne,
Victoria 3004, Australia and

Broadway House, Newtown Road,
Henley-on-Thames, Oxon RG9 1EN, England

Phototypeset in Plantin by
Input Typesetting Ltd, London
and printed in Great Britain

© Jocelyn Powell 1984

No part of this book may be reproduced in
any form without permission from the publisher,
except for the quotation of brief passages
in criticism

Library of Congress Cataloging in Publication Data

Powell, Jocelyn, 1938–

Restoration theatre production.
(Theatre production studies)
Bibliography: p.
Includes index.
1. English drama—Restoration, 1600–1700—History and
criticism.   2. Theater—Great Britain—History—17th
century.   3. Dramatists, English—Early modern, 1500–1700.
I. Title.   II. Series.
PR691.P68   1984   792'.0942   83–27250

British Library CIP data available

ISBN 0-7100-9321-7

This world is a comedy to those that think,
a tragedy to those that feel.
HORACE WALPOLE

Contents

Illustrations

Plates

Figures

Acknowledgments

Many of my students and colleagues have encouraged me in the writing of this book by their interest and criticism. I would particularly like to thank Terry Johnson, Fidelis Morgan, Jane Wymark and Jane Wynn Owen, whose enthusiasm got it under way; Professor John Russell Brown, whose advice has been invaluable in helping me to focus the particular theatrical problems of the period; Colin Bailey, for tracing Jordaens's picture to the Hamburger Kunsthalle; Clive Barker for helping me obtain photographs of the Berliner Ensemble; Eric Ljungkvist, who guided me round the theatre collections in Stockholm, especially the Drottningholm Court Theatre; Per Bjurström and his assistants at the National Museum, Stockholm; Barbro Stribolt of the Drottningholm Theatre Museum; Elaine Williams and Ron Hallmark, who assisted me in obtaining pictures from Paris collections; Jean Dowling, for drawing the maps; Lesley Skeates for wrestling with my somewhat clumsy sketches for figures in the text, and making sense of them; Jane Slowey, for typing the manuscript, and my secretary, Elaine Harwood, for thereafter keeping pace with my frequent corrections; and finally, from Routledge, Philippa Brewster and Harriet Griffey for obtaining illustrations and permissions, and Melissa Brooks for working her way meticulously through the maze of complications provided by the manuscript.

I am grateful also to the following for permission to reproduce plates and figures: Her Majesty the Queen for Plates 1 and 37; The British Library for Plates 8, 10, 11, 12, 17, 18, 19, 20, 27, 28, 29, 30, 31 and 32, and Figures 3, 4, 5, 6, 11, 12, 13, 14, 15, 16, 17, 18, 19 and 20; The British Museum for Plate 5; The Trustees of the Chatsworth Settlement for Plates 13, 14, 15 and 21; The Museum of London for Plates 3, 4 and 6; The Kungliga Biblioteket, Stockholm for Plates 23 and 24; Percy Paukschta for Plates 38 and 39; The National Maritime Museum, London, for Plate 2; The Provost and Fellows of Worcester College, Oxford for Plate 9; The Warden and Fellows of All Souls College, Oxford for Plate 16; La Documentation Française for Plate 22; Nationalmusie,

Stockholm for Plate 26; Hamburger Kunsthalle for Plate 33; Réunion des musées nationaux for Plate 34; Lady Teresa Agnew for Plate 35; The Theatre Museum, Harry R. Beard Collection for Plate 36. Plate 25 is from the Devonshire Collection, Chatsworth, reproduced by permission of the trustees of the Chatsworth Settlement; photograph Courtauld Institute of Art.

A note on the references

Anyone writing on the Restoration theatre is necessarily indebted to a number of full-scale studies that may be said to have established a basic picture of the Restoration playhouses, their plays and audiences. Chief among these are Leslie Hotson (*The Commonwealth and Restoration Stage*, Cambridge, Mass., and Oxford, 1928), Allardyce Nicoll (*A History of English Drama 1660–1900*, vol. 1: *Restoration Drama 1600–1700*, Cambridge, 1952), Montague Summers (*The Restoration Theatre*, London, 1934, and *The Playhouse of Pepys*, London, 1935), and there are also, more recently, R. D. Hume's important *The Development of English Drama in the Late Seventeenth Century*, Oxford, 1976, and the indispensable first volume of *The London Stage (1660–1700)* with a critical introduction by Emmett L. Avery and Arthur H. Scouten, edited by William van Lennep, Carbondale, Ill., 1960. My dependence on these works is so continuous that I have not attempted to document it in detail below, and references are given only when concerned with complex problems the reader might wish to follow up.

There are difficulties of edition when quoting from, or referring to, Restoration texts. The original spelling and punctuation is essential in my view, also the capitalisation and other graphic vagaries of the period. The suggestions of phrasing and emphasis to be derived from this evidence are invaluable, and the complex sentence structure is often easier to follow. I have therefore tried to assist the reader by using critical editions in old spelling of works frequently cited (Davenant's adaptations, the plays of Congreve, Wycherley and Otway, the plays and poems of Dryden) in order to give as close a reference as possible. Other Restoration texts are quoted from the original quartos. In both cases, I have allowed myself occasional silent editorial emendations, usually to take an edition back to the original or to correct a misprint in a quarto. The convention of italics for songs, prologues, epilogues, etc. is not employed. Speech prefixes are given in full.

It may be as well to comment here on the sources for the illustrations.

Authentic designs and working sketches, such as those of Inigo Jones for his masques at court in the earlier part of the century, have not survived for the main body of the Restoration period. There are not even sets of engravings, such as were made in France and Italy of Giacomo Torelli's stage designs. The only exceptions here are the crude engravings for Settle's *The Empress of Morocco* and the frontispiece to the anonymous *Ariane*. Both of these publications were intended to commemorate specific productions, and so may be assumed to represent what was seen on the stage, at least to some extent; but both present problems of interpretation, particularly as to scale and proportion. It is, however, possible to supplement this meagre information. Jones's Italian style was developed and subjected to influence from France and Italy, so both Jones's own designs and those of Torelli may be considered relevant where their iconography is appropriate; while contemporary painters employed the same theories of expression and conventions of costume. This is argued in the text, and illustrated not merely from portraits, but also from paintings not of theatrical subjects but using theatrical styles, and again from illustrations to later play texts, such as those accompanying the works of Shakespeare and of Beaumont and Fletcher. In these cases, the editions do not commemorate any particular production and care is needed in the interpretation of the prints, in which evidence of dramatic traditions is frequently, though not always, perceptible. It will be remarked that the Frontispiece to *Macbeth* (Plate 31) hardly reflects playhouse conditions, though it captures the atmosphere of a Restoration presentation of the play, while that to *Hamlet* (Plate 30) contains, in the detail of the fallen stocking, an emblem of his madness and disarray that seems to owe more to the traditions of the stage than to the text of the play as we know it. It is therefore appropriate to assemble this variety of evidence, in order to give the reader assistance in imagining the very particular presentational style the period evolved for itself.

The following abbreviations, mostly for periodicals, are used in the notes: *ELH, Journal of English Literary History; HLQ, Huntingdon Library Quarterly; Mod. Phil., Modern Philosophy; MQ, Musical Quarterly; PMLA, Publications of the Modern Language Association of America; PQ, Philological Quarterly; Stud. Phil., Studies in Philology; TN, Theatre Notebook.*

Part One

A period and a style

They who have best succeeded on the stage
Have still conformed their Genius to their Age.

DRYDEN

1. Catherine of Braganza as
   Saint Catherine. Jacob
   Huysmans. Reproduced by
   gracious permission of Her
   Majesty the Queen.

2. James, Duke of York, as
   Lord High Admiral. Gascar.
   Courtesy of the National
   Maritime Museum.

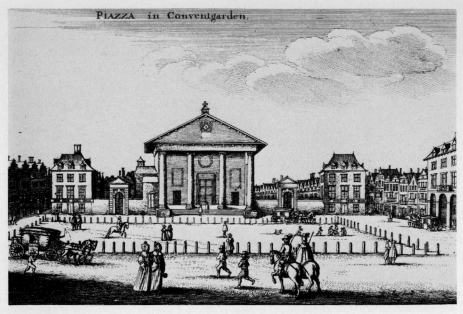

3. The piazza at Covent Garden. Wenceslaus Hollar. The Museum of London.

4. The Royal Exchange. Wenceslaus Hollar. The Museum of London.

5. A Coffee House. Anonymous water-colour, circa 1700. The British Museum, Department of Prints and Drawings.

6. Rosamond's Pond, St. James's Park. The Museum of London.

7. (Above left) Jo Haines in the Ass Epilogue. Thomas Brown, *Works,* IV, 1744. Author's collection.

8. (Above right) Nell Gwyn in the Epilogue to *Tyrannick Love. The Key to the Rehearsal,* frontispiece. Buckingham, *Works,* II, 1714. The British Library.

9. (Left) William Harris as the Empress in Duffet's burlesque of *The Empress of Morocco.* Courtesy of the Librarian of Worcester College, Oxford.

1 · Riding the audience

On 29 May 1660, John Evelyn noted in his diary:[1]

This day his Majestie Charles the Second came to London after a sad and long exile and calamitous suffering both of the King and Church, being 17 yeares. This was also his birth-day, and with a triumph of above 20,000 horse and foote, brandishing their swords and shouting with inexpressible joy; the wayes strew'd with flowers, the bells ringing, the streetes hung with tapissry, fountaines running with wine; the Maior, Aldermen, and all the Companies in their liveries, chaines of gold, and banners; Lords and Nobles clad in cloth of silver, gold and velvet; the windowes and balconies all set with ladies; trumpets, music, and myriads of people flocking, even so far as from Rochester, so as they were seven houres in passing the Citty, even from 2 in ye afternoone till 9 at night.

The king returned to his capital with a pomp and a pageantry reminiscent of an earlier period. Evelyn was partial; but his account captures the euphoria of a people welcoming both old and new together. 'I stood in the Strand and beheld it, and bless'd God.' Perhaps the promise of that day was not to be fulfilled; but it was a splendid show, and seemed to herald a new age.

It was an age of particular promise for an excited and ebullient minority. The theatres of England had been dark since 1642, when Parliament decreed the stoppage of all dramatic performances. The restoration of a monarch seemed to herald a restoration, or even a resurrection, of the stage. Like the monarch himself, it came again in glory. There were now actresses to play the women's parts, instead of boys or men; pictorial scenery, offering the illusion of changing places, where before the war there had been merely the structure of the playhouse and a few machines and scenic emblems. As Killigrew, manager of the king's new company, remarked to Samuel Pepys:[2]

Now, all things civil, no rudeness anywhere; then, as in a bear-garden. Then, two or three fiddlers; now, nine or ten of the best. Then the

Queen seldom, and the King never would come; now, not the King
only for state, but all civil people do think they may come as well
as any.

Killigrew was boasting. The Restoration playhouse could be at least as
much of a bear-garden as that of Charles I; but in the new theatres, the
music was certainly frequent and fine – people assembled early to hear
it, foreigners reported it and noted not ten, but twelve, of the royal violins
playing in the gallery.[3] They also noticed how the fine wax candles 'did
not offend the nostrils', and in their soft and flattering light the playhouse
itself became a fashionable meeting place under the direct patronage of
the monarch, who not only lent his name to one of the companies but
spent much time at the playhouse, taking an interest in many practical
questions of repertoire and production. It was, indeed, a new kind of
theatre, and the introduction of scenes and actresses, the delight in music
and spectacle, and the determination to appeal to an educated and fashionable audience created a new style in English drama.

The use of the term 'Restoration' in English theatre history seems to
have become extraordinarily flexible. It is used to refer to events not
simply of the reign of the 'restored' Charles II, but to that of his brother
James, and even of his brother's daughters. It has been employed to
distinguish editions of plays, in collections of the drama from 1660 to the
Stage Licensing Act of 1737 in the reign of George II, and on theatrical
posters advertising the performances of comedies written in the late eighteenth century.[4] It bids fair to be considered meaningless jargon; yet the
term has preserved a meaning – an association with the particular style
of the drama that emerged during those pioneering years of the reign of
Charles II. The heyday of the style was brief. It flowered in the late 1660s
and early 1670s, producing such masterpieces as Etherege's *The Man of
Mode*, Wycherley's *The Country Wife*, Dryden's *The Conquest of Granada*,
Marriage à la Mode and *Aureng-Zebe*. Then, times and tastes began to
change and the essence of Restoration theatre was gradually whittled
away, physically and spiritually, its brilliance, precision and intelligence
making occasional comebacks, mainly in the comic mode, into the early
eighteenth century. There is a value in associating some of these later
writers, Fielding or Gay, for example, with the earlier style, for though
it was very much of its time, it was a striking and original theatrical
experiment which has, in fact, a hold on theatre even today. To understand this experiment, it is vital for us to consider the audience for whom
it was originally undertaken and the world in which those men and women
lived.

It is not easy to imagine London as it must have been in those days. It
was small, but densely populated, and its importance was out of all

proportion to its size. It was already the second largest city in Europe and its population of just under half a million was 7 per cent of that of the whole of England. The population of Paris, the largest of the European capitals, was only 2¹/₂ per cent of that of France. London contained fifteen times as many inhabitants as Bristol or Norwich, the next greatest cities in England, and by the end of the century had outstripped even Paris itself.[5] All these people were contained in a small but expanding strip of land between Westminster and the Tower of London (see Figure 1).

At that time there was little south of the river, across London Bridge lined with its shops and houses, apart from the borough of Southwark and some ribbon-development along the south bank where the Elizabethan and Jacobean bear-gardens and playhouses had stood. London Bridge was the only road-bridge across the river. Other crossings had to be made by boat or by horse-ferry from Westminster to Lambeth, where the palace of the Archbishop of Canterbury was situated. Pepys died at Clapham, in the country house of his friend, William Hewer.

On the north there was little more. The French traveller, Sorbière, said he would allow three-quarters of an hour to walk across the city at its widest, from St George's Fields beyond Southwark over London Bridge to Shoreditch.[6] Hampstead and Islington were villages, and the actor Clunn was killed by highwaymen while he was riding home to Kentish Town after a performance of *The Alchemist* (Pepys, 4 August 1664). Beyond Westminster, field and marsh stretched down towards the village of Chelsea, already becoming both fashionable and notorious. Further west, the country stretched away past the old palace of Kensington to Hampton Court and Windsor.

London itself was in reality not one but two cities – the city of London and the city of Westminster.

The city of London lay in the main within its ancient walls, clustered on the north bank of the Thames between the Tower and Temple Bar. It was already the City, the stronghold of mercantile England, with its Guildhall, banking houses and liveried companies, its Royal Exchange (see Plate 4), a market for both money and fine English and foreign goods, and its thriving port. The Great Fire of 1666 gutted the city, and the rebuilding, though slow, was splendid. The dereliction must have hovered as a spur to new vitality. The old cathedral was devastated and pulled down to be rebuilt to Sir Christopher Wren's triumphant design, not finally finished until 1711. But meanwhile new streets rose, wider and more substantial in deep red brick, a growing symbol of sobriety, enterprise and prosperity.

Over against the city, Westminster ranged itself about the ancient abbey and the Parliament House at Westminster Hall. This was on the edge of the old palace of Whitehall, a shambling labyrinth of buildings badly

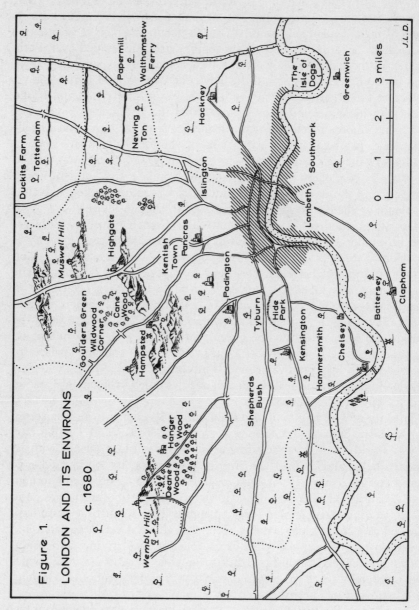

Figure 1 London and its environs in the later seventeenth century. (*Map drawn by Jean Dowling*)

constructed at different times and for different purposes, without design or comfort. Nevertheless, Charles was in residence here during the winter months, while James lodged across the park in the palace of St James. Whitehall stretched down King Street (now called Whitehall itself) to Charing Cross, lying between the street and the river on the south and between the street and St James's Park on the north. On the river side were the Water Gate, the old Hall which Charles had refurbished for theatrical performances, and the magnificent Banqueting House designed by Inigo Jones. On the park side lay the Cockpit in Court, a curious little theatre that had also been designed by Inigo Jones, but which Charles soon abandoned, since he preferred more modern spectacles.

Between Westminster and the city lay a curious no-man's-land. Immediately beyond the city walls this lay in the Liberties of London; the rest of the conurbation, which was beginning to develop rapidly in the seventeenth century and to draw the two cities into a single whole, came under the jurisdiction of Westminster. It was in this area that fashionable London began to arise, and it became known as the Town.[7]

To the west of the city, along Fleet Street, which joined the city gate at Temple Bar to Charing Cross and Whitehall, the peers of the realm had built palaces down to the water. The river itself was a crucial thoroughfare. It could sometimes take two hours to ride in a coach from Westminster into the City, and it was easier to slip down by water when the tide was right. North of the Strand lay more noblemen's estates and the Inns of Court, their pleasant and secluded yards giving towards Lincoln's Inn Fields and the open country.

In the 1620s the nobility began to realise the potential value of this land, and to circumvent government regulations about the expansion of London in order to sell to developers. The outbuildings and the gardens of the palaces were built over with shops, houses and apartments in spite of continuous attempts to prevent it. In the 1630s, perhaps in the hope of better building, the Earl of Bedford obtained permission from the Privy Council to develop land in Long Acre, Covent Garden, into a grand piazza of shops and apartments after the Italian manner. It too was designed by Inigo Jones (see Plate 3). The piazza itself was surrounded by arcades on two sides only. To the south were the gardens of Bedford House, to the west St Paul's Church, a centre for fashionable worship. The piazza was 'the Heart of the Towne',[8] and was rapidly surrounded by new streets of shops and houses, taverns and coffee-houses. Before the Restoration, a new Exchange had been built on the Strand, in imitation of the Royal Exchange in the City. It was built of black stone, and consisted of 'two long and double galleries, one above the other, with eight rows of shops'.[9] At first, it did poorly compared with its grander rival; but, with the growth of the Town, took on a new lease of life as a covered walk where ladies could cheapen lace and taffeta and gentlemen browse among its book-stalls. It was here in the Town that the managers, Killigrew and Davenant, established their new theatres (see Figure 2).

Restoration theatre is virtually London theatre – more than that, the theatre of the Town. Tudor and Stuart legislation had, to a great extent, suppressed provincial dramatic activity, though it was beginning to show some signs of new life.[10] In 1660, Sir William Davenant, Poet Laureate to Charles I, and Thomas Killigrew, the new king's friend and Court Jester, had established between them two theatre companies only, the King's and the Duke's, under the liveries of Charles and his brother. They suppressed all rival managements by a mixture of bribery, skulduggery and force, and began playing in temporary accommodation while they made new homes for themselves.[11] Davenant opened his new playhouse, converted from Lisle's Tennis Court in Portugal Street, Lincoln's Inn Fields, in 1662, combining the wide fore-stage of the Jacobean and Caroline private theatres with full sets of scenes where the old tiringhouse and musicians' gallery had been. There he soon revived, with additions, his 'opera', *The Siege of Rhodes*, with which he had introduced such scenery to the public stage in the last years of the interregnum. The new house was a success and drew audiences from the other company. Killigrew, not to be outdone, leased a plot of ground between Drury Lane and Bridges Street and was able to open in similar splendour in May of the next year. The companies were now on a par, but the managements were not content. Killigrew was widening Drury Lane in 1665, while the theatres were closed during the plague, and in 1671 Thomas Betterton, the leading actor of the Duke's Company, who took over as manager for Lady Davenant after her husband's death, built a fine new playhouse at the bottom of Salisbury Court with a river frontage at Dorset Stairs. In 1672 the Theatre Royal was destroyed by fire, and Sir Christopher Wren designed a new theatre for Killigrew on the same site. This, the Theatre Royal, Drury Lane, was opened in 1674, and it, the Dorset Garden, and Lincoln's Inn Fields may be considered the major playhouses of the Restoration.[12]

The Dorset Garden and the Theatre Royal were very different in style, and the contrast between them is an apposite sign of a tension in Restoration life as well as drama. The Dorset Garden was the most magnificent theatre London had seen, and was proud of the fact. Soon after it opened, the management celebrated its splendour by publishing one of its major successes, Settle's *The Empress of Morocco*, with a frontispiece depicting the outside of the playhouse and a set of rather crude engravings of the most spectacular scenes (see Plates 10, 11, 12, 18 and 19). This is the only set of such pictures published in England at the time, and it illustrates the nature of the competition between the two

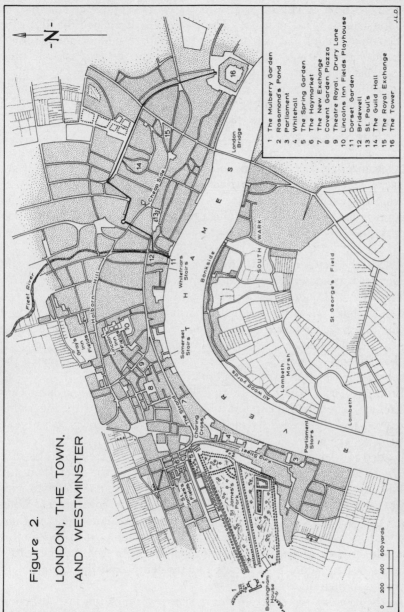

Figure 2.
LONDON, THE TOWN.
AND WESTMINSTER

1 The Mulberry Garden
2 Rosamond's Pond
3 Parliament
4 Whitehall
5 The Spring Garden
6 The Haymarket
7 The New Exchange
8 Covent Garden Piazza
9 Theatre Royal. Drury Lane
10 Lincolns Inn Fields Playhouse
11 Dorset Garden
12 Bridewell
13 St. Pauls
14 The Guild Hall
15 The Royal Exchange
16 The Tower

Figure 2 London and Westminster, c. 1680. *(Map drawn by Jean Dowling)*

companies. Both attempted in different ways to capture the attention of London and its varied audience. The Dorset Garden gilded the lily, with its elaborate scenes and machines and its superb auditorium, adorned with the busts of the poets around the galleries. In contrast, the king himself had suggested that the new Theatre Royal should be a 'plain house', and at its opening, Dryden, who was under contract to the King's Company, gibed at the gaudy entertainments of the rival theatre:[13]

Though in their House the Poets Heads appear,
We hope we may presume their Wits are here.

On the surface the two playhouses opposed spectacle and intelligence, extravagance and style. Their policies seemed to emphasise either culture or excitement as alternative theatrical experiences. But in reality both were striving for a reconciliation of the two, and their dilemma in attempting to bring together sensuality and intellect echoes the dilemma of Restoration society.

The City, the Town and the Court all possessed distinctive lifestyles, and these were to some extent at odds with each other.[14]

The City of London was strongly puritan. The centre of trade and capital, it built its wealth upon the puritan virtues of thrift, piety and profit. The great merchant families both lived and worked there, heading its liveried companies and confirming its commercial identity. The spirit of the capitalist stronghold was fiercely independent, and dominated the economics and politics of the kingdom.

From the earliest times the English king had been a visitor to his City of London. The City had charters of independence, and guarded its rights fiercely. The king needed its support for government policy to promote its growth. The power of the kings of England in the seventeenth century depended to a large extent on the delicacy with which they could balance the financial interests of the merchant classes against the interests of the nobility and landed gentry. These interests were to become polarised with the expansion of trade and the development of party government. Whig peers like Buckingham and Shaftesbury made their homes in the City, and Charles asserted himself, when the Whigs attempted to exclude his Catholic brother James from the throne, by an attack on the City's charters, a revocation of London's independence, and the appointment of Tories to high offices in the City.

As the City was the centre of the business world, so, in their different ways, the Court and the Town were centres for the world of fashion and society. Charles II was a shrewd enough man with a head for business, but he liked his pleasures laid on and saw that they were so. He also liked to share them with others. He took great pains for instance in the improvement of St James's Park as a public pleasure garden.[15] James I had planted an avenue of elms and a garden of mulberry trees at the top, where Buckingham Palace now stands. Charles channelled the stream that ran through the park into a Grand Canal with a decoy for water-birds. He made an enclosure for deer and drained and refurbished Rosamond's Pond at the head of the canal, transforming it into a secluded, wooded spot with a covered walk that became a favourite place for assignations (see Plate 6). The Park, the Mulberry Garden and the Spring Garden (contrived from the formal garden before St James's Palace), became the resort of fashion, as did Hyde Park beyond.

The culture of the Court as well as its openness gave a lead to the Town, which similarly catered for people of leisure. The houses around Covent Garden took to providing lodgings for the gentry, and for their wives and families, visiting London on business or to attend Parliament, and also for a rising class of people who have been termed the pseudo-gentry – leisured inhabitants of towns, gentry by lifestyle rather than by the ownership of property, families or individuals who had, by marriage or speculation, acquired money without land.[16] It was to provide pastime for such people that the coffee-houses grew up, typical of the period in their combination of stimulants, tobacco, gambling and conversation (Plate 5), and also the new taverns and the ordinaries in the parks and gardens. For them also, experiments began to be made in new kinds of entertainment. John Bannister, 'one of the King's band of Violins who had a singular talent at . . . composition as well as performance'[17] opened a 'Musick School' in Whitefriars and presented public concerts. Later, concert houses combined with pleasure gardens grew up beyond the Town. Mr Sadler opened his Music House in Islington, and in Chelsea was the notorious World's End.[18] Situated as they were in the Town, the theatres formed a natural part of this leisure activity.

Their placement, however, has wider implications. In easy reach of the City, yet well situated for fashionable patronage, the managers were very naturally trying to tap the wealth of all three areas. The social orientation of London into City, Town and Court lies at the heart of their policy. The Court and the Town stuck closely together. The social ties were strong and so were those of class. It appears from Sorbière that fashionable visitors to London often did not set foot in the City.[19] Between the City and the Court there was a spiritual gulf their physical proximity did little to conceal. The life of the City centred on money and work, that of the Court on money and leisure. The Town grew up around the commercial pressures of leisure as the City had grown up around the commercial pressures of profit. Significantly, the puritan Milton depicts the devils in hell passing the time of Satan's absence in the pursuit of culture (*Paradise Lost*, Book II, 500-). Yet the Town also acted, to some extent, as a buffer between the two opposed worlds. It was a place where they could meet each other. Charles's Court, compared with those of Europe, was curiously easy-going. His courtiers at Whitehall mingled freely with the professional classes, and even with the upper ranks of the merchants. The only criterion for admission to the gallery at Whitehall was the dress of a gentleman.[20] The City also had a diversified upper stratum of society, involving merchants, nobles and professional men. It was at such men and their families, as well as at courtiers and gentlemen, that the Restoration managers aimed – men who had an eye to business but also an eye to the glamour of Court connection.

The contention that the audiences at the Restoration theatres were merely a rowdy Court coterie has now been sufficiently disproved.[21] The king and his friends were of course important to the playhouses. They were the stars of the audience and did a good deal for the box-office. The constant presence of Prince Rupert contributed much to the success of Ravenscroft's *The Cit Turned Gentleman*, foreign travellers all note the fashionable tone of audiences, and Pepys amply shows how important the air of fashion was to the theatrical occasion (cf. 12 June 1663). The fellow auditors are as important to the event as the play. Pepys observes with interest that the king now makes signs to his new mistress Moll Davies in the very presence of Lady Castlemaine, who looks fire. He is irritated with Sir Charles Sedley who talks during the action, but irresistibly amused at his comments. The presence of the mighty is part of the entertainment value and a stimulus to theatre-going. The bread and butter of the actors must however have derived from a wider range of persons. Mrs Pepys visits the theatre as often almost as her husband. She goes there with her husband's friends, and sometimes by herself, accompanied by her maid for decorum and company. Pepys is often accompanied by senior and junior colleagues. There was a freedom among the men and women who sat together in the pit that became notorious and was eventually banned, but the licentious element of the audience was leavened by sober persons, among whom might be found lawyers, merchants, Parliament men and men of letters. Robert Hooke, the scientist, a rather dour gentleman, went sometimes to the theatre, and Sir Christopher Wren, John Evelyn and Judge Jeffries, men of very different temperaments, were also in frequent attendance there.

But though it was not the mere plaything of the Court, the theatre was not for the people either. The prices were in themselves fairly prohibitive.[22] The cheapest seats (at a shilling) got you into the upper gallery. A shilling would also buy you a couple of chickens in the market. For the middle gallery the price was eighteen pence, and for the best seats in the lower gallery and the boxes, and in the pit immediately before the stage, it was two shillings and six pence. Two and six could also buy you a woman. It was a farm-worker's average weekly wage. The two and six provided only a single seat in a box, and Pepys, coming late to the theatre on 6 January 1668, had to take a whole box for himself and his companions and was much disturbed that for the box and fruit for the ladies he was set back twenty shillings. He seemed similarly disturbed on 26 March 1663, when he took on a new cook-maid for £4 per annum. One can also see why Pepys felt that the presence of his clerk in the two-and-sixpenny seats lowered the tone of his theatre-going. Even the presence of 'citizens' made the occasion less pleasant for him from this point of view. The citizens attended the theatre, in the main on public holidays, but the money-lending or shopkeeping classes, true tradesmen, were not very welcome in the playhouse.[23]

The audience catered for by the Restoration theatres had at least a strong pretension both to style and class. Led at first by the Court, it was never entirely dominated by it. John Dennis, writing in the early part of the next century and contrasting the Restoration audience with that of his own day, significantly remarks that the former was characterised by the fact that it understood what it saw and heard.[24] It was not only their status but also their taste that set the cits apart. Dryden scoffs again and again, in his prologues and epilogues for the plain Theatre Royal, at the admiration shown by the citizens for the empty spectacles on the Dorset Garden stage. He juxtaposes the wit and the intelligence of his professional audience with the vulgarity of that at the other house. This is special pleading, of course, but it is amusing to note that Pepys reflects the same attitude. When he goes to see *The City Gallant* on 12 September 1667, he remarks that 'the play is a very silly play methinks, for I and others that sat by me, Mr Povey and Mr Proger, were weary of it; but it will please the citizens.' Mr Proger was a Groom of the Bedchamber to the king, and Mr Povey a fellow member with Pepys of the Royal Society.[25]

The intellectual calibre of the audience is fundamental to the whole experience of Restoration drama. This may seem paradoxical. Its behaviour was notoriously casual and often brutal. The play was accompnied by the chat of the audience and the cries of the orange-wenches. Pit and gallery were known for the presence of masked women openly selling themselves. The gallants challenged each other for their favours, and the servants outside waiting for their masters disputed so loudly that, as Dryden put it, 'Oft the play is silenc'd by the farce.'[26] In *A True Widow* (Act IV), Thomas Shadwell draws a scathing picture of the callous behaviour of self-important men, trying to enter the house without paying, and taking the best seats to display themselves rather than listen to the play. Of course, these are dramatists speaking, but outside evidence supports them. Pepys reports such conversations and disputes, and the Frenchman, François Brunet, remarked that he and his company, when they visited the Dorset Garden on 6 October 1676, had to leave at the end of the second act because 'they could hear nothing'.[27] The bullying atmosphere often led to actual violence. On a famous occasion in June 1679, the poet Otway challenged and fought with John Churchill, later Duke of Marlborough, on the latter being insolent to an orange-woman,[28] and there was enough physical violence to necessitate the lining of the stage with spikes to prevent the audience clambering up, and even to station soldiers in the auditorium (Plate 7).[29] Charles and James had to issue edicts to prevent gentlemen seating themselves on the stage (incidentally, a common practice in French theatres).[30]

This rowdyism is important, but it must be appreciated as the darker aspect of a complex and dynamic theatrical atmosphere. It reflects that strange and squalid undertow of the age of reason that flowed alike beneath the intelligence of Charles's Court, the elegance of the Town, and even the thrifty prosperity of the City itself. Culture and wealth floated on the surface of violence and poverty. When Sir William Coventry spoke roughly in the House of Commons of the king's mistresses, Moll Davies and Nell Gwyn, he was set upon in the Haymarket and his nose slit to the bone, probably on the orders of the king himself. Dryden was soundly beaten one night in Rose Alley, going home from a tavern, by order of the notorious Earl of Rochester, for composing a satirical poem against him. (The poem was in fact written by someone else.) Rochester himself could attempt the rape of an heiress in broad daylight from her carriage in Charing Cross, and Sir Charles Sedley and his friends roamed the city at night, screaming drunken songs and breaking windows.

Violence and squalor, however, were not an upper-class prerogative. The City itself reflected the same ambivalence. As well as its fine new houses, it preserved crowded tenements and plague-breeding slums, particularly in the Liberties of London. There in the Barbican was the area of the stews, convenient yet easily overlooked except on holidays when the virtuous apprentices were allowed to ape their betters and storm through the streets breaking the windows of the brothels. Crime was rife despite severe penalties, and the appalling conditions in Bridewell, Newgate and the Fleet. Restoration society embodied an extreme of a common form of social schizophrenia. Idleness was in a sense as brutalising a factor as poverty. The consumption of leisure in thought, reading and conversation had its darker side in riot, atheism and curious forms of nerveless despair. Inigo Jones's fine new church in Covent Garden was as notorious a pick-up place as the playhouse itself.[31]

There is a side of human experience with which rationalism has never been able to cope. It tries to cover it up, but it breaks out nevertheless with startling ferocity, despite all the controls the intellect can bring to bear. Intelligence easily breeds insolence and despotism. But there is another side to it that, rather than aggression, breeds irony and self-questioning. A critical detachment was as much a part of the chatting, fidgeting and commentating of the Restoration audience as was casual self-indulgence and triviality; and this paradox carried over into their drama, which operates in a fascinating area of experience, between the virtues of contemplation and the vices of off-handedness. The superficial and the perfunctory combine with inquiry, objectivity and intelligence to create a dialectic between the formal art of the dramatists and the conscious life of their public which is the life-blood of the Restoration stage.

Nowadays we consider the play to be the proper focus of attention in the theatre; then, they did not do so. They came to the same play often, and saw no reason to sit through it in silence or in its entirety. Pepys and his friends would frequently take in one act at one theatre and another at the other, not because it was cheaper merely, but out of the same curiosity that made them move about sampling sermons in different churches of a Sunday.[32] The play was more the focus for a social occasion which began as the audience arrived well before the start of the show, to meet, converse, observe the company, and listen to the music provided. Society was the essence of recreation. When Sorbière noted that the playhouses were more convenient for social intercourse than the parks, he was making an important point: they were indeed the same kind of social club as a coffee-house and with the advantage of a mixture of the sexes; in those lit auditoria the 'gallant company', upon which Pepys so often remarks, must have been even more important. Today such an attitude may seem trifling, yet it is precisely this aspect of the theatre that gave Restoration drama its special power. Theatre is a collective entertainment, and the Restoration playhouses had a vital informality that we have lost.

In the light from the candles that gild the auditorium, a curiously close relationship is established between the audience and the dramatic event. Anticipation mounts as footmen enter on the forestage to light the chandeliers and draw them up over the stage. A formal overture gathers the attention, and then before the curtain a leading actor enters to speak the Prologue:[33]

> How comes it, Gentlemen, that now aday's
> When all of you so shrewdly judge of Plays,
> Our Poet's tax you still with want of Sence?
> All Prologues treat you at your own Expence.
> Sharp Citizens a wiser way can go;
> They make you Fools, but never call you so.

Dryden's Prologues show a mastery of elegant, ironic banter. The actor greets the audience on behalf of the company and the poet. He warms them up with wit, perhaps abuses them, gibes at their fashions and behaviour, comments on their taste or the events of the week. Under all the satire, however, sharply observant as it is of the abuses of the day, lies the essential compliment to the audience's present importance. Whether a Prologue is for the house or against it, it is a direct acknowledgment of their presence and of their lives beyond the theatre's walls.

The Prologue acts as an appetiser and creates the sense of a particular occasion. They were spoken only on the first three nights of a piece – after that they lost their topicality – and were considered of sufficient importance for such poets as Dryden to be given fees of £6 for their composition. For revivals with a particular topical significance new Prologues might be contrived, as Dryden did for the visits of the Duke and Duchess of York to Otway's *Venice Preserv'd*. The Prologue provided novelty, wit, immediacy. To open *The Wild Gallant*, Dryden showed two astrologers prognosticating the play's horoscope; for his improved version of *Troilus and Cressida* the Ghost of Shakespeare rises through the stage. Whether literary, imaginative or political, the Prologues set up a pattern of present thought that at the same time marks the separation of stage and audience and stimulates a dialogue between them which continues throughout the play.

The audience clapped a lot, and their clapping seems to have constituted an act of judgment as well as of appreciation and excitement. Applause gave the performances of the period a particular dramatic rhythm as well as achieving a continuous statement of involvement on the part of the spectators. The Prologues are clearly intended to initiate this participation. Exclamations of appreciation, in the conversational ambiance of the auditorium, would have been natural greetings to the elegantly turned couplets and sophisticated wit of these pieces, as well as deprecatory hisses, playful rebukes and appreciative guffaws at the dirty bits. Even audience interruption would become a natural part of such a rhythm, as when an actor, making a meal of a love-scene, ranted out[34]

My wound is great because it is so small,

and the Duke of Buckingham responded from the audience

Then 'twould be greater were it none at all,

presumably drawing more applause than the stage.

The auditoria of the Restoration theatres were not large, holding around 500–800 people, and the audience were all close to the actors.[35] There is no need therefore to think of applause in terms of a modern ovation. It was a light, appreciative punctuation of the actors' lines, prolonged only at the climax of a speech or scene. In his Prologue to *The Gentleman Dancing Master*, the first new play on the Dorset Garden stage, Wycherley addressed the citizens, who may well have found the building closer to their homes as well as the spectacle closer to their tastes.[36] He carefully calculated his lines to provoke a continuous and lively rhythm of differing response from various areas of the house. Here, his Prologue cries:

> we shall be heard, be understood,
> If not, shall be admir'd, and that's as good;

a smattering of applause, perhaps, which the actor caps

> For you to senseless Plays have still been kind,

silence from the citizens, laughter from the gentry

> Nay where no sense was, you a jest would find:

more genteel laughter, jeers from the broader cits

> And never was it heard of, that the City
> Did ever take occasion to be witty
> Upon dull Poet, or stiff Players Action,

gathering laughter, jeers, hisses – the actor continues in a hurt tone:

> But still with claps oppos'd the hissing Faction.
> But if you hiss'd, 'twas at the Pit, not Stage . . .

The jeers and hisses are now a two-way dialogue within the audience, and the actor rides the sounds to a climax:

> So, with the Poet damn'd the damning Age,
> And still we know are ready to ingage
> Against the flouting, ticking Gentry, who
> Citizen, Player, Poet wou'd undo.

Here surely full applause breaks out, and Wycherley wittily 'profits' by it to round off his speech with an ambiguity that both sides can claim as a victory:

> The Poet! no; unless by commendation,
> For on the 'Change, Wits have no reputation;
> And rather than be branded for a Wit,
> He with you, able men, would credit get.

The Prologue, with a ceremonious bow, ends in flattery to the citizens, and yet his metaphor, throughout the speech, has really upheld the superior intellect and cultural values of the gentlemen themselves. They would have particularly appreciated the paradox that it was the thrifty City that liked expensive shows, the extravagant Court that appreciated plain sense.

Wycherley manipulates his audience with great skill. Sharp reference to observed behaviour, metaphor, wit and humour, are expertly deployed and play into the hands of the actor, whose gesture and deportment can easily exploit positive or negative reaction as it arises at a particular moment from the audience's mood or taste. Of course, actors and authors responded readily to the opportunities of such an atmosphere, and not always for the best. Such behaviour was parodied by Jo Haines in a delightful little play, *The Female Wits*, a charming cross between *The*

Rehearsal and *Les Précieuses ridicules*. He shows an authoress coaching her actors for such a claptrap:[37]

> Dear Mrs. Knight, in this Speech, stamp as Queen Statira does, that always gets a Clap; and when you have ended, run off, thus, as fast as you can drive . . .

But the satire is surely at an exaggerated response and a causeless seeking of it, rather than at the general interaction of audiences and stage. Haines's parody actually provokes a fresh response from the parody itself, for the great stamp was given by Mrs Barry in *The Rival Queens*, a popular play in the repertoire of the rival company, and Haines was himself courting applause, first for his reference, and then for Mrs Knight's doubtless malicious imitation of the other actress's passionate style. Such claptraps could be crude – the audience loved burlesque, and loved to recognise public figures in coarse postures; but it could also be highly sophisticated. The best authors used all their skill to stimulate the excitement of comment and applause for moments of intelligence and irony. They did not let the public lose themselves in the action (in such circumstances it would be difficult anyway) and the audience made capital from the alternative, spurring on the action and holding it back at pleasure, while the artists – authors, actors, machinists, designers – courted their reactions.

The plotting of the plays and the structuring of scenes were arranged for claptrap climaxes. In *The Country Wife*, Act IV, when Lady Fidget pretends she is tickling Horner to avert the suspicions of her husband, her ingenuity would be applauded. Similarly, in Otway's *Alcibiades* (Act II), when the King offers Tissaphernes in honour the cup which the latter has poisoned in order to murder the monarch, the audience would applaud the biter bit, and might even laugh in approbation at the neat turn of events, especially when Tissaphernes immediately feigns a swoon of joy and spills the wine on the ground. Congreve almost certainly expected such a reaction at the revelation of the contents of the notorious black box in the last act of *The Way of The World*; and changes of dramatic direction, as when Belvidera embraces Jaffeir as he is about to kill her (*Venice Preserv'd*, Act IV), are also designed for this kind of response, which is as apposite to serious as to comic moments of apprehension when given in such an atmosphere. Cibber recollected Kynaston eliciting such laughter of approbation in sinister parts in tragedy.[38] It was the consequence of aptness of the observation, the justice of the performance, and Cibber felt that his contemporary Booth was wrong to seek to hide it. Even the designer might expect to be appreciated for a brilliant or apposite effect, especially at the climax of an action. The gory revelation of the impaled bodies at the end of *The Empress of Morocco* was obviously intended to bring the house down (see Plate 12).

The audience's constant emphasising of its presence by laughter, comment and applause was not, therefore, entirely gratuitous. The density of the texts to which they listened, and their extraordinary subtlety of verbal detail, suggest a sharpness of attention and an informed response which could be directed at all aspects of stagecraft. By allowing the audience its head and encouraging it to flex its intellectual muscles in this way a good deal was gained. The Restoration theatre does more than permit, it makes time for reaction and comment. Sorbière despised English dramatic structure, remarking: 'They do not matter tho' the play be a hodge-potch, for they mind only the parts as they come on one after another, and have no regard to the whole composition.'[39] The Frenchman had a rather modern view of the theatre. He did not realise that here the unity of a play lies as often in the occasion and in the incidental pattern of current ideas it arouses as in the plot itself.

In comedy, this was emphasised by the locations represented in the scenery. The playhouse was a popular environment for the characters, and must have given a particularly wry and ambivalent effect, but so were many other actual places of leisure in the Town or business in the City. In Shadwell's *The Squire of Alsatia* a crucial setting represented a particular square in that area of London, while the parks, the piazza and the New Exchange were other favourites. Wycherly uses the last two in *The Country Wife*, and *Love in a Wood* suggests that it was the Rosamond's Pond area in St James's Park that was represented by the scenery. Sir Charles Sedley makes an entire comedy revolve around assignations in the Mulberry Garden. This is a more striking relationship of action to life than we find in modern comedy of manners, where the appropriate areas in Chelsea or Bayswater are mentioned but not actually presented on the stage. The latter presents the illusion of life, the former makes it self-conscious and so a joke or a matter for applause. The prints of London scenes in Plate 3 to 6 could easily function as designs for the Restoration stage. The first act of *The Way of the World*, for instance, is set in a chocolate-house, and its second act by Rosamond's Pond. Such pictures could form an appropriate painted background, and the appearance of a new scene of this nature would be a sure claptrap. The New Exchange was modelled on the Royal Exchange, and a painting of such an open court, even with its crowd, would again be suitable for Wycherley's scenes, while a scenic presentation of Hollar's engraving of Covent Garden, seen behind the proscenium arch of a Restoration theatre would have given the impression that Alithea in *The Country Wife*, Act V, was crossing Russell Street between the two arcades on the square's eastern side.

This self-conscious dialogue between life and the stage was completed by a continuous flow of incidental allusion that could be political and literary as well as personal. In *The Gentleman Dancing Master*, Wycherley contrives for the actor Nokes, in character, to compare himself to a rival comedian, to his own advantage, as he makes Olivia, in *The Plain Dealer*, discuss the notorious 'china' scene in *The Country Wife*. Such scenes can be effective only when the audience can be relied on to enjoy the references, and they are not always so straightforward. Nokes apparently played Duncan in *Macbeth*. In *The Soldier's Fortune*, Otway has him as a foolish, mild man who undertakes a murder, and allows his presence and his dialogue to be full of parodistic references to Shakespeare's play. In another scene, he has the hero, Courtine, discovered bound to a bed – a parody of the famous bedroom scene in *The Maid's Tragedy*. This is neither derivative nor plagiaristic, and is highly suitable to the atmosphere of the Restoration playhouse. Such reminiscences would gain applause or encouraging groans, as when Otway makes his Malagene, echoing Falstaff, refuse to co-operate 'upon compulsion'. When Dryden copies the Lorenzo–Jessica episode from *The Merchant of Venice* in *The Spanish Friar*, he even calls the young man Lorenzo, and Tate naughtily allows Edmund to die with the couplet:[40]

> Who would not chose, like me, to yield his Breath,
>
> T'have Rival Queens contend for him in Death,

thus placing his adaptation of *King Lear* in direct competition with Lee's hugely successful tragedy *The Rival Queens*, to which it bears no resemblance whatever.

Every average satirist is aware that if you get in something from today's newspapers the audience goes overboard. The dramatists of the Restoration knew this too, and interwove continuous hints at the current political scene into the pattern of allusions, alongside the people and the plays. Such plays as Crowne's *The Destruction of Jerusalem* and Lee's *Lucius Junius Brutus* cunningly satirise the relations of church and state in the guise of the doings of Jews and Romans; when Otway's Caius Marius hides from his pursuers in a wood, and so escapes them, the Court part of the audience at least would applaud the memory of Charles' famous escape after the battle of Worcester. Not, of course, that Caius Marius is either royal or especially meritorious, but Dryden could similarly design his St Catherine as a compliment to the queen whose patron saint she was, and his Almanzor as a compliment to the Duke of York (see Plates 1 and 2), without expecting the intimate details of either characterisation to be taken too literally. Every level of the house would delight, during the Dutch Wars, in Stephano in *The Tempest* knocking back his brandy with the toast, 'Up se Dutch!'

The arbitrary nature of these allusions is particularly important. They act as a counterpoint, giving the audience a double experience. The play is made to touch their emotional lives one way, and their intellectual lives in another. When, in *The Conquest of Granada*, Dryden makes a hero and heroine from fifteenth-century Spain elaborate an image from the fire of London as a climax to a scene of amorous renunciation, he is not, there-fore, flying in the face of emotion, but playing with this dialectic of drama and audience, present and fictional time. His audience know all too well the story of the fire, the king's intervention and the decision to blow up property to stop the spread of the conflagration, of the excitement of rebuilding, particularly of the new St Paul's, and the depression and frustration of those without capital to redeem their losses. The actor and actress play on the audience's awareness of their sharing of this experience as well as that of the underlying emotion of the situation in the play itself:[41]

ALMANZOR: My joyes indeed are dreams; but not my pain:
          'Twas a swift ruin, but the marks remain.
          When some fierce fire lays goodly buildings wast,
          Would you conclude
          There had been none, because the burning's past?
ALMAHIDE: It was your fault the fire siez'd all your brest,
          You should have blown up some, to save the rest.
          But 'tis, at worst, but so consum'd by fire,
          As Cities are, that by their falls rise high'r.
          Build love a Nobler Temple in my place;
          You'l find the fire has but inlarg'd your space.
ALMANZOR: Love has undone me; I am grown so poor,
          I sadly view the ground I had before,
          But want a stock; and ne'r can build it more.

The gap between the real experiences described in the images (with the direct emotion the recollection must have aroused in contemporaries) and the ideal rationalisation of the emotional predicament of the dramatic characters is oddly touching. The scene rides to its climax on waves of applause that follow almost every couplet and draw their strength from the recognition of immediate reality rather than involvement in the imagi-native fiction.

A play concluded with an Epilogue that returned the audience to the real world. In the last Act of Dryden's *Tyrannick Love*, Nell Gwyn as Valeria comes to a sticky end, and lies out the rest of the play with others who have met similar fates, elegantly disposed as images of destruction. At the play's end, as was the custom, footmen come on with biers to remove the bodies. When they come to Nell, the corpse sits up abruptly:[42]

          Hold, are you mad? you damn'd confounded Dog,
          I am to rise, and speak the Epilogue.
          (see Plate 8)

The final scenes of *Tyrannick Love* are serious, lyrical, moral and intense. This brings us back to the world of the stage with a vengeance. Nelly leaps from the bier, clutching the instrument of her self-immolation and knocking the wig off one of her bearers in her haste and annoyance. Away from the character she returns to the actress. She mocks the play, the poet, herself. She flirts suggestively with the gallants, and flies rapidly from heroic virtue to open invitation. 'I am the Ghost', she says, 'of poor, departed Nelly.'

> Gallants, look to't, you say there are no Sprights;
> But I'll come dance about your beds at nights,
> And faith you'l be in a sweet kind of taking,
> When I surprise you between sleep and waking.

It might seem at first sight that this whole concept is a complete under-mining of what was at any rate a mechanical and half-hearted attempt at serious drama. Seen in the context of Restoration theatre production, this is not so. Throughout the performance the audience are in two minds about the play – their own, and that of the plot of the drama. Even a play of heroic virtue must be played out against an awareness of current life and so necessarily with a consciousness of its extreme difference from the ideals and perfections described. The comic Epilogue (this is particularly good, but they are quite common) is a brilliant acknowledg-ment of this awareness. It emphasises the natural dialectic between ideal and reality, part irony, part grief. Fiction and reality are matters of conscious separation in Restoration drama. Such contrast heightens our detachment. It does not undermine the ideals, it rather celebrates the fiction.

In one of the most famous and popular Epilogues of the period, Jo Haines rode onto the stage on a donkey. Haines was dressed as a Horse-Officer and the donkey wore a fashionable peruke (Plate 7). As a climax to his verse, Haines remarked:[43]

> Now some have told me this might give offence,
> That *riding* my *ass* thus, is *riding* the *audience*:
> But what of that? The *brother* rides the *brother*;
> The *son* the *father*; we all ride one another.
> Then for a jest for this time let it pass;
> For he that takes it ill I'm sure's an ass.

Playing with the multiple meanings – social, sexual, scatological – Haines also makes a neat comment on the dramatic techniques of his time, for the Restoration actor and dramatist, constantly aware of the audience's sometimes unruly presence, were continuously riding their responses, teasing, coaxing, dominating, creating a vigorous and present dialogue between reality and imagination. Brecht said that good theatre should be like sport:[44]

When people in a sporting establishment buy their tickets they know exactly what is going to take place; and that is exactly what does take place when they are in their seats: viz. highly trained persons developing their special powers in a way most suited to them, with the greatest sense of responsibility yet in such a way as to make one feel that they are doing it primarily for their own fun.

The audience at a sport is an audience of connoisseurs. They follow and judge the skill of the participants. They applaud their virtuosity, and are involved and excited by their tactics. Such were the audiences at the Restoration, and both theatres and plays were constructed with this in mind.

2 · New forms

The conscious separation of the audience from the play produced a kind of involved detachment that permeated the new dramatic forms the age created for itself. The most important of these were a very special kind of comedy of manners, the egregious heroic tragedies, and the hybrid semi-opera, though more usual forms – farce, burlesque, satirical comedy and comedy of intrigue – ran in and out of the repertoire.[1] The new forms, naturally, did not spring up overnight. The theatres took time to discover their audience and the possibilities of their new playhouses. At first they played revivals of pre-Restoration successes, and the two companies divided between themselves the best of Shakespeare, Jonson, and Beaumont and Fletcher,[2] and the work of the latter especially remained staple diet for the rest of the century; but as new dramatists emerged, they began to take the qualities of tried and successful plays and turn them into something rather different. The comedy of manners mixed the social observation of Jonson with the easy repartee of Beaumont and Fletcher. Heroic tragedy took the dilemmas of love and honour that delighted the Carolines, and spiced them with dialectic and mordant irony. Semi-opera elaborated the masque-like spectacles so often found in Jacobean and Caroline tragedy and comedy, blended them with a new variety and created a strange and haunting, if thoroughly hybrid, theatrical experience. The new forms of the Restoration theatre seem at first sight to be astonishingly different. Heroic tragedy is notorious for rant and melodrama, semi-opera seems to drag in music to decorate any needy script, while comedy of manners is known for the brilliance of its wit and the indecency of its action: yet these differences are in important ways superficial. All these new methods of organising theatrical experience aim at a rational and objective exploration of life, and have a common style derived from the deepest and most characteristic feature of the society they set out to entertain.

Clarity was the god of Restoration thought and became both the curse and the glory of Restoration art. This should not surprise us. The brilliance of the period was rooted in paradox. The greedy, almost predatory, intensity of act and emotion was coupled with an obsession for definition, lucidity and proof. Men were newly and fundamentally sceptical and enquiring. The king's exile in France and Holland had brought him and his companions in contact with the major cultural influences in Europe, and this contact encouraged a less provincial idea of the position of England, questioned current values, and fed men's minds with a fascination for variations of custom, thought and behaviour about the world. There was a consuming interest in the details and discrepancies of human life and thought that could be both intimate and exotic. The care of and pleasure in the minor accidents of human life that leap from every page of Pepys's marvellous diary are echoed in the numberless books and pamphlets that describe, explore and satirise the nature of London and its daily actions with a loving delight, while there was also a considerable market for such works as John Ogilby's translation of *An Embassy from the East India Company of The United Provinces to the Grand Tartar Cham, Emperor of China* (1669), with its descriptions of society, wealth and custom, and its engravings of pagodas, palm-trees and fringed umbrellas. In *The Indian Emperor*, Dryden tries to excite his audience with a spectacular glimpse of an exotic past to create a background for a discussion of reason and faith in contemporary religious belief.[3]

But this omnivorous curiosity was balanced by an equal need to observe, categorise and define. Much as men enjoyed and indulged the pleasures of life, they also needed to comprehend and analyse them, making the very act of living one of fascinating self-consciousness. The Restoration is a period when to call something artificial is to bestow upon it a high compliment – it draws attention to both ingenuity and truth. Among the delights of his Court, the king kept his own laboratory, and extended his patronage to the newly founded Royal Society whose avowed aim was to clear natural philosophy of superstition and the false dogma of the past by the right use of reason and by practical experiments with the material world. In this way, the true workings of the universe were to be established without question, both in its cosmic and in its domestic operations. The society set up an enormous number of committees to this end, and on a huge range of subjects. There were committees on mathematics and astronomy, chemistry, optics, agriculture and the history of trade. Papers were presented for discussion on mechanics, the weather, architecture, ship-building, monsters – any matter that caught its attention and seemed susceptible to investigation. It received its Charter on July 15 1662, and from 1665 onwards its work became generally known through the publication of its *Philosophical Transactions*.

The attitude of the Royal Society to its investigations embodied a typically English compromise. On the one hand, its members set up laboratories to weigh, measure, and number the material world, to test action and reaction according to the experimental methods advocated by Bacon. Experiment and inductive reasoning were at the very heart of the society's beliefs. On the other hand, they developed and explored the more abstract logic of mathematics. The society encouraged the thought of Descartes, whose work was quite generally available in England.[4] In him, it found a mathematician, a scientist, who could demonstrate the truths of the spirit as well as of matter. Descartes and his method of doubt undermined the truth of sense-experience, but could be made to reassert it again through mathematical hypotheses. Fontenelle, in an essay on *The Utility of Mathematics*, had pointed out that the 'geometric spirit' could be transported to other branches of knowledge. The English had taken this up with glee. In his inaugural lecture as Professor of Astronomy at Gresham College in 1657, Christopher Wren had remarked:[5]

> Mathematical Demonstrations being built on the impregnable foundations of Geometry and Arithmetick, are the only Truths that can sink into the mind of man, void of all uncertainties; and all other Discourses participate more or less of Truth, according as their Subjects are more or less capable of Mathematical Demonstration.

For curiosity to be satisfied, truth must be established, and so every subject worthy of curiosity must be made capable of mathematical demonstration. The weighing and measuring of the material world discloses its inner design.

The means to this end was the grounding of argument in the definition of experience, and so words, the currency of communicated thought, must be made as absolute as numbers, so as to be capable of reaching 'that condicionall knowledge, or that knowledge of the consequence of words, which is commonly called science'.[6]

> The Light of Humane minds is Perspicuous Words, but by exact Definition first snuffed and purged from ambiguity; *Reason* is the *pace*; *Encrease* of *Science*, the *way*; and the Benefit of man-kind, the *end*. And on the contrary, Metaphors, and senseless and ambiguous words, are like *ignes fatui*; and reasoning upon them, is wandering among innumerable absurdities; and their end, contention, sedition, or contempt.

Only a language of mathematical precision can present a clear and distinct idea, and the value of a clear and distinct idea is that it is or at least appears to be a thing in itself, an object of the mind. In this almost tangible separateness it becomes susceptible to the operations of science and also appeals to that essential virtue of the gentleman – rational detachment.

This idea was important to the Royal Society. Sprat points decisively to the need for its members to reform language and behaviour, and attain coolness of thought and utterance. 'All the enchantments of *Enthusiasm*' must be resisted, for in enthusiasm lies fanaticism, and there the causes of the late Civil War. Sober and judicious men dispute without 'the Easie Vanity of *fine speaking*'. They avoid 'this vicious abundance of *Phrase*, this trick of *Metaphors*, this volubility of *Tongue*, which makes so great a noise in the World'. At society meetings there was 'no room left, for any to attempt, to heat their own, or others minds, beyond a due temper'.[7] Therefore[8]

> They have exacted from all their members, a close, naked, natural
> way of speaking; positive expressions, clear senses; a native easiness:
> bringing all things as near the Mathematical plainness, as they can:
> and preferring the language of Artizans, Countrymen, and
> Merchants, before that, of Wits, or Scholars.

Hobbes derives the word 'idea' from the Greek word meaning 'to see'. The men of the Restoration wanted to know, and to do so they wanted to see clearly. They carried this desire into almost every aspect of their life. Not only would clear ideas turn thoughts into objects for the mind, objects which they could examine with the same loving care as they could monsters, or the behaviour of ladies in the Strand, but rules and regulations of conduct – definitions, one might call them, of truth and error in behaviour – would articulate and clarify the true relations between men. Accuracy of language and correctness of manners are both projections of the mathematical demonstration of truth.

All this may seem a long way from the theatre: it is not so. The lists of members of the Royal Society overlap very significantly the classes that went to the playhouse, and the effect of such a climate of opinion on the dramatic art of the period was profound. It moulded not merely the language of the plays, but their plots as well, and even extended into concepts of characterisation, staging and musical accompaniment, as well as into the art of acting itself. The relation between hypothetical and experimental science, between abstract argument and concrete example, is implicit in the sharpness and wit of the comedy of manners, in the ironies of heroic tragedy, and the peculiar logic of semi-opera. It is as if the theatre is striving for its own synthesis, preserving for the purpose the enthusiasm tempered with informed detachment of a scientific experiment.

Drama in the later seventeenth century became a pseudo-science. Poetry ceased of its own nature to be a means to truths; its methods had to be justified, its theories proved. Dryden wrote: 'A man should be learned in several sciences, and have a reasonable, philosophical, and in some measures a mathematical head to be a complete and excellent poet.'[9] The poets became obsessed with the laws of art and the principles by which they might be established and a work judged absolutely as good or bad. Ironically, the chief means at their disposal was that very classical authority that science was striving to throw off, so it was fortunate that in their *Philosophical Transactions* the Royal Society seriously attacked only Aristotle's *Metaphysics*, leaving intact the value of his *Ethics*, *Logic* and *Rhetoric*.[10]

In the attempt to establish the science of art, almost all authors wrote copiously about their works, and engaged in ferocious critical wars in which the cool detachment of the gentleman is notably absent. The basic methods employed were personal insult, classical authority, accompanied with many tags in Latin or Greek to add weight to the argument, and venomously close textual analysis. The reduplication of such writings is significant. Dryden prefaced most of his published work with long discourses on the nature of his art, and his engagement with such questions in a busy literary life shows not only the artist's need to defend his art but also the potential readership value of their presence. The works obviously sold well, and it is fair to assume that the majority of those that bought them were potential if not actual members of the audience. The theory of drama was part of that body of response the audience brought to a play and articulated while it watched, and cross references and theoretical dispute, echoed as they so often are in Prologues and Epilogues, were a genuine part of the entertainment.

The central problem of the criticism of the period is the problem of form. The elaborated plots and comic interludes of English drama came from a tradition which had no authority in the ancient world. On the other hand they worked, and they pleased their audience. Restoration critics were in pursuit of truth, like their scientific friends, but like the scientists also they were practical men and most of them wrote for the stage. They enjoyed experimenting and were opportunist about satisfactory results. Dryden upholds the English tradition against Thomas Rymer whose work returns again and again to the superior clarity of the ancients and of French rules of unity and propriety. Rymer was not a dramatist, and his criticism is as consistent as it is often dull: Dryden, Settle, and even Tate producing classical authority for farce, are as disingenuous as they are often lively. The difficulties are most successfully articulated in Dryden's *Essay of Dramatic Poesy*, which employs the form of a dialogue to throw into opposition the essential theories of the day. His contestants argue the relative merits of traditional narrative forms of drama against the rules deduced by neoclassical critics in France from the works of Aristotle and Horace. The dialectical form of the piece reflects his own practice as a playwright, giving each style its independent value.

Dryden's theatre practice contrives a new principle of dramatic construction which is a synthesis of contradictory methods, and this principle dominated the theatre of his day. It was that the truth of a drama depended upon the truth of its design; that such a design was like a geometrical proof, and must operate from the logic of its own propositions, which are valid independently of the deceitful observations of the senses. The senses, as the philosophers tell us, delude us as to the true nature of reality. Truth is embodied in clarity of idea, and the design of the play must make perspicuous a clear and distinct idea of life.

The operation of this theory can be seen in the way in which the plays of Shakespeare were consistently 'improved' during this period. There were three clusters of such adaptations. The first by Davenant in the 1660s, the second in the difficult period between 1677 and 1683 and the third at the turn of the century. Davenant's *Macbeth* and Nahum Tate's notorious *King Lear* may serve as examples of the creative processes involved.

Tate found *King Lear*: 'A Heap of Jewels, unstrung and unpolish't; yet so dazzling in their Disorder, that I soon perceiv'd I had siezed a Treasure.'[11] It was his pleasant task to create a design from this disorder, to exercise the proper judgment of the poet in building his poem, so as to make its true beauty clear to the spectator. ' 'Twas my good Fortune to light on one Expedient to rectify what was wanting in the Regularity and Probability of the whole, A *Love* betwixt *Edgar* and *Cordelia*, that never chang'd word with each other in the Original.' This happy thought at once clarified Cordelia's attitude to her father in the first act and explained her crossing him – the young woman was naturally distressed at being asked to marry another. It further motivates Edgar's disguise and more importantly ennobles the action. He is protecting Cordelia, which 'makes that a generous Design, which was before a poor Shift to save his life'. Under the circumstances, it became necessary to give the play a happy ending in order to conclude 'in a success to the innocent distrest Persons'. Tate's changes form a remarkable example of the meaning of the phrase 'to reduce to order'. They may destroy *King Lear*, but they make it make sense.

To the same end, William Davenant provides *Macbeth* with a moral:[12]

> Ambition is a tree whose roots are small,
> Whose growth is high, whose shadow ever is
> The blackness of the deed attending it,
> Under which nothing prospers. All the fruit
> It bears are doubt and troubles, with whose crowne
> The overburdened tree at last falls down.

An irreproachable sentiment, which renders the hesitance, weakness and superstition of Macbeth's character and the dark fate which overtakes him and his wife entirely perspicuous. The action is further clarified by the development of a contrast that is barely present in Shakespeare's text as we have it: Lady Macduff and her husband are built up as a truly loving counterpart to the Macbeths, and the opposition is emphasised by a new scene, early in the drama, between Lady Macduff and Lady Macbeth. While her loved husband is away at the war, Lady Macduff cannot sleep for fear. Lady Macbeth's sleep-walking scene becomes no longer an image of disintegration but a part of an orderly pattern of moral comment. Davenant would have doubtless justified his image of ambition by the honoured authority of the Emblem books.

The need to organise dramatic structure as a demonstration, almost an experiment, in moral argument is crucial to the style of the period. The poet contrives an object for the audience's contemplation, an object that operates by recognisable laws. It is an independent fiction that the poet has feigned to enact his moral purpose, and its laws are to be those of the moral rather than those of the subject. When Rymer criticises the works of Beaumont and Fletcher, his criticisms are aimed at their lack of art in turning the action towards a just moral. Their characters lack truth because they behave as people do:[13]

> Many are apt to mistake *use* for *nature*, but a poet is not to be an Historiographer but a Philosopher, he is not to take *Nature* at the *second hand*, soyl'd and deform'd as it passes in the customs of the unthinking vulgar.
>
> The (a) *Phedra* in *Euripides* told us truly that it is *not Natural to do evil when we know good*. Therefore vice can never please unless it be painted and dress'd up in the colours and disguise of virtue, and should any man knowingly and with open eyes prefer what is evil, he must be reckon'd the (b) greatest of Monsters, and in no wise be looked on as any image of what is Natural, or what is suitable with humane kind.

Rymer's argument rests on his stated assumption that moral truths are absolute and can be universally recognised by men of any country, race or creed. A true action depends on the truth of its moral essence, and this must govern the accidents of the plot.

Inevitably, the effect of making idea the ruling power in the construction of a fiction is the opposite to that intended. The attempt to create mathematical demonstrations of moral truth in the context of a human action produces palpable falsehood. That this should happen is ironical; but it is not necessarily as disastrous as one might suppose.

In *Marriage à la Mode*, Dryden proposes the following design: Polydamas, the usurper of the throne of Sicily, lost a child in infancy; he discovers two children, a boy and a girl, one of which is his; he is told it is the boy, which he naturally is inclined to believe, but meets trouble when he tries to arrange the child's marriage to an important lady in the court – the boy is in love with the shepherdess with whom he was brought up; a crisis is avoided by the revelation that it is not the boy but the girl who is the royal offspring, but the situation then repeats itself the other way about. Finally, the young man is proved to be the son of the true king, the girl the true daughter of Polydamas, and they can both marry and so resolve the contrived political conflict. This is a silly story. It is strictly 'possible', I suppose, but hardly 'probable'. As presented, however, it becomes rather moving. The metamorphoses of the plot juxtapose images of different kinds of virtue and truth. They pinpoint ideas of fatherhood and of royal authority, and contrast them with the duties of children to their parents, to their king and to each other. They manifest different concepts of love and of moral purpose in such a way that they can be readily compared. The truth of Dryden's characters and the truth of their behaviour lie in his accurate observation of the nature of the different roles people play. He is demonstrating ideas as absolutes of right and wrong and so is untroubled by the fact that the ideal is seldom actually true – it is simply ideally true, and he can organise the design to present a hypothesis of ideal behaviour and demonstrate its consequences.

In this case, of course, he goes further. The story of Polydamas of Sicily, with its echoes of *The Winter's Tale*, is set against a pure comedy of manners, a series of intrigues among a quartet of ladies and gentlemen of the usurper's court. The whole of this part of the play, with its parks, grottos and taverns, is clearly London oriented, 'Scene: Sicily' notwithstanding. In it, a young man who has been ordered by his father to marry a certain heiress tries to seduce his friend's wife in the few days left him of freedom, while, for his part, the friend has a go at the heiress. Dryden neatly juxtaposes the ideal with the real. Leonidas and Palmyra will die rather than change their love: Palamede and Melantha will marry anyone rather than lose their estate, but will none the less try to have their own way on the side. In this very fetching play, Dryden uses the two kinds of truth to counterpoint each other. His accurate observation of how people really behave is the inversion of his mathematical demonstration of how they should behave. Experiment confronts hypothesis, the flesh, the spirit. The play is almost an embodiment of the 'method of doubt', and the two kinds of truth are made to work together dramatically because Dryden accepts the crucial fact – whether you are presenting what you consider to be real life, or whether you are demonstrating a moral hypothesis, you are constructing a fable. Either way, it is artificial. Both are fictions.

The abstract stylisation of the plot is heightened by the depiction of character. Today actors and audiences think of character in terms of individual psychology. In the seventeenth century it was seen as a moral concept. Character, in fiction, made a selection from the accidents of life to present the moral essence of a person. Psychological insight and the observation of behaviour were means for the incarnation of this 'idea'. This attitude had been fostered by a long tradition which flowered at this period into a number of fine collections of what has come to be known as 'Character' literature, delightful assemblages of thumbnail sketches of men and manners, perhaps best represented in England by the *Characters* of Sir Thomas Overbury and his friends, and the *Microcosmographie* of John Earle, and in France by the acid and elegant *Caractères* of La Bruyère. These works all derive in the long run from the *Ethics* of Aristotle and the *Characters* of his pupil Theophrastus, which La Bruyère in fact translated as a preface to his own book. Aristotle had remarked that each individual possessed a particular physical disposition, and was therefore inclined by nature to particular kinds of behaviour. Behaviour that was frequently indulged would become habitual, but the individual could discipline himself to curb the extremes of his disposition and form right habits. To do so or not was a matter of moral choice, and a man's moral character was therefore articulated by the choices implicit in his habitual conduct. So Theophrastus tells us, according to La Bruyère, that stupidity is a habitual heaviness of mind, and a stupid man is one who getting up to relieve himself in the middle of the night, goes outside and trips over the dog, who bites him. His habit of mind has engendered lack of foresight and lack of care.

The appeal of this consonance of idea and act to the Restoration mind will be apparent. It combines practical observation with mathematical truth, and man's curiosity at the forms of outward existence is placed at the disposal of a higher concept. The character-writers of the seventeenth century, many of whom were clergymen, could use the pithy form to demonstrate extremely neatly the interconnection of outward behaviour and inward worth. A covetous man, writes Overbury, pinning the vice down like a butterfly on a board, 'never spends candle but at Christmas (when he has them for new-yeeres gifts) in the hope that his servants will breake glasses for want of light, which they doubly pay for in their wages.'[14] As La Bruyère developed as a writer he began to go even further in the process of abstraction, producing a purer truth. His 'characters' become 'maxims' that give simply the moral essence, formulated towards the idea even more than the behaviour: 'To bear with both her flirtations and her religion is more than a woman can expect of her husband; she had better choose between them.'[15] Newton stated his famous Laws as formulae by which certain phenomena might be measured, not as matters of cause and effect. The character-writers observe the same style – they measure moral worth; they do not motivate it.

The use of such characterisation is distinct in both comedy and tragedy, comedy tending towards the observational and tragedy towards the more hypothetical, essential form. Thomas Shadwell, imitating Ben Jonson, frequently prefaced his plays with 'characters' of the *Dramatis Personae*. Young Maggott, in *A True Widow* (1679), is: 'An Inns of Court-Man, who neglects his Law, and runs mad after Wit, pretending much to Love, and both in spite of Nature; since his Face makes him unfit for one and his Brains for the other.' The method is clear: the collection of a set of behavioural characteristics, which are recognisible from life and may be demonstrated in action but which are centred on a specific moral weakness which gives the observations unity and truth – in Maggott's case a pretension to things of which his disposition is incapable. It is the same method that creates such fools and fops as Etherege's man of mode with his substitution of forms for feelings, or Wycherley's Sparkish, whose easiness is the mark of self-satisfaction rather than of respect for others. The very names of such characters declare their *ethos*, even when no 'character' is given in the *Dramatis Personae*.

In serious drama, especially in tragedy, it was the idea itself that dominated. The idea becomes the ideal. The epigrammatical quality that captures a character's essence in words is transferred to a conceptual absoluteness of behaviour. This of course gains even greater authority from classical precedent: Horace wrote:[16]

> Describe *Achilles*, as *Achilles* was,
> Impatient, rash, inexorable, proud,
> Scorning all Judges, and all Law but Arms;
> *Medea* must be all Revenge and Blood,
> *Ino* all tears, *Ixion* all Deceit,
> *Io* must wander, and *Orestes* mourn.

Character was consistent, total, an incarnate idea, and if a poet ventures on a new one it must remain within the general truths of the human personality. Such 'generalisation' does not exclude particularity, but it must be an example of the moral ethos. In any case, the ethos must take precedence over observed or empirical fact in the interests of higher truth. When drawing the character of Henry III of France from history in *The Duke of Guise*, Dryden remarks: 'We were indeed obliged by the Laws of Poetry, to cast into *Shadows* the *Vices* of this *Prince*; for an excellent Critique has lately told us, that *when a KING is nam'd, a HEROE is suppos'd*: 'tis a reverence due to Majesty, to make the Vertues as conspicuous, and the Vices as obscure as we can possibly.'[17] The behaviour of even historical figures must be controlled by the nature of their disposition and the character of their role in society. The decorum of truth demands it because it is the essence that is true, not the accidents.

This is why, as Aristotle said, poetry is more philosophical than history. Character in its moral sense becomes as knowable as anatomy.

This is a limiting view of characterisation. The concept of the moral essence, and its corollary, that of decorum, reduce complex human nature to a clear idea that can seem lacking in life and can too easily become conventional. But it is also a method that has a certain dramatic force. Man's moral nature was understood to lie in the strength with which he succeeded in controlling with his will the habits provoked in him by his passions.[18] Passion is suffered by the soul and then moves outward, as emotion, into action. A dramatist designs his scenes to embody these 'motions of the mind', as Dryden calls them.[19] The structure of each scene is a function of the relationship of the ideas implicit in the characters, rather than an imitation of dealings between men. This is why the dramatists are on the whole content with conventional patterns of action – the concealments, disguisings, and gullings of comedy, the battles, the betrayals, the dilemmas of love and honour in tragedy. They are mere mechanisms for bringing out the moral idea of the drama, and the closeness of such accidents to the conduct of daily life is less important than the significance with which they arrange their ideas.

For such selective lucidity and pointedness of action, Brecht coined the word *gestus*. A *gestus* is not just any act or gesture, but one which conveys 'particular attitudes adopted by the speaker towards other men'.[20] In other words, in Restoration terms, it conveys 'character'. The effect of the *gestus* is to alienate or objectify the action itself so that it may be judged or questioned. The design of Restoration drama operates in a very similar manner. Through the shape of his scenes and the organisation of his plot, the dramatist focuses each moment or episode into an action that embodies an idea of his characters. Significantly, the actor's incarnation of such moments was known at the time as an 'attitude'. Furthermore, as also with Brecht, the whole effect is controlled by a *gestic* use of language. It is this language, as I suggested in the first chapter, that creates through its pointed and easily grasped phrases that dialogue of judgment and applause that is fundamental to the Restoration theatrical experience.[21]

Wit and judgment are the mainstays of writing in the age of reason, and the former is necessarily the handmaid to the latter. Wit, Hobbes tells us, is a property of quickness of the imagination, the ability to perceive likeness between things unlike. This celerity of thought is sometimes called 'fancy'. Judgment, on the contrary, is the ability to distinguish between things, to tell them apart.[22] The impropriety of metaphor arises precisely because it confuses two different objects together. It employs celerity of imagining at the expense of clarity of judgment. A quick wit, however, also assists understanding, as John Dennis noted in a letter to Wycherley, carefully carrying out his own prescription:[23]

> By a man of Wit, I do not mean every Coxcomb whose Imagination has the Ascendent of his little reason; but a Man like You, Sir . . . in whom Fancy and Judgment are like a well-match'd Pair; the first like an extraordinary Wife, that appears always Beautiful and always Charming, yet is at all times Decent, and at all times Chast; the second like a Prudent and well-bred Husband, whose very Sway shows his Complaisance, and whose very Indulgence shows his Authority.

Unlike a metaphor, a similitude is both cool and perspicuous. Thus Dryden, in *The Hind and the Panther*, chooses to argue with tremendous and rather underrated wit on behalf of the Catholic Church, a subject then like tinder to a conscience, by framing his discussion in the similitude of an animal fable, gaining capital for his judgments through the witty conception of his animal protagonists, and attempting to calm faction through an exercise of the mind.

At the Restoration, comedy of manners is really quite as much comedy of ideas. Its style is an intellectual one which seeks to impose clarity on the vagaries of feeling, sensation and action, through the power of the mind. It is a theatre of words. There is a Shavian coolness about it. The Restoration audience listened to a play as they listened to a sermon, appreciating the sense of the line, its moral implications and the elegance of its phrasing – the accuracy and virtuosity with which it captures its ideas. Repartee becomes a vehicle for the description of life:[24]

COURTALL: Well, *Franck*, what is to be done to-day?

FREEMAN: Faith, I think we must e'ne follow the old Trade; eat well, and prepare ourselves with a Bottle or two of good *Burgundy*, that our old acquaintance may look lovely in our Eyes. For, for aught I see, there is no hopes of new.

COURTALL: Well, this is grown a wicked Town! It was otherwise in my memory; a Gentleman should not have gone out of his Chamber, but some civil Officer or other of the Game wou'd have been with him, and have given him Notice where he might have had a course or two in the Afternoon.

FREEMAN: Truly, a good motherly woman of my acquaintance t'other day, talking of the sins of the times, told me, with tears in her Eyes, that there are a company of higgling Rascals, who partly for themselves, but more especially for some great friends, daily forestall the Markets; nay, and that many Gentlemen who had formerly been Persons of great worth and honour, are of late, for some private

reasons, become their own Purveyors, to the utter decay
and discouragement of Trade and Industry.

COURTALL: I know there are some wary Merchants who never trust
their business to a Factor; but for my part, I hate the
Fatigue, and had rather be bound to back my own Colts,
and man my own Hawks, than endure the impertinences
of bringing a young Wench to the Lure.

With all its studied ambiguity and easy precision of utterance, this
dialogue is simply a 'Character of the Town'. It does not imitate a conversation between two men, though its language is characteristic enough.
Rather is the image set up apart from the characters. They become the
agents for our understanding. Author and actors present the lifestyle of
the characters by describing it, not by enacting it. The dialogue is a
convention that acts as a vehicle for the description.

This verbal centre for dramatic art is essentially an objectifying factor.
It separates action and feeling. The emotions implicit in the dramatic
situation are seen from a distance, as it were through the microscope of
wit and with the eye of judgment. They are described to be observed.
For this very reason Dryden applauds the practice of giving a 'character'
in words before the entrance of the actor, so that the audience may miss
nothing of its meaning,[25] and prepares us for the arrival of Melantha in
Marriage à la Mode by a neat dialogue between the play's two rakes.[26]

With all this, she's the greatest Gossip in Nature, for besides the
Court, she's the most eternal Visiter of the Town: and yet manages
her time so well that she seems ubiquitary. For my part, I can compare
her to nothing but the Sun; for like him she takes no Rest, nor ever
sets in one place but to rise in another.

When she does appear, she is indeed a whirlwind, flitting on and off
stage, and from man to man, like an ecstatic bird, a direct incarnation of
the words that first conjure her up. And the effect is as Dryden suggests:
one looks on at her humour, and does not participate in her feelings. One
applauds author and actress for the truth of their idea.

In the rhymed heroic play, the same taste for description and definition,
the determination to approach the intelligence rather than the apprehension of the audience have a particularly characteristic effect. Nowadays
we conceive of tragedy as an emotional form, and the obviously satirical
dimension of heroic tragedy seems extremely peculiar. Since this combination of formality, wit and magniloquence is never far from the surface
in any Restoration tragedy, it is important to grasp its significance.

Dryden, attacking Settle about *The Empress of Morocco*, complains:
'This fellow has a Buzz of Poetry in his head; and never thinking clearly,
can never express himself intelligibly.'[27] He goes on to demonstrate his
point in venomous detail, quoting Settle's lines out of context:

> *Hell, no of that I scorn to be afraid:*
> *Betray, and Kill, and Damn to that Degree,*
> *I'le crowd up Hell till there's no room for me.*

'It seems [the Queen-Mother] is exactly informed of the Dimensions of Hell, what numbers it will hold, and what it wants to fill it. How she should come by this knowledge I cannot tell.'[28] Settle of course replies in kind and accuses Dryden of the same tricks. What is arresting is that neither poet ever suggests that characters in a high state of tension might well talk nonsense. To neither critic is this a proper justification, for it is not the poet's business to imitate speech but to describe its underlying moral or emotional significance.

The concept that ideas are moving makes sound dramatic sense, but it also creates a very different tone for a tragedy. Dryden, and indeed Settle and Sir Robert Howard, though not with such spectacular success, use the pungent form of the couplet to articulate their thoughts and make them palpable. The heroic couplet does not imitate speech. It crystallises the motives for action and the general principles involved. It 'discriminates between notion and notion, word and word, with the exactness of a chemist's balance'.[29] When Almahide has been left behind in the captured citadel of Granada, the Moorish king, Boabdelin, who is betrothed to her, fears for her safety and her honour. Her father, however, is sanguine, if severe. He remarks:[30]

> One of my blood, in rules of virtue bred;
> Think better of her, and believe she's dead.

This sharp summation of the heroic absolute is dangerously close to comedy, but it may draw a gasp, followed by applause, rather than a laugh. Feeling is not absent, but it is implicit in the nature of the thought rather than in the passion of the emotion. It lies in fact in our own feeling toward the 'attitude' of the character that has been presented for our observation. The implicit abstraction from the emotional or physical realities of the situation make possible the sustaining of a mood of continuous irony which goes far beyond the usual function of comedy in tragic drama. The villainous Zulema, having got away with treasonous behaviour informs us:[31]

> Forgiveness to the Injur'd does belong;
> But they ne'r pardon who have done the wrong.

It is a true and frightening psychological perception, rendered cool, but not less dangerous, by its utterance from the lips of a pardoned traitor. It is also a style perfectly suited to that dialogue with the audience described in the first chapter. It exploits to the full the dialectic of fiction and life the conditions of performance created. The onlookers can note with detachment the wickedness of the character, while gleefully acknowledging with their applause the accuracy of the perception, bestowing upon the idea 'the laughter of approbation'.

In response to the questing and defining habit of mind that dominated the period, the great Restoration dramatists do not try to give the illusion of events actually taking place before our eyes. Their method is perhaps more subtle. The language of their characters describes the nature of the experiences in which they are involved, while the structure of the action presents observations of the behaviour of men, selected by a discriminating judgment to present the audience with an idea of society or of life. The plays proceed by 'mathematical demonstration', and present not a developing action but a pattern of related ideas brought into significant juxtaposition by the often conventional mechanisms of the plot. The structures of Restoration drama are musical, not narrative. They depend on contrast and variation, on analytical relationships. Clash of personality and developing conflict is replaced by the clash of ideas incarnated in character, physicalised in 'attitude' or gesture, and described in words. The character images brought together in this way articulate the design of the drama. Each scene in fact, presents a moral image, and each act a unified pattern of such images.[32] It was this method of theatrical organisation that served to bring the more affective elements of the plays within the pale of reason. It says a great deal for the strength and consistency of the Restoration attitude to dramatic art that ways were found to turn the sensuous excitements of music, dancing and painted scenes to the ends of design and perspicuity.

3 · Music and spectacle

When Sir William Davenant circumvented the Commonwealth ban on dramatic performances in 1656 and presented *The Siege of Rhodes* in specially prepared apartments at Rutland House, he introduced for the first time to the English public stage the scenic apparatus of the Court masque and the musical conventions of the Italian opera. To celebrate the occasion the text was printed in the same year, and sold by Henry Herringman from his shop in the lower walk of the New Exchange. The titlepage read:[1]

> *The Siege of Rhodes.*
> *Made a Representation by the Art of Prospective in Scenes,*
> *and the Story sung in Recitative Musick.*

The music is unfortunately lost, but drawings for the scenery do exist. It was designed by John Webb, a pupil of the great masque designer and architect, Inigo Jones, and though much reduced in scope from the glories of pre-war days – the stage at Rutland House was only 11 feet high and 15 feet deep – these designs provide a good starting-point for understanding the scenic effects in operation on the English stage in the second half of the seventeenth century, and the spectacular music-drama which they supported.

The little stage was framed by a special 'frontispiece' or proscenium arch, which both concealed the workings of the machinery and masked the sides of the stage from the auditorium. It was designed specially for the opera, and displayed the trophies and ensigns of those defending the city supported by 'divers habiliments of war' (Plate 13). Behind the proscenium came three sets of wings, representing 'a maritime coast, full of craggy rocks and high cliffs, with several verdures growing naturally upon such situations'.[2] At the back of the stage to close the scene (see Plate 14) was

the true prospect of the City of Rhodes, when it was in prosperous estate; with so much view of the gardens and hills about it, as the narrowness of the room could allow the scene. In that part of the horizon terminated by the sea, was represented the *Turkish Fleet*, making towards a promontory some few miles distant from the town.

The rock wings were arranged in pairs, and placed further onto the stage as they were further from the audience (Figure 3); the upper part of the scene was masked by borders representing clouds, and the stage sloped gently upwards. This enabled Webb to create a false perspective that could considerably enhance the apparent depth of the tiny stage, while the prospect behind was simply a two-dimensional painting, again giving an illusion of depth. This painting was not a backcloth, in the modern sense. The room was low, and it was not convenient to lower or unroll cloths. Instead, the picture was painted on a pair of flats, held upright in a grooved frame, similar in principle to a pair of sliding doors, only with a single groove for each pair of flats so that they would meet

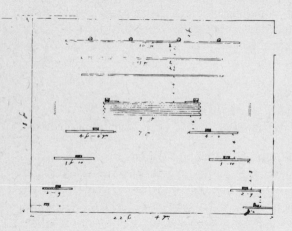

Figure 3   *The Siege of Rhodes.*
Ground plan. Webb.
(*The British Library Department
of Manuscripts, Lansdowne
MSS 1171*)

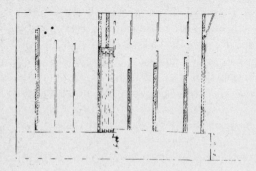

Figure 4   *The Siege of Rhodes.*
Elevation. Webb.
(*The British Library*)

flush in the middle. The picture could therefore divide in the centre and slide apart into the wings, revealing a new prospect behind. Such pairs of flats were known as shutters, and soap was used to lubricate the wooden grooves so that they would slide smoothly along them. The floor-plan and elevation for *The Siege of Rhodes* shows space for four pairs of shutters, set directly behind each other (Figures 3 and 4). This allowed for immediate and striking changes of scene without the curtain being lowered, so that the scenic images transformed before the audience's eyes to a series of pictures like the prospect in Plate 14, but showing the progress of the siege.

As well as this series of military spectacles there was a further scene, differently contrived and in marked contrast to the others. The plan shows three more lines running the width of the stage behind the set of shutters, and they coincided with the three uprights at the rear of the elevation (Figures 3 and 4). These were the marks for a scene of 'relieve', which in the cramped circumstances of the hall had to be kept permanently in place, hidden by the closed shutters in front. The 'relieve' provided the stage with a yet greater illusion of depth rather on the lines of a child's pop-up picture book (Plate 15). The scene was clearly an important one:

> The further part of the Scene is open'd and a Royal pavilion appears
> display'd, representing Solyman's Imperial throne; and about it are
> discern'd the quarters of his Bassas and inferior officers.

From John Webb's drawing, it is possible to see how this scene was contrived. First comes a cut-out frame – the two sets of columns and the step beneath them, probably joined above by the drapery and the canopy that surmounts the throne; next, the chequered floor, drawn in false perspective, runs the width of the stage and supports the painted cut-out throne, its cushion and scimitar, all two-dimensional and not practical; finally, behind both these, hangs the permanent backcloth, showing the circle of the Bassas' tents. It is the series of 'cut-out' effects that gives the contrivance the name 'relieve' or 'relief' scene.

Davenant's introduction of such scenery to the stage was a sensational success, and the King's Company swiftly followed suit at their own theatre. The combination of the painted scene with its wings and shutters giving the illusion of depth, and the relieve scene giving further depth behind, became basic to the scenic design of the Restoration, and the interaction of deep with comparatively shallow scenic effects gave the plays much of their rhythmic impulse. The great curtain in the Restoration theatres rose at the beginning of the play and generally did not fall till the end, so that the swift and startling changes of scene, which grow more elaborate as the period progressed, had a dynamic visual energy.[3]

A comparison of the plan for *The Siege of Rhodes* (Figure 3) with

Wren's section of a theatre (Plate 16) shows the similarity of principle and its development. The scenic stage stretches to the right of the double pilasters in the centre of the drawing, and vertical grooves are drawn for four sets of wings and three pairs of shutters. Beyond, under the floor of the dressing-rooms, there seems to be further space for a deep-scene, or relieve, though the wings and shutters are not marked. It is generally thought that Wren's design was for the Theatre Royal, Drury Lane, though it is torn across and may never have been executed in quite this form. It shows a stage of 20 feet in depth, and a deep-scene of 25 feet. The width of the Drury Lane stage has been estimated at about 25 feet, and it was proportionately high. The frontispiece to the opera *Ariane*, one of the early productions there, would seem to represent the proscenium and stage in action (Plate 17).[4]

Drury Lane was, of course, Charles's 'plain House'. The Dorset Garden was susceptible of more elaborate effects, as shown in the designs for *The Empress of Morocco*, but though grander in scale, the designs can be interpreted according to the same principles. The opening scene is a prison (Plate 10). It seems to show three sets of wings, with borders to match, and back-shutters in false perspective showing the depths of the dungeon. I would interpret the shutters as incorporating everything behind the hanging lamp and chains, which would be painted upon them, but it is arguable that the whole vista-stage was employed for a grand opening effect. The use of a complete set of wings, borders and shutters in combination give a magnificent sense of illusion. This is increased in the picture by the floor-covering, but the latter is probably a product of the engraver's imagination. The stage at the time was covered with a cloth of green baize.[5]

Another illustration shows what is apparently a 'relieve' scene in which 'is represented the Prospect of a large River, with a glorious Fleet of Ships, supposed to be the Navy of Muly Hamet' (Plate 11).[6] This engraving is less easy to interpret. The architecture at either side and the great ships immediately behind could be painted on the same wing, or the architecture could be cut out in relieve and the ships painted upon a wing behind. The sea, with the rest of the fleet and the boat coming ashore, might be painted on shutters, as in *The Siege of Rhodes*, or might be practical, with the ships passing on grooves between the turning waves (Figures 5 and 15). In the latter case, the perspective would be created by conventional cloud wings and borders as in Torelli's design for *Les Noces de Pélée et de Thétis* (Plate 22).

Such an interpretation demonstrates a number of the developments in design during the period. In the first place, the whole scene, including the side wings, had been changed, as was the practice in the baroque theatres of Europe. The great Italian designer, Giacomo Torelli, a magical

Figure 5   Machine for a ship. Sabbattini.
BC is the groove. DE and FG are wave profiles (*The British Library*)

innovator in stage machinery, was working in Paris in the 1640s and 1650s, and King Charles may well have seen and enjoyed these elaborate presentations. Certainly the king sent Betterton to France in the early 1670s, and he went again in the 1680s to find out about developments in stage spectacle. Killigrew also visited France and Italy during his years of exile. Torelli invented mechanical means of changing borders and side wings, and it is probable that his method of changing scenery by mounting it on trucks descending through slots in the stage, enabling all the wings to move together by the operation of a single capstan may have been employed in at least the deep-scenes of the Restoration theatres.

Another of Torelli's specialities was the split-scene.[7] In the masque in *The Empress of Morocco* (Plate 18), the arch of Hell, with Cerberus in full cry, is surmounted by a further blazing structure, giving the effect of two levels at the back of the stage. The whole scene could easily have been painted on a pair of shutters, but the deep-scene could alternatively and more spectacularly have been divided into an upper and lower part (Plate 24).[7] If so, the proscenium arches of the theatres must have been sufficiently high. Even French visitors to London reported that the scenes were fine,[8] so perhaps the extreme difference in sophistication between Torelli's design and those for *The Empress of Morocco* may be ascribed to the engravers rather than to the designers themselves.

A third and crucial point is that the area behind the proscenium arch was capable of taking additional sophisticated machinery. These added a further visual dynamic to the already exciting alteration of the scenes. The simplest machines were the traps for the raising of ghosts or devils and the engulfing of the wicked; the most spectacular were the various kinds of flying-machines for humans, Gods, spirits and even flaming monsters. The masque from *The Empress of Morocco* reached its climax as 'several infernal spirits rise from under the stage and dance', a couple apparently flying off at the corners of the stage.

Interestingly enough, the basic principle for such machines was also the groove. The basic trap was a square of the stage that descended into a frame made from four trunks of wood with their corners cut out to take the corners of the trap. This was supported on a frame with a centre batten, from either side of which ropes were stretched upwards to raise the mechanism. The chariots rise from the sea in a similar fashion (Plate 22). The deities descending at the side of the stage in Plate 24 are seated on saddles supported by frames in the shape of right-angled triangles, the back-sides of which run up and down vertical grooves concealed behind the wings (Figure 6). While the flight of devils or angels across the stage was usually supported by parallel beams, near-side corners grooved and placed very close together, which made a slotted groove (sometimes a strengthened rope was employed) for the passage of a little truck which

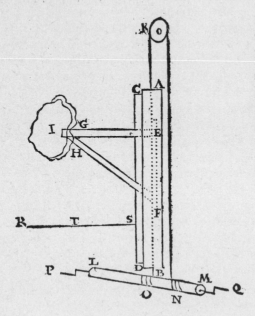

Figure 6 Cloud descent at the side of the stage. Sabbattini.
ABCD are the two sides of the groove, EFG the arm for the cloud (I) in the groove. FO is a rope to lower cloud when windlass is wound to the right. EKN is the rope to raise cloud when the windlass is wound to the left. A similar principle was used for shifting side wings on and off the stage, the capstan being in the centre, below the stage itself. For the effect cf. Plate 24 (*The British Library*)

supported in its turn the pulleys from which the trapeze or belt could descend towards the stage.

The pulley systems for such descents were of varying complexity. The simplest was the cloud-machine or 'glory'. A 'glory' was a platform that would make a vertical descent from above the stage, and was frequently found in the Court masques of the Caroline period. It was large enough to contain one or more people, and had its own proscenium, usually a circlet of clouds, within which the apparitions sat, backed by a diminishing cloud-perspective (Figure 7). It was lowered by ropes from pulleys in the flies. The operation of the trapezes for solo flying was more elaborate. They possessed at least a double mechanism, and required some sort of counterweighting if they were to be fully effective. A capstan at one side of the stage ran a rope across to the truck at the other. If this were on the left, the truck would travel from right to left as it was wound in. With a counterweight on the right-hand side of the stage, it would be possible to release the brake on the capstan and allow the truck to travel back to the right. The spirits or devils on the trapeze below would thus fly backwards and forwards across the stage. For vertical movement, another mechanism was required. A rope or ropes bearing the trapeze ran through the truck from a capstan at one side of the stage. By coordinating the two systems a variety of aerial movement becomes possible. The spirit can descend at any point at which the truck stops on its journey across the stage, but even more magically, it can fly down or up on a diagonal track, when the trapeze is raised or lowered as the truck travels

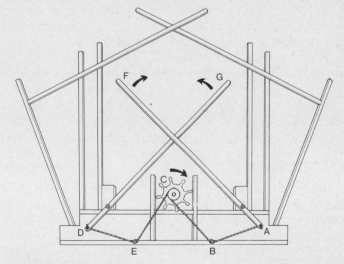

Figure 7   A machine for opening a Glory.
The frame is faced with clouds. When a windlass is wound clockwise, the frame opens at AF/GD. (*Drawing by Lesley Skeates after a sketch in the Nationalmuseum, Stockholm*)

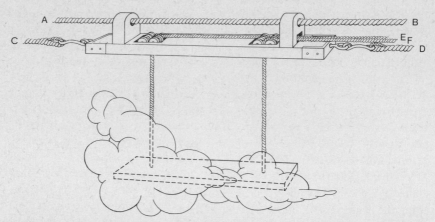

Figure 8   A flying track with vertical, lateral and diagonal movement. The heavy rope
AB supports the wooden car. If the rope CD is pulled right or left the car runs laterally
in the given direction. If the ropes EF are let out the trapeze is lowered. If they are taken
in, it is raised. If the car is pulled across while the trapeze is raised or lowered, a
diagonal track is achieved. (*Drawing by Lesley Skeates after machinery in the Court Theatre,
Drottningholm and plates in Diderot's* Encyclopedia)

across the stage (Figure 8). If two such tracks are used together, spirits
on the ground at either side of the stage can rise suddenly, 'crossing in
the air', to disappear aloft at opposite sides of the stage. The two Devils
in the masque from *The Empress of Morocco* may be flying out after such
a manoeuvre, which was a favourite with audiences at the time. The co-
ordination of such movements was clearly a tricky business, and the stage
crews must have been very skilled, for the elaboration of such effects in
important scenes is as astonishing as it is exciting.

The scenes and machines of the Restoration stage were matter for great
wonder and delight, and the theatres competed with each other in
displaying them. Even Dryden, scornful as he liked to be of such empty
shows, incorporated them in his plays with considerable skill and elegance. Their transformations and magical defiance of human limitations
provided a play of fancy that counterpointed the intellectual astringency
of the plays' construction, and, in tragedy, the superhuman ideals of the
protagonists. This magic was usually enhanced by the use of music, which
added aural to visual splendour and conveniently covered the natural
creaking of the ropes and wires. The result was a magnificent interaction
of sound and vision, which is typically baroque in its blending of music
and machines, songs and dances, to evoke a sensuous fantasy to astonish
the mind. But for all its sensationalism, baroque art has another dimension. It operates by 'extreme contrasts woven together by the style of the
artist into an organic whole',[9] and yet the appreciation of that whole
becomes a game for the intellect, an exercise in wit as well as in fancy;

the juxtaposition of spectacular images builds its own design, its own vision of moral order. The images form a pattern of feeling that is itself accessible to the understanding.

In the early 1670s, the Duke's Company began to exploit the resources of the spectacular Dorset Garden stage with a series of musical and dramatic spectacles. Not to be outdone, the King's Company, as well as burlesquing the genre, attempted the staging of a genuine opera in the French tradition, and presented *Ariane, ou le mariage de Bacchus* in *their* new theatre. It was published in both French and English, emulating the printed libretti of the rival company, and given a showy frontispiece (Plate 17). This depicts the scene of the Prologue, in which the rivers of Europe come to London to praise Charles and his Court. They rise one by one from the waters of Thames (London Bridge can be seen in the background), and sing from their chariots. The Seine praises the Court because valour rules there, the Tiber because justice rules there, the Thames itself because love rules there, and finally comes the river Po to celebrate a royal alliance.[10] The scene has all the absolutism of European high baroque art, but in fact it simply provides the occasion for a more secular celebration in which the arts of valour, justice and love come together in the marriage of a hero.

The opera itself provides just the kind of fanciful, classical allegory so popular in seventeenth-century painting. Bacchus is a hero and conqueror, the darling of Mars and Bellona. Venus and Euphrosyne determine to subject him to the pangs of love. He sees Ariadne and is enraptured, but she has been deserted by Theseus and will not trust to love again. Mars tries to wean him back to war with the full assistance of drums and trumpets, but Venus gives her girdle to Ariadne to assure the continuance of love. The Graces tie it about her waist, and she consents. The final act celebrates the marriage.

This is a straightforward enough design, but it is wound about with a whole galaxy of enchanting and complementary images in action, dance and music, and each act assembles them by law of variation and contrast about the next strand in the main design, culminating in danced intermezzi. The piece is a series of divertissements linked by a central theme. There is a pastoral sub-plot, accompanied by recorders, in which the shepherd Damon, rejected by Chloris and Philis, tries to forswear love, but fails to do so. There are a swarm of contrasted allegorical figures – Thetis, Megaera, Bellona – with their respective Waves, Furies or Soldiers in attendance. And Bacchus has two differentiated choruses to accompany him – the Corybantes, whose music is dominated by hautboys, and the comic Silenes. The latter have a sub-plot of their own. When Bacchus resolves to marry, his drinking companions are in despair and lament his loss to the bottle. They bury their bottle in a tomb, and cover it with cypress boughs. Venus, however, consoles them, and Euphrosyne informs them that love and wine are not incompatible. The bottle is resurrected in triumph and placed on a 'Throne made of Green Turff strowed with flowers'. The Satyrs dance about it, and then, 'the Triumph ending, a small Cloud comes down from above that steals away their Bottle up into Heaven, leaving the Satyrs gazing with admiration.'[11] The delicacy and ingenuity of the contrasts is delightful (starting with the careful orchestration of the Shepherds, Corybantes and Soldiers), and dominates the architecture of each act. In this way, each step of Bacchus' progress is given its varied inflections to his final apotheosis (neatly anticipated by that of the Bottle) as he ascends in a radiant palace, leaving the clowns dancing below.

Ariane was not a success. The English did not take to baroque opera, in spite of the managers' repeated attempts at it. When Davenant first revived his operas at the Restoration, the scenes were much admired, but the presentation of the story, expressed, as he put it, 'in vocall and instrumental musick',[12] fell oddly on English ears. In the French and Italian operas of the period, as in *Ariane*, the whole piece is sung, including dialogue passages. These are declaimed, with various accompaniments to fill in the harmony, in a free rhythm that is responsive to the words, while the airs are more elaborately vocalised and accompanied, and focus climaxes of feeling as they occur during the action. This continuous flow of music is frequently enlivened in the French operas of the time, as in *Ariane* by extended movements for dancing. The English clearly enjoyed the sensuous elements of song and dance; but the declamation or 'Recitative Musick' appeared absurd. Gildon, writing in the early eighteenth century, quotes Saint-Évremond on the matter:[13]

Can any Man persuade his Imagination, that a Master calls his Servant, or sends him on an errand *singing*? That one Friend communicates a secret to another *singing*? That Politicians deliberate in Council *singing*? And that Men are *melodiously kill'd with Sword, Pike and Musket*?

The English could not so persuade themselves, and since the catalogue covers almost every activity required of the characters of *The Siege of Rhodes*, Davenant found himself obliged to omit the sung dialogue at the Restoration and substitute a spoken text. The result of this attitude was that music in the English theatre came to provide moments of entertainment or of heightened feeling interspersed in the course of an ordinary play and was not admitted to a central part in the conduct of the drama. The action of the second part of *The Siege of Rhodes* is carried on entirely in spoken dialogue. What began as music-drama becomes simply a play with music, and it is as plays with music that Davenant continued with his operatic and scenic experiments.

There is a problem implicit in this attitude that is crucial for Restoration dramaturgy. Dryden pinpoints it in his Prologue to his own first real attempt at opera, *Albion and Albanius*:[14]

> Some hopeful Youths there are, of callow Wit,
> Who may one day be Men, if Heav'n think fit;
> Sound may serve such, ere they to Sense are grown;
> Like leading strings, till they can walk alone.

The power of music to convey emotion is a snare and a delusion. It tickles the fancy, but does not address the mature understanding. Meaning escapes it and so, in employing it, the dramatist had the problem of harnessing this enchantment so as to maximise its sensuous impact while minimising the distraction caused to the clear stream of his design. In short, he had to attempt to make music rational, to create areas of the drama where music could be employed in such a way that the presence of song was not absurd in action, and the presence of emotion did not lead to a loss of sense.

With the solo song this was not too hard. *Marriage à la Mode* begins with the entry of Doralice and Beliza. Doralice says:[15]

Beliza, bring the Lute into this Arbor, the Walks are empty; I would try the Song the Princess *Amalthea* bad me learn.

(*They go in, and sing.*)

The excuse is palpable, but it accomplishes the necessary rationale: songs may be introduced when people might naturally sing them, or call for them to be sung. The reasonableness, however, disguises a considerable complexity of function. Doralice sings:

> Why should a foolish Marriage Vow
>   Which long ago was made,
> Oblige us to each other now
>   When Passion is decay'd?
> We lov'd, and we lov'd as long as we cou'd,
> Till our Love was lov'd out in us both:
> But our Marriage is dead, when the Pleasure is fled:
> 'Twas Pleasure first made it an Oath.

This level-headed attitude to life and love is the core of the action, the 'idea' of the singer's situation as we are to see it unfold in the play. As the lady sings, young Palamede enters and 'hears the song':

> If I have pleasures for a Friend,
>   And farther love in store,
> What wrong has he whose joys did end,
>   And who cou'd give no more?
> 'Tis a madness that he should be jealous of me,

> Or that I shou'd bar him of another:
> For all we can gain, is to give ourselves pain,
> When neither can hinder the other.

This second verse carries the idea a step further, and introduces us to the design of the first action of the play at the moment when the young man who is to carry it through makes his appearance. The wiles of music are not simply excused but are employed to announce the shape and significance of what is to follow. Doralice sings from an arbour. Her absence may have been because the actress could not sing, but it has a useful function anyway. It focuses attention on the meaning of the song and the action of the listener, rather than upon the art or personality of the singer. It is a kind of 'voice-over' effect, which was extremely popular, and effectively employs the emotional medium of music as part of that intellectual dialogue with the audience that was basic to the performance. It is a juxtaposition of significant images for ear, eye and mind.[16] Another singer may have sung the song from the wings; but it is just as likely that the separation was complete and that it was in fact sung from the gallery above the stage where the instrumental musicians were located, as shown in the engravings of the Dorset Garden (Plates 10 to 12).[17] The Restoration dramatists use song in a way similar to Brecht: not simply to create moods, but to reflect ideas. Palamede's mime, as he listens to the sentiments of the free-thinking lady, articulates his response to the idea, while the female voice and the male presence create a witty image of the forthcoming action. Only one thing may perhaps be thought of later on: the stern virtues of the Princess Amalthea would hardly have drawn this song to the attention of a young married woman.

The incidental music which was so much a part of Restoration performances also assisted the detached dialogue of stage and auditorium. The concert before the show probably consisted of popular medleys, since none of the extant performance music is sufficiently extensive for the reported 'concerts'; but specially written pieces often preceded the Prologue and were played at beginnings and ends of acts. Such pieces are usually in the dance forms of the period, which with their simple binary and ternary structures and traditional rhythms provide sharply etched and contrasted mood pictures. In his incidental music for *The Tempest*, Locke provides a vigorous Rustick Air for the entrance of the comics at the beginning of Act II, a stately Minuet for the scene between Prospero and Miranda that opens Act III, a Corant for Act IV and a curious 'Martial Jigge', half-heroic and half parodistical, to precede the scraps and disorders of Act V. The music provides a series of gestures in sound that prepare the action and emphasise its design and orderly division into five acts.[18] These pieces are probably the more important in that the brief intervals between the acts were sometimes filled with comic turns of small

10. (Above left) *The Empress of Morocco*.
    A Prison. The British Library.

11. (Above right) *The Empress of Morocco*.
    A Prospect of a River. The British
    Library.

12. (Left) *The Empress of Morocco*. The
    Gaunches. The British Library.

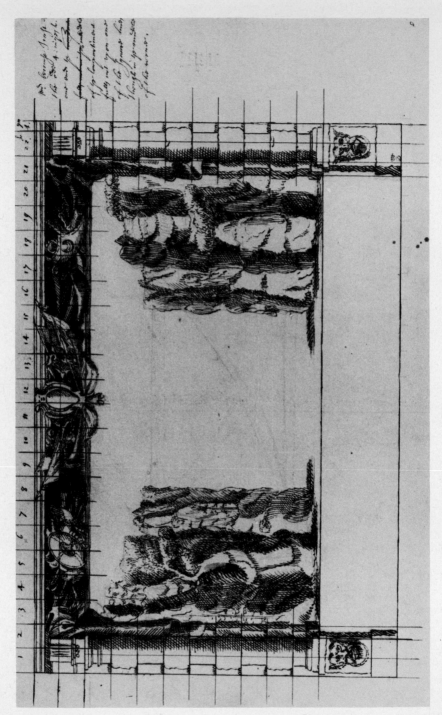

13. *The Siege of Rhodes*. Frontispiece and wings. Webb. The Trustees of the Chatsworth Settlement.

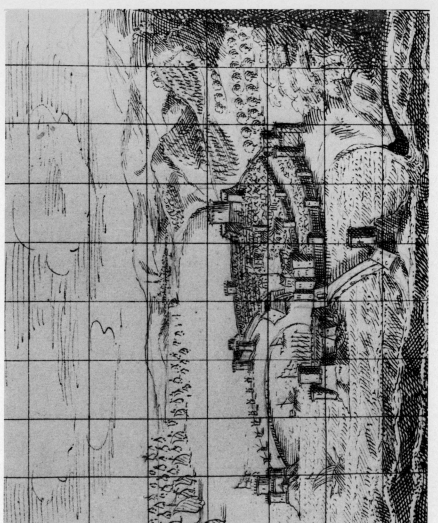

14. *The Siege of Rhodes*. Design for shutters. Webb. The Trustees of the Chatsworth Settlement.

15. *The Siege of Rhodes*. Scene of 'relieve'. Webb. The Trustees of the Chatsworth Settlement.

16. A section of a theatre. Wren. Courtesy of the Warden and Fellows of All Souls College, Oxford.

17. *Ariane*. Frontispiece, showing Wren's proscenium. The British Library.

18. *The Empress of Morocco*. The
    Masque of Pluto. The British
    Library.

19. *The Empress of Morocco*.
    Moorish Dance. The British
    Library.

20. *Wit at Several Weapons*. Tonson's Beaumont and Fletcher, 1710. The British Library.

relevance to the play itself. The Jacobean and Caroline theatres had given jigs (narrative and character dances, almost small musical farces) during and after performances, and the Restoration saw a gradual growth of such entertainment.[19] Davenant's early shows had contained spots for tumblers and 'Somersautes', and Charles was said to have been first attracted to Nell Gwyn on seeing her dance a jig. Dances were given between the acts of Betterton's *Hamlet* in the 1670s, and Cibber refers rather scathingly to the old practice of 'brightening the audience with a dance between the acts' (p. 264). We are likely to agree with him if we do not remember the detached excitement of Restoration audiences. In such a context a jig during *Hamlet* was probably less distracting than the fight for a stiff gin in the interval in the darkened theatres of today. The Act Tune was there to bring the audience back to the business in hand.

In this rational atmosphere the fully affective uses of music and dance had to be carefully placed and justified. The justification was found in ceremonial, ritual and magic, and in the energetic gesticulations of farcical comedy. Court entertainment becomes a common excuse for sung masques like that in *The Empress of Morocco*, or smaller interludes that often echo the exotic settings of the plays in which they occur. Settle also managed to include a Moorish Dance '*presented by Moors in several Habits, who bring in an artificial Palm-tree, about which they dance to several antick Instruments of Musick*' (II, i.; Plate 19). Some of the exotic effect of this scene can be caught from a burlesque of it by Thomas Duffet, who devises[20]

> *a Heathen dance . . . presented by Tinkers and Jack-puddings, who bring in an artificial broad spreading broom about which they dance to Drumstick and Kettle, Tongs and Key, Moorish Timbrel and Salt-box, &c. . . .*

Restoration dancing was characterised by a confluence of traditions.[21] Besides the jigs, there were the old English country dances and songs, collected and published during the interregnum in Playford's *The English Dancing Master*. These could be used in various guises; most often as a festive conclusion to comedy. Then there were the new French social dances, sarabande, courante, minuet, that Charles and his courtiers had learned in exile, and which were taught to the actors by dancing-masters, and to the public by newly opened dancing-schools. The French dances gained a specifically theatrical extension, formalised with the founding of the Académie Royale de Musique et de Danse by Louis XIV in 1661. The Académie proceeded to lay down rules for the sort of dancing, analysing and noting steps and jumps, and, above all, the positions of the feet – the turn-out of the leg that was anatomically necessary for its high positions and to raise it above the hip-joint – which in the five true positions of the *danse noble* became the basis for elegant deportment. They also became the basis for the virtuoso art of professional dancing.

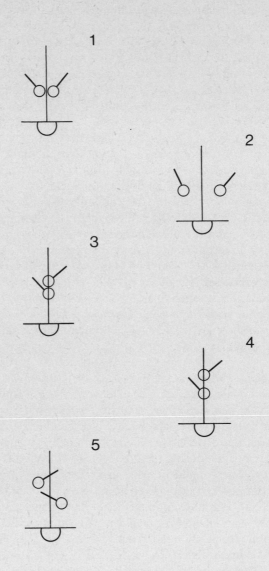

True Positions

Figure 9   The five positions of the feet for the *danse noble* (*After Feuillet*)

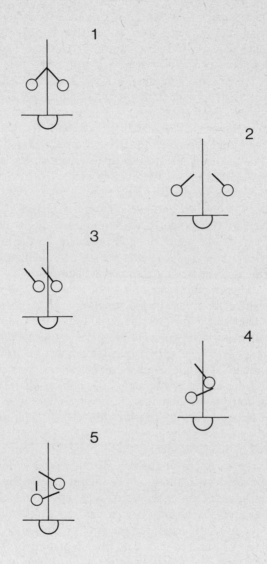

False Positions

Figure 10   The five 'false' positions

But five false positions were also defined, turning the toes in with an air of comic insufficiency as a basis for grotesque characters (Figures 9 and 10). Such dancing links the *danse noble* with the other crucial tradition, that of Italian dance and mime exported to the rest of Europe by the touring companies of the *commedia dell'arte*, who made a home in Paris and visited London on a number of occasions.[22] The flamboyant movement of these masked comedians, with their brilliant *lazzi* and juxtaposition of slapstick, acrobatics, and high comedy moved the old traditions of the comic mime into a new tradition of character dancing.

These dance-traditions created together a rich texture of movement for the stage that is nicely illustrated in the frontispiece to *Wit at Several Weapons* by Beaumont and Fletcher (Plate 20). The danced part of the masques gave opportunity for contrasted sequences of movement, as in the interludes of *Ariane*, and the juxtaposed images of the old masque and anti-masque were perpetuated by the interlinking of these traditions. The last act of *Ariane* is full of such contrasts. In the midst of the noble wedding celebrations, rustics bring presents to the happy couple; but the Silenes torment them by 'Turning their Sausages to Eels and their Eggs to Froggs'. This is pure *commedia* – the same kind of trick that Otway creates for the actor Leigh in his adaptation of Molière's *Les Fourberies de Scapin*. The same principles can be found in the contrasted movement sequences of many comedies. Etherege's *Love in a Tub* is a particularly good example. Here the sprightly masquerades of Sir Frederick Frolic and his retainers are contrasted with the farcical prancing of the comic servants and the heroic posturing of the nobles, characterising different kinds of action by different styles of movement, the bumbling 'false' postions of farce continually mocking the elegant bearing of the idealised gentry.[23]

Such masque-like episodes as these, serious or comic as the case may be, are clearly intended for the role of intermezzi within the play itself; but it was really only in those scenes that employed the apparatus of the supernatural that the full richness of stage effect and musical splendour could find excuse. Davenant in particular had a sense of such things. He not only elaborated and extended the witch scenes in *Macbeth* but greatly developed the musical episodes in his adaptation of *The Tempest*, and even added a dance of angels around the death-bed of Queen Catherine in *Henry VIII*, which contributed much to the success of that entertainment. The other theatre was not to be outdone. Dryden illuminated his tragedies in particular with touches of exotic enchantment. In *Tyrannick Love*, Nigrinus summons spirits to seduce St Catherine, in a scene that deploys a number of resources. The spirits descend in the clouds and sing. The clouds part. One flies up, the other down. St Catherine is raised through a trap, in her bed, and the scene is changed to a paradise, which was painted specially by Isaac Fuller, and a court of law valued his work at no less than £335.10s.[24] Finally, St Catherine's Guardian Angel '*descends to Soft Musick*, with a flaming Sword', and sends the evil spirits away. Dryden's scene is really a miniature opera. Music and spectacle act together as strongly affective elements, raising wonder and delight in the hearts of the spectators; but all this is still controlled by the design: the scene projects the heroine's moral struggle into a pleasing allegory.

Such operatic excursions were admissible because the subject was, as Dryden put it, extended 'beyond the limits of human nature'. Under these circumstances 'human impossibilities are to be received as they are in faith; because where Gods are introduced, a supreme power is to be understood, and second causes are out of doors.'[25] In such spectacles as these, the period was able, at last, to go beyond reason, specious as their reasons were, musical and spectacular elements being introduced rationally or semi-rationally within the action of ordinary dramas. It is a hybrid form; but it has immense significance. The musical scenes are devised to form an amalgamated logic of thought and feeling which produces a sensuous enrichment of the idea through an interplay of mood and emotion.

The Restoration used the affective devices of music, machinery and scenic spectacle to complement one another and the design of the whole. The objectivity that made such detachment possible was implicit in the organisation of the stage itself. The Wren drawing (Plate 16) shows a fore-stage of 20 feet between the audience and the proscenium, to which entry can be obtained from two doors on each side. This effectively meant that any actor playing within the scene, that is behind the proscenium arch, was at least that distance from the nearest member of his audience. The effect of such a distance would, of course, depend on the height of the proscenium in relation to that of the galleries; but it would also be dependent on the sightlines from the side-boxes as the stage deepens. These are, to say the least of it, poor, and it is significant that Cibber remarked that when the patentee removed half the fore-stage in the 1690s in order to get more people into the pit, the resulting relationship with the audience was weaker both in the actors' ability to dominate the house, and in the impressiveness of the scenes themselves.[26] It was necessary for the actors to come as close as possible to the audience in order to preserve the intimacy of their performances, hence the doors to give them a direct access; but it was also helpful to the illusion of the scenes that they were at a distance and separated from the house. Implicit in this dialogue of stage and fore-stage lies one of the major problems of Restoration stagecraft.

In Shadwell's *The Virtuoso* (II.ii), Sir Nicholas Gimcrack is discovered '*learning to swim upon a table*'. If he were so discovered in a theatre built according to the Wren drawing, he would be behind the shutters, 40 feet or so from the front row. Now the other actors are given an opportunity to come forward on to the fore-stage and make their comments to the audience, but these would surely lose their effect if Sir Nicholas remained so remote. He needs to be much nearer if the audience is to get the benefit of his antics:[27]

> Ah! well struck, *Sir Nicholas*; that was admirable; that was as well swum as any man in *England* can. Observe the Frog. Draw up your Arms a little nearer, and then thrust 'em out strongly – Gather up your Legs a little more – So, very well – Incomparable –

The swimming-master's exclamations each suggest attempts on the part of his pupil that must be seen, and dialogue is also involved:

LONGVIL: Have you ever tri'd in the Water, Sir?

SIR NICHOLAS: No, Sir; but I swim most exquisitely on Land.

BRUCE: Do you intend to practise in the Water, Sir?

SIR NICHOLAS: Never, Sir; I hate the Water, I never come upon the Water, Sir.

LONGVIL: Then there will be no use of Swimming.

SIR NICHOLAS: I content myself with the Speculative Part of Swimming; I care not for the practick.

The combination of politeness and irony is not built for distance. Sir Nicholas needs to be discovered – and as near the audience as possible.

Richard Southern solved this problem with a theory of 'dispersed' shutters.[28] This allows for a single pair of shutters at each wing position, and would certainly be handy; but the front shutters would then be about 15 feet by 20 feet, very unwieldy, and impossible to draw off into the wings. To counter the difficulty, Edward Langhans proposed an arrangement with shutters at the third and sixth positions, and John Spring proposed to reduce the probable width of the proscenium arch to make shutters immediately behind the curtain possible.[29] The measurements of the Dorset Garden theatre are so conjectural that it is not easy to make a judgment, but it does seem likely that a compromise is necessary. The third shutter seems still too far away, the proscenium position ideal, but to narrow the acting area undesirably. Shutters at the second wing position and at the fourth, however, with a deep scene beyond and with a stage width only slightly narrower than that suggested by Langhans, would allow more intimate work to be performed near enough to the audience and still have the possibility of a discovery, preserving the deep stage for spectacular and operatic effects where appropriate.

The effect of such an arrangement would be highly characteristic. The scenic illusion is not an environment for the actors, as in the modern theatre: it is simply a background for them – an effect clearly to be observed in Plates 27, 28 and 29. When actions do appear within the scene, they are either presented to the audience as a framed 'gesture', as is Sir Nicholas Gimcrack, or gain from the distance a remote and dreamy quality which can enhance the magic of the spectacle. The apparitions in Davenant's *Macbeth* may well have appeared behind their tiffany gauze at the front of the deep-scene itself (Plate 31).

The distance of the scenes from the audience and the natural gravitation of the actor to the fore-stage created a role for the scenery that the authors much enjoyed, particularly in juxtaposition with discovered tableaux or other stage action. They compete with the scenic effects, matching trick with word. The scene of the ships in *The Empress of Morocco* is accompanied by an extended description of the fleet sailing homeward[30] as they

in a solemn and triumphant pride,
Their course up the great River *Tensist* guide.

The language duplicates the scene, as it does also in Lee's *The Rival Queens*, where an elaborate series of portents is 'described' both by the set and the characters. A fine elaboration of effect can be achieved in this way. In Act IV of *Lucius Junius Brutus*, also by Lee, conspirators on the stage prepare the slaves for a human sacrifice. Then 'The *Scene draws, showing the Sacrifice; One Burning, the other Crucify'd: the Priests coming forward with Goblets in their hands, fill'd with human blood.*'[31] The rite and the discovery presumably occupy the shallow and middle stages, with the sacrifices in the deep-scene and some actors forward on the fore-stage; while all the time, with truly baroque juxtaposition, the comedian Nokes comments on the horrors '*from a window*' above one of the fore-stage doors.[32] His words form a series of 'captions' for the action, bringing out the anti-catholic innuendos in the conduct of the priests and presenting it for the audience's contemporary disapproval.

For all its elaborate illusion – and Wren appears to have tried to increase this in his theatre by creating a false perspective even in the auditorium, articulated by the pillars of the galleries – the Restoration playhouse preserved a presentational ambience. Glynne Wickham and Richard Southern both noted that the scenic effects of the Restoration theatre were in the emblematic tradition of the Elizabethan stage, for all their grander scale.[33] It therefore seemed quite logical, in *The Siege of Rhodes*, not only that the besieging Turks should be present on the back-shutters well before they are announced, but that a background representing the city besieged should form the setting for scenes both in the city and outside. The scenery presents the idea of the action as much as its location. This is, of course, entirely consistent with the detached attitude the audience held to dramatic fiction, and its effectiveness was enhanced by three further aspects of production practice: the lighting, the costumes and the use of stock scenery.

The fore-stage was illuminated by chandeliers hanging above it, and by light spilling from the brackets around the auditorium. It is unlikely there were footlights.[34] The scenes were lit by candles fixed in vertical rows behind each wing position. As a consequence of these arrangements the focus on the fore-stage was naturally heightened, while the effect of separation between fore-stage and scene would be made more striking by the different qualities of illumination in the two areas.

Such lighting was, of course, constant, and because of the difficulty of varying its intensity, the imitation of different kinds of light, the contrast between day and night, for instance, had to be effected by other means. It became the property of the scene-painter. For Act V of *2 The Siege of Rhodes*, Davenant presented 'A prospect of Rhodes by night, and the Grand Master's palace on Fire' (p. 351). This effect would have been simply painted on the back shutters, contrasting the dark tints of the night sky with an ebulliently flaming palace. When the King's Company revived Fletcher's *The Island Princess* in an attempt to win audiences from the other company, a spectacular presentation of a city in flames was one of the attractions of the new production. Tonson's Beaumont and Fletcher of 1710 very possibly shows how it was done – a painted shutter of the disaster in action before which the actors could play their scenes (Plate 27).[35] The graphic presentation was, in fact, a kind of witticism – a juxtaposition of reality and illusion, emphasised by the presence of the turbulent crowd at the bottom of the picture. As in *The Siege of Rhodes*, the action was not left only to supers, but given an added dimension by the presence of painted figures.

Again, the piquant artificiality of the juxtaposition of moving actors and a static, or emblematic crowd pleased rather than disturbed the audience, as did the pictorial presentation of a change of light. In Act IV of Dryden's *Amboyna*, the scene is a dark wood, and by and by the moon glimmers through the trees. Moonlit scenes were painted in blue, night colours, but such mobility of light was not generally available at the time: either the wood scene was already painted with the glimmering moon, or the actor suggested it by his action; in either case, the lighting itself did not alter.[36] In fact, the miming of darkness and its comic consequences, a commedia tradition, was particularly enjoyed, for the wit of seeing those who cannot see.[37] The old Elizabethan tradition was still observed. A daylight street becomes a night street by the carrying of a torch, a daylight room a night room by the lighting of a candle – so night is coming when Margery lights a candle to write a letter in the scene that has represented Pinchwife's lodging throughout *The Country Wife*, and by entering with a link-boy Alithea convinces us that though Covent Garden is painted bright as day night is in fact upon us.

With the same reasoning, it seemed unnecessary to go to the great

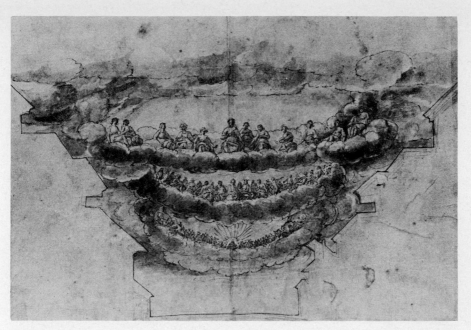

21. *Salmacida Spolia*. Design for the whole heaven (detail). Inigo Jones. The Trustees of the Chatsworth Settlement.

22. *Les Noces de Pélée et de Thétis*, Third Entry. Paris, 1654. Torelli. La Documentation Française.

23. *Les Noces de Pélée et de Thétis*. Prologue. Torelli. Kungliga Biblioteket, Stockholm.

24. *Les Noces de Pélée et de Thétis*. Act V. Torelli. Kungliga Biblioteket, Stockholm.

25. *Salmacida Spolia*. The Storm. Inigo Jones. The Trustees of the Chatsworth Settlement.

26. *La Finta Pazza*. Cypress Walks. Torelli. Paris, 1645. Nationalmuseum, Stockholm.

27. (Above left) *The Island Princess*.
Frontispiece. Tonson's Beaumont and
Fletcher. The British Library.

28. (Above right) *Love's Cure*.
Frontispiece. Tonson's Beaumont and
Fletcher. The British Library.

29. (Left) *Measure for Measure*.
Frontispiece. Rowe's Shakespeare.
1709. The British Library.

expense of producing new scenes for every play. The formulae of tragedy and comedy played games with the same locations – palaces, city walls, tombs, temples, prisons, in the one; lodgings, streets, gardens, in the other; rural prospects, groves, forests, and deserts in both.[38] All these would do duty in almost any play, and could be trotted out as necessary, while cloud-wings and cloud-borders could fill in any gaps. Even the wings might be left in place, as in *The Siege of Rhodes*, while shutters only altered; and certainly stock-wings could be employed in conjunction with special effects, as in *Albion and Albanius*, where a street of palaces leads to the Royal Exchange, or *Ariane*, where just such a street leads to old London Bridge (Plate 17).

Such combination and repetition inevitably emphasises the emblematic nature of each scene, and gives the presence of new effects in a sequence of stock pictures an interest that is important to the play's meaning as well as to its visual excitement. Davenant makes constant play with his 'Heath' scene in *Macbeth*, using its pictorial barrenness as an appropriate emblem of evil, and emphasising this by its rhythmic recurrence. He even brings Lady Macduff there to meet with her husband. The contrivance is not entirely happy. As the Lady remarks upon her entrance:[39]

> Art sure this is the place my Lord appointed
> Us to meet him?

To which her servant replies:

> This is the entrance o'th'Heath; and here
> He order'd me to attend him with the Chariot.

The excuse is palpable, but the Macduffs must encounter the witches and so clinch the contrast between them and the Macbeths. The visual presence of the scenery helps the audience to understand the play's pattern, and for this end abstract may take precedence over imitative truth.

This reasoning also explains the Restoration's curiously eclectic attitude to costume. Like the Elizabethans and Jacobeans, the Restoration actors wore basically contemporary dress in tragedy and comedy alike. This was added to or varied with a similarly emblematic logic. The characters of tragedy were nobler, so wore the grander clothes given by members of the aristocracy to the playhouses, adorned with high feathers on their heads and, for the women, long trains borne by attendants. But the basic wardrobe owned by the theatres was still near enough street-dress to require a rule docking actors of a week's salary if they wore their clothes out of the theatre.[40] These clothes did not change very much either, whether the location was London or Peru. The extras might wear exotic clothes for Indian dances or masques, but the principals rarely went further out of their way than to put on a turban instead of a peruke. Pepys said, of the opening of *Heraclius*, that it was done in habits 'like

Romans, very well'; but the Roman costumes were probably only adapted according to the baroque conventions of the period, as in the portrait of The Duke of York as Lord High Admiral, where James's heroism is symbolised by his Roman armour, but his wig and the fleet behind show that it is to modern times that his Roman virtue appertains (Plate 2).

To this end, details were picked out in the actor's costume to emphasise the 'idea' of the character and its contemporary relevance. Hamlet's father's ghost is armed cap à pied in a Renaissance style, but Hamlet himself and his mother appear in Restoration clothes, a Restoration Macbeth turns away from timelessly robed witches, and Henry VIII and Wolsey argue in front of a group of Restoration dandies (Plates 30, 31 and 32). Such disjunctions are of the same order as the presence of Dryden's Restoration gallants in the Court of Polydamas of Sicily. When Genest criticises Lee severely for anachronisms in his *Sophonisba*, he really misses the point. 'Sir, Madam and other improper expressions occur,' he says, 'particularly *Cards*.'[41] But as with Dryden, Lee is intending a similitude between ancient and modern. He is wanting the worlds to clash because he is using history as an emblem to throw modern behaviour into relief. Such ironies are part of the general pattern of incidental reference, the dialogue between fiction and contemporary life that was so crucial to the Restoration style. The comic irony that Duffet parodies in the frontispiece to his *Empress of Morocco* was intended by the original (Plate 9).

Music and spectacle on the Restoration stage operate in the same manner as the plays themselves. They provide similes for experience, clearly distinguished from life and illusion by their own artificiality as is an author's fiction. The actors appeared in front of the painted scenes, their disjunction from them undercutting the illusion of the stage as the writer's wit undercut the heroics of their plots. It is significant that when Brecht adapted *The Recruiting Officer*, he employed the same kind of disjunction for his own purposes, sharpening the artificiality of the action to point the question it raises by the juxtaposition of flesh and blood actors with a two-dimensional, painted scene (Plates 38 and 39).

The art of the Restoration stage is a baroque art. The baroque work invites you into it as does the Restoration prologue, and plays with feeling constantly; but this play of expression is controlled by a structure of ideas which is intended to be understood. The audience is excited by sensationalism; but this excitement is both intellectual and physical, it comes not only from the expression but from the conception of the work. The experience is shared through a shared perception of its idea, its truth.

The consequence of such an idea of a theatre is curious. The different elements of dramatic art, scenes, actors, music, give separate performances in their separate areas, controlled in their divergence by the author's overall design, the plan of his experiment, only rarely, at climaxes, coming together to incarnate his idea. When Dryden and Davenant adapted Shakespeare's *The Tempest*, in 1668, they exploited this interrelationship and independence of dramatic elements to the full. They deployed the new, detached, intellectual style with clarity and vigour, touching it with song, fancy and spectacle, and, when Betterton revived the piece in 1674, he built up the elements of sensuous excitement, but preserved and enhanced the play's design. The result was an entertainment both intimate and extravagant, 'all things perform'd in it so Admirably well, that not any succeeding Opera got more Money.'[42] *The Tempest* is in fact a classic example of Restoration style in action.

4 · *The Tempest, or The Enchanted Island*

The curtain, flying up,[1]

> *discovers a new Frontispiece, joyn'd to the great Pylasters, on each side of the Stage. This Frontispiece is a noble Arch, supported by large wreathed Columns of the* Corinthian *Order; the Wreathings of the Columns are beautify'd with Roses wound round them, and several* Cupids *flying about them. On the Cornice, just over the Capitals, sits on either side a Figure, with a Trumpet in one Hand, and a Palm in the other, representing* Fame. *A little farther on the same Cornice, on each side of a Compass-pediment, lie a Lion and a Unicorn, the Supporters of the Royal Arms of* England. *In the middle of the Arch are several Angels, holding the King's Arms, as if they were placing them in the midst of that Compass-pediment.*

The opening of *The Tempest* at the Dorset Garden on the afternoon of 30 April 1674 was manifestly a royal occasion. The new frontispiece, similar to those of *The Siege of Rhodes* and the masques at Court, was in the first place a spectacular piece of baroque painting, creating on its flat surface a sense of airy spaces by the movements of the cupids and angels. But this pictorial extravagance was also significant politically. The king's own arms are supported by the lion and unicorn of England and given divine sanction by the angels. It is obviously intended to frame the whole performance with a gesture of loyal deference.

For this splendid revival Dryden's play had been made into an opera by Thomas Shadwell.[2] For the music, the management had followed the advice of their founder and 'the most transcendent in that art in England'[3] had been engaged to compose and play it. John Bannister's songs were retained from the earlier production, but there were many important additions. Special incidental music had been composed by Matthew Locke, new dances by Giovanni Battista Draghi, master of the queen's music, and more and more elaborate masques by Pelham Humfrey, who had trained as a composer in France and had recently been made master of the children of the Chapel Royal. There were also additional numbers by Pietro Reggio, Shadwell's friend and music-master, and the amateur composer, James Hart.[4] All this was to be performed by the king's twenty four violins augmented by other instruments, and the masques to be sung by the gentlemen of the Chapel Royal, who were to be permitted, during the weeks of performance, to remain in London and not return to their duties at Windsor until the week-ends.[5] An even greater importance was lent to this aspect of the performance, too, by a change in the seating of the orchestra. Instead of playing from the gallery, the front of the stage was opened and '*the Band of 24 Violins, with the Harpsicals and Theorboes which accompany the Voices*' were placed between the pit and the stage.

The full and sonorous effect of such an assembly of instruments would have delighted the ears of the audience with the opening of Locke's 'First Music'. This consisted of an Introduction and two dances, and the noble harmonies of the opening carried by strings supported by the continuo instruments must have provided a riveting contrast to the popular medleys that had gone before. The Introduction is a beautiful, and original movement, with a curious and heart-catching single contrast of soft and 'Lowd' near its beginning, the ensuing Galliard is made pleasantly piquant by its uneven phrase-lengths, and the sequence closes with a sprightly Gavotte. With his first three musical gestures Locke has brilliantly suggested a scale of moods, from the grand to the comic and light-hearted, which is entirely proper to the experience that is to follow.

After the chandeliers had been lighted on the fore-stage, the Second Musick began. Only two pieces, this time, a beautiful, touchingly mournful Saraband, creating yet another mood, abruptly set off by a vigorous dance movement, oddly entitled Lilk, whose strong accents gather the excitement, and the sudden ending of which, with two accented quavers on the last beat of the bar, would give the actor tremendous impulse as he strides onto the fore-stage to start his Prologue on the first beat of the following bar, which the orchestra never plays:[6]

> Wee, as the ffathers of the Stage have said,
> To treat you here a vast expense have made;
> What they have gott from you in chests is laid,
> Or is for purchas'd Lands, or houses paid,
> You, in this house, all our estate may find,
> Wch for your pleasures wholly are designed.

With their display of Royal bounty in the orchestra pit, and Locke's splendid opening music, the Duke's Company start their part of the entertainment with an act of open war against the other theatre. Shadwell provides a commentary on Dryden's famous Prologue for the opening of the new Theatre Royal (see above p. 10). The Dorset Garden's show is a projection of the players' generosity – the Theatre Royal's plainness a projection of the company's meanness. The other company is old and impotent – Killigrew took the older actors and the best older plays. Their company is vigorous, youthful and original. Finally, he tries to turn aside Dryden's accusations of the triviality of show. It is not witless, but a new form of wit with all the *joie-de-vivre* of the young in heart:

> With the best Poets heads our house we grac'd
> Wch we in honour to ye Poet's plac'd.
> Too much of the old witt they have, 'tis true:
> But they must look for little of the new.

It is a splendidly contentious piece of writing, beautifully calculated to rouse the audience's participation in its argument while neatly vindicating their taste. The king's presence in the theatre clinches the matter. It was Charles who sent Betterton to France to research the elaborate scenery of the new theatre, so the splendour of the performance becomes an image of the splendour of the monarch and of the nation, a reflection of the greatness of king and kingdom. It is also a way of implicitly asserting the Divine Right of pleasure and of art.

The curtain rose to one of the most original pieces in the opera – Locke's brilliant and evocative Curtain Time. Over a series of intense harmonies above a falling bass-line, the violins seem to rise from nothing in slow suspensions. The middle parts move into a wavelike motion which gradually quickens. The effect is strange and stormy, though quiet – at once tranquil and threatening. The rhythm sharpens suddenly, and Locke notes 'lowder by degrees' (this is probably the first marked crescendo in music). Flurrying scales stir up the music still further, and the sound grows to a violent climax and suddenly is quiet again, like the distant rumble of the storm. Again with extraordinary suddenness, the music bursts out anew, with hammering repeated notes in the violins, and again subsides into tranquillity. The little movement lasted barely two minutes, but has set the heavy atmosphere of the on-coming storm, in a piece of graphic description.

Shakespeare began in the middle of his storm. In accordance with the longer lead up to the performance, the Restoration adaptors take their time. The dialogue starts quietly, with the entrance of two mariners, Mustacho and Ventoso, closely followed by Trincalo, who has become the Bosun in Davenant's version, and Stephano, promoted to the Ship's Master.

VENTOSO: What a Sea comes in?
MUSTACHO: A hoaming Sea! We shall have foul weather.
Enter Trincalo
TRINCALO: The Scud comes against the Wind, 'twill blow hard.
Enter Stephano
STEPHANO: Bosun!

TRINCALO: Here, Master, what say you?
STEPHANO: Ill weather! Let's off to Sea.
TRINCALO: Let's have Sea-room enough, and then let them blow the
Devil's head off. (I.i.1–8)

And so, with a call to the cabin-boy Stephano sets in motion the ship's
seaward manoeuvres and commences the brilliant crescendo of noise and
movement which gets the drama under way.

The general effect of this crescendo is given in Shadwell's opening
stage direction. The scene represents

*a thick Cloudy Sky, a very Rocky Coast, and a tempestuous Sea in
perpetual Agitation. This Tempest (suppos'd to be rais'd by Magick) has
many dreadful Objects in it, as several Spirits in horrid Shapes, flying
down amongst the Sailors, then rising and crossing in the Air. And when
the Ship is sinking, the whole House is darken'd, and a Shower of Fire
falls upon 'em. This is accompanied with Lightening and several Claps
of Thunder to the End of the Storm.* (p. 117)

Obviously all the flying machinery described in the previous chapter is
gradually brought into play. It seems from the other requirements of the
opera that there must have been four fly-tracks available for its conduct.
The interaction of the four figures moving vertically, laterally and diagon-
ally in carefully co-ordinated manoeuvres must have been very spectacular
as set against the increasingly anxious movements of the sailors, passing
backwards and forwards across the stage with the implements of their
work, and accompanied by shouts and screams off stage, and finally by
rhythmic chanting as they all pull together on a great rope to cries of
'Haul catt, Haull catt!' The scene was punctuated throughout by blasts
on the Bosun's whistle.[7]

The movements of these sailors and the spirits were extremely
important to the general effect of the scene. The ship, it will be noticed,
is not mentioned by the author as being represented on the stage. Its
presence had to be suggested by the miming of the actors. The scene
itself, of a rocky coast, was probably similar to that devised by Inigo
Jones for the opening of the masque *Salmacida Spolia* (Plate 25). Here
there is in fact a ship on the waters, and such a thing would be perfectly
possible in the emblematic tradition of *The Siege of Rhodes*, and may be
implied by the reference to '*when the ship is sinking.*' In any case, the
action of the scene would be played in the main on the fore-stage. This
would act, as it were, as the deck of the ship, looking out to sea beyond.
Here, Stephano and Trincalo give their orders, and the courtiers curse
and complain, enabling Gonzalo's asides ('I have great Comfort from this
Fellow; methinks his Complexion is perfect Gallows') to be given directly
to the audience, establishing a certain objectivity even amid the excitement. The sailors' activities, however, would have to move between fore-

stage and scene, for it is there that the fly-lines operate, enabling the spirits to fly down among them and increase their confusion. The dialogue is played out against a choreographic storm.

We can get some idea of the verve of this action from the hilarious parody Thomas Duffet provided the Theatre Royal to riposte with. *The Mock-Tempest, or The Enchanted Castle* passes in Bridewell Prison, of which Prospero proves to be the keeper; but its opening takes place in one of the notorious brothels of the Barbican. Here the courtiers, played in travesty by the women of the company, are enjoying the facilities of the redoubtable madam Stephania, played by a man, and her Ladies, also men. But Stephania's house is besieged by a hoard of apprentices, up to their traditional amusement of window-breaking and brothel-baiting, and so threatened with immediate invasion by those horrid shapes or devils, the City watch. Duffet's development of this situation is clearly a direct parallel to the action in *The Tempest* itself, but his stage directions are more explicit.

To begin with:

'*A great noyse heard of beating Doors, and breaking Windowes, crying a Whore, a Whore, &c.*' (p. 63).[8]

The whores, Beantosser and Moustrappa erupt onto the stage:

BEANTOSSER: What a noyse they make!

MOUSTRAPPA: A roaring noyse, we shall have foul weather.

      Enter Drinkallup

DRINKALLUP: The Dogs have us in the Wind, 'twill go hard. (I.i.1–3)

Stephania enters, to dominate the proceedings like the ship's Master, blowing whistles on her fingers and sending them about and about to bar the doors and windows. To her screams and whistles, '*The Wenches run on and off again.*' They come back with '*Spitts, Tongs, Chamber Potts, &c. They pass over the Stage.*' They are running about with their implements as the sailors in *The Tempest* must have been running about with the tackle, 'Vials', and 'Nippers' the text calls for. As they run, they repeat each other's lines in mounting confusion:

STEPHANIA: Stir, Wenches, stir, bring out all the Jourdans full of Water.

ALL: The Jourdans, the Jourdans, &c.

      Beantosser, Drinkallup, and Moustrappa run off several ways crying the Jourdans

      A great noyse within, all crying a Whore, a Whore, &c.

      (44–5)

Clearly the crescendo of the storm was assisted by ad lib repeats from the mariners, to support their complex visual manoeuvres, which employ every area of the stage to create a sense of space and confusion. At one time '*The Wenches run down the Trap Door . . .*', later '*Stephania whistles and the Wenches come up from the Trap Door.*' Similarly, Davenant's sailors are sent severally to the hold and up the mast, and the cries and screams on and off-stage drive the scene forward, as surely did the '*several Claps of Thunder*' in *The Tempest*, probably made by the rolling of canon balls down a stepped run over the stage (see Figure 11).[9] Excuse for the same noise is provided by Duffet in the whores' attempts to drag the sweat-tub and the great chest to block the doors, to cries of 'Heave all together, heave Cats. Heave . . . Cheerily, cheerily,' from off the stage. At last

> *A great noyse of fighting, crying Fire, Murther, &c. The Rabble and Wenches enter fighting. It Rains Fire, Apples, Nuts – A Constable and Watch enter and drive all off.* (p. 70)

So Duffet concludes a marvellously lively scene with a parody of the famous shower of fire as the ship sank in *The Tempest*.

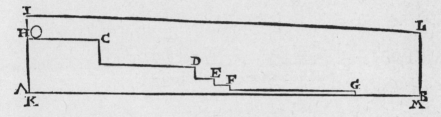

Figure 11 A thunder-run. Sabbattini. (*The British Library*)

This final, climactic effect, which was a favourite with audiences,[10] is in fact very carefully calculated. The general light on the Restoration stage was not very intense, but it would have been augmented in this scene by occasional vivid flashes of lightning – a dangerous process that involved powdered resin held in a metal box and shot forward through a candle flame to give a vivid explosion of light. There might also have been the more subtle effect of a streak of lightning, a squib sent down a wire across the stage and ignited by ordnance to make it shoot.[11] It is notable that Duffet includes dialogue about making noises to sound like guns. At the moment of the shower of fire however, the whole house was darkened. This could not include the auditorium (the word house usually includes this in such a context, but does not always do so,) since the lights on the galleries could not be got at in a performance, but shields would have been put over the lights in the wings, and the chandeliers on the stage drawn up (Figure 12). This would make a sudden and considerable drop in light, and the final shower of St Elmo's fire would have emphasised this with its gentle golden rain at the front of the stage, which darkened behind it.

The moment of darkness was important, because it ushers in one of those exquisite contrasts so beloved of the baroque theatre.

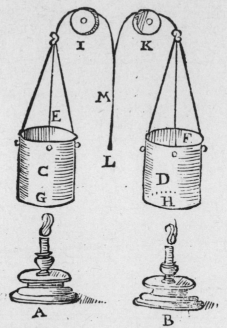

Figure 12   Shields for lights within the scene. Sabbattini.
The letting out of the cord L lowers the cylinders over the candles, keeping light off the
wings behind. (*The British Library*)

> *In the midst of the Shower of Fire, the Scene changes. The Cloudy Sky,*
> *Rocks and Sea vanish; and when the lights return discover that Beautiful*
> *part of the Island, which was the Habitation of* Prospero; *'Tis compos'd*
> *of three Walks of Cypress Trees, each Side-walk leads to a Cave . . .*
> *The Middle-Walk is of great depth and leads to an open part of the Island.*

There is stillness after the storm, the light slowly dawning on a new and
tranquil image, some of the effect of which can be gauged from Torelli's
beautiful cypress garden for *La Finta Pazza* (Plate 26). The scene in *The
Tempest* may have been yet more elaborate, being a triple perspective with
divergent walks to show the two caves (Figures 13 and 14). In the moment
of silence before the burst of applause its effect must have been breathtaking. Rightly so, because the two contrasted images, the roaring, violent
storm and the tranquil order of the garden, present in essence the whole
design of the play.

The Enchanted Island is essentially a series of moral emblems projected
into action and grouped around a theme, enhanced, in a typically baroque
way, by the splendours of music and spectacle. The theme is closely
related to that of Shakespeare's play, but the Restoration need for precision and clarity of idea requires alteration of the whole tone of the play

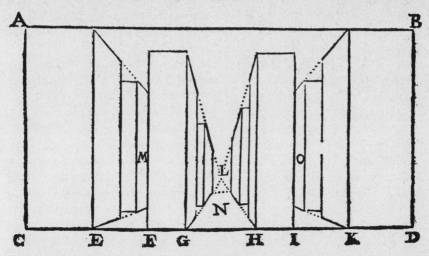

Figure 13   Triple perspective – convergent. Sabbattini. For the effect, see Plate 26 (*The British Library*)

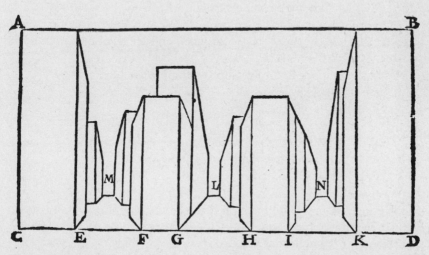

Figure 14   Triple perspective – divergent. Sabbattini. For the effect, see Plate 23 (*The British Library*)

in a most unexpected direction. The responsibility for this, Dryden tells us, lay with Davenant. Shakespeare's design, he says, is formed around the idea of a woman who had never seen a man.

> *But* Sir William Davenant, *as he was a man of quick and piercing imagination, soon found that something might be added to the Design of* Shakespeare . . . *and therefore to put the last hand to it, he design'd the Counterpart to* Shakespeare's *Plot, namely that of a Man who had never seen a Woman; that by this means those two characters of Innocence and Love might more illustrate and commend one another.*

To fulfil this design the original adaptors created the character of Dorinda, Miranda's sister, as the 'character of innocence', and a young prince, Hippolito, rightful heir to Alonso's kingdom, and brought up by Prospero in seclusion on the island, for the 'character of love'. The quartet of lovers thus contrived take over the play. A dialectic of innocence and experience is played out between them, and Prospero becomes above all a foolish father who pits himself in vain against the promptings of nature. This idea is certainly not absent from Shakespeare, but in his play it involves complex interaction between Prospero, Ariel and Caliban, as well as between Ferdinand and Miranda. Indeed, it is difficult to see how anyone could think the design of *The Tempest* was based on the idea of a woman who had never seen a man, although Miranda provides the play with a telling image. To make way for their lovers, Dryden and Davenant severely reduce the roles of Caliban and the comics, and leave the courtiers almost entirely out of account. Instead we witness a witty experiment in social ideas, and the darkness of the power struggle that lies at the heart of *The Tempest* is argued in the clear light of reason.

The rationalisation of the play commences with Prospero's first great scene. It sticks fairly closely to the original, and seems at first sight to be merely mangled Shakespeare:

MIRANDA: You often, Sir, began to tell me what I am,
But then you stopt.

PROSPERO: The hour's now come;
Obey and be attentive. Canst thou remember
A time before we came into this Cell?
I do not think thou canst, for then thou wert
Not full three years old.

MIRANDA: Certainly I can, Sir. (I.ii.17–22)

The expurgation and simplification disturbs the rhythm and completely removes the subtle, lyrical quality of Shakespeare's scene. In what follows, the passion is missing from Prospero's narrative, which becomes a simple tale and speaks like prose, and the dialogues with Caliban and Ariel are subtly distorted in a similar manner, so as to remove the mystery of these creatures. Though the shape of the scene is preserved it has a new tone, and an emphasis on pattern and idea. Prospero must say:

> I have done nothing but in care of thee,
> My Daughter, and thy pretty Sister (I.ii.9–10)

and further prepare the audience for another of the contrived symmetries of the new design, arousing, one may suppose, delighted anticipation:

> Save for two Brats that she did Litter here,
> The brutish *Caliban*, and his twin-sister. (188–9)

It is not difficult for Shadwell to add more felicities of the same kind, and allow Ariel to call for applause by saying:

> I did flame distinctly.
> Nay once I rain'd a shower of Fire upon 'em. (110–11)

And bring his scene to its climax with:

> I know that this day's business is important,
> Requiring too much toyl for one alone.
> I have a gentle spirit for my Love,
> Who twice seven years has waited for my freedom:
> Let it appear, it will assist me much,
> And we with mutual joy will entertain
> Each other. This I beseech you grant me. (212–18)

This must have been a pleasing surprise for the first audience. Dryden preserved Ariel's beloved Milcha for the final sarabande in his version. Now she flies down to applause in the very first scene, and they cap it inevitably by flying up and crossing in the air. Here, of course, is the real reason for the inclusion of Milcha. Much as baroque theatre loves symmetry, it is absolutely essential here. The new flying machines cannot be used to their full effect unless Ariel has someone to cross in the air with! To the balance of the design they add a pictorial balance, a diagrammatic harmony that is a fanciful comment on the new, mathematical tone of the play. The plot, Prospero's joint scheme to unite Miranda and Ferdinand and so reclaim his kingdom, and Dorinda to Hippolito and restore the prince to his, is treated as a matter of little emotional importance. It is simply a formula for presenting certain juxtapositions of idea.

Under these circumstances, the comedy of manners with which the act ends is a not unnatural inflection on what has gone before. Dorinda, the 'character of innocence', comes bouncing in, full of excitement about the ship which she thinks is a 'huge great creature'. Miranda helpfully informs her that far from being a creature itself there are creatures inside it:

> And shortly we may chance to see that thing,
> Which you have heard my Father call, a Man. (311–12)

Dorinda is intrigued at once:

DORINDA: But what is that? for yet he never told me.

MIRANDA: I know no more than you: but I have heard
                My father say, we Women were made for him.
DORINDA: What, that he should eat us, Sister?
MIRANDA: No sure, you see my Father is a Man
                And yet he does us good. I would he were not old.
DORINDA: Methinks indeed, it would be finer
                If we had two young Fathers. (313–20)

It is perhaps surprising to find a 'character of innocence' so very lubricious, but that is, of course, Dryden's rather cynical point. The idea of 'natural instinct' is made perspicuous. It is also boldly objectified. The women who have never seen a man are standing in fact in front of rows of them clearly visible in the auditorium. It seems likely that the more improper lines were given in open invitation to the nearest gentleman.

This play with the actresses both as characters and as experienced women known to many in the audience governs the way in which this part of the action unfolds, and is given a further twist. The part of the prince, Hippolito, was played by a girl – possibly by Charles's mistress, Moll Davies. The role is in many ways like that of Cherubino in *The Marriage of Figaro*, but Dryden again makes use of the audience's presence and awareness of the nature of actress and character. In his very first scene, Prospero warns Hippolito to beware of women:

HIPPOLITO: Sir, I have often heard you say, no creature liv'd
                Within this Isle, but those which Man was Lord of;
                Why then should I fear?
PROSPERO: But here are creatures which I nam'd not to thee,
                Who share Mans Sovereignty by Nature's Laws,
                And oft depose him from it.
HIPPOLITO: What are those creatures, Sir?
PROSPERO: Those dangerous enemies of Men call'd Women.
HIPPOLITO: Women! I never heard of them before.
                What are women like? (II.ii.25–33)

Dryden was clearly disingenuous in apologising in his prologue to the 1667 performance that 'one of our women must present a boy'. The whole part is set up for it, as the woman on stage asks the mixed audience what women are like. By having the boy played by a girl, the audience is made continually aware of the ideas involved in the encounters of the 'characters', while any exploration of the emotional basis of these ideas is avoided. To make the ideas perspicuous, individual complexities of relationship must be omitted, but these are compensated for by the fun that can be had with the ideas. The scenes are designed as emblems that hold up the characters' nature for the audience's contemplation. Audience and actors have a dialogue, as it were, over the characters' heads.

Dryden and Davenant are using their quartet of lovers to discuss the relationship of nature to nurture, a favourite question of the day. Through the development of their plot, they demonstrate a series of propositions behind which lurks the somewhat cynical idea that most of the nurture given the children by Prospero is of little use. Their understanding, and the taming of their natures, must come from within them. Each time they appear on the stage, a new catalyst is added to the situation, in order to push its argument one stage further. The girls find Hippolito in his cave, and he and Dorinda fall in love. Miranda, as in Shakespeare, is given to Ferdinand, but the two relationships are made to complement each other. Dorinda's love is an innocent and guileful yielding to desire, and is matched by that of Hippolito. Miranda is older, and realises that love must depend on mutual attraction and sacrifice and is not the work of a moment. To teach Hippolito this, Prospero involves the experienced Ferdinand, with disastrous results. No sooner does the 'character of Love' learn that there are more women in the world than his simple Dorinda, than he determines to have them all, including Ferdinand's Miranda. To defend his right Ferdinand fights and kills Hippolito, and Miranda and Dorinda's natural love for each other is destroyed. The sequence depicts very clearly a series of movements of the mind, an interplay between instinct and self-control, and Ariel provides a caption for the situation from his vantage-point on his flying-machine:

> Harsh discord reigns throughout this fatal Isle,
> At which good Angels mourn ill Spirits smile;
> Old Prospero, by his Daughters robb'd of Rest,
> Has in Displeasure left 'em both unblest.
> Unkindly they abjure each other's Bed,
> To save the Living, and Revenge the Dead. (IV.iii.222–7)

Never in a thousand years could Shakespeare's Ariel have referred to his master as 'Old Prospero'.

The resolution of this fatal situation is brought about by the adaptors' one attempt to introduce some fantasy of their own. The result is characteristic. The revival of Hippolito is accomplished by a weapon-salve, which Ariel has prepared after being chidden by Prospero for his failure to prevent the disaster. The effect of this fancy is to create an image which, with all the detached style of the previous scenes, manages to make explicit the complex sexual sub-text hitherto unexpressed. Ariel tells Prospero to 'annoint the Sword which pierc'd him with this Weapon-salve, and wrap it close from air till I have time to visit him again.' It is a simple enough instruction; but it is not what takes place. Prospero sends Miranda to Hippolito, and she arrives 'carrying Hippolito's Sword wrapp'd up'. It should be Ferdinand's sword, and it should not be wrapped up until it has been anointed with the salve. The conduct of the scene itself makes clear the reason for this Freudian slip on the adaptor's part. Although repentant, Hippolito is still promiscuous, and attempts to make love to Miranda:

MIRANDA: But, Sir,
            I am another's, and your Love is given
            Already to my Sister.
HIPPOLITO: Yet I find
            That if you please, I can still love a little.
MIRANDA: I cannot be unconstant, nor should you. (V.ii.54–7)

A correct moral line has been firmly established. It is then countermanded by the action:

HIPPOLITO: O my Wound pains me.

Miranda is instantly repentant:

MIRANDA: I am come to ease you. *(She unwraps the sword)* (58–9)

What follows, played one must suppose with wit and gusto by the two actresses, is really quite breathtakingly indecent:

HIPPOLITO: Alas! I feel the cold Air come to me,
            My Wound shoots worse than ever.
            (She wipes and anoints the Sword)
MIRANDA: Does it still grieve you?
HIPPOLITO: Now methinks there's something
            Laid just upon it.
MIRANDA: Do you find no Ease?
HIPPOLITO: Yes, yes, upon the sudden all the Pain
            Is leaving me: Sweet Heav'n, how I am eas'd! (60–7)

This emblematic presentation of masturbation and orgasm could be most embarrassing on the stage if not played with great frankness. It must also be played for its concept rather than as an imitation of the experience. It says much that Pepys found it 'the most innocent play that ever I saw' (7 November 1667). His judgment also suggests that throughout the performance the sexual doubles entendres were played for wit rather than for smut. The detachment necessary for such an approach is here provided by the sense of a clever similitude, a play of fancy with oddly dialectical implications. The curing of Hippolito by Miranda through her physical ministrations to Hippolito's sword contradicts the scene's explicit moral. Apparently, for the 'character of love' to learn to govern his instincts both the experience of the 'wound' and of the 'cure' are necessary. Well, such is the idea Dryden addresses to our judgment.

The moral of the new design is that the instincts cannot be arbitrarily controlled, but that right habits must be cultivated by the will, informed by the understanding. Prospero's educational tyranny therefore acquires some force as a political analogy, and this aspect of the theme is carried through into the other two strands of the action. Hippolito's lust for possession was aptly demonstrated in his determination to 'have' all the women in the world. In the other plots this lust is for power and land and leads to a similar loss of control with consequent disorder. The mariners' plot is farcical in tone, and the monsters, Caliban and Sycorax, become little more than absurd catalysts to the sailor's struggle to dominate the island. That of the Courtiers is rather melodramatic, and is used to motivate the musical elements of the play. This is very proper, since the adaptors emphasise not action but re-action. Gone are Antonio's attempts to persuade Sebastian to kill Alonso (as are Caliban's to persuade Stephano to cut Prospero's throat), and Sebastian is in fact omitted altogether. Instead, the focus is on the feelings of remorse brought out in Alonso and Antonio by their wreck and the loss of Ferdinand, which leads them to repent the usurpation of the dukedoms of Prospero and the infant Hippolito. The two styles, operatic and comic, are interwoven with some skill with the comedy of manners that is the essence of Dorinda's and Hippolito's behaviour, and creates a dramatic counterpoint of considerable richness.

The mariners are given three scenes. In the first, Mustacho and Ventoso have been thrown on to the island with a runlet of brandy. Stephano appears and claims possession of it and the island as Ship's Master. They dispute, but he gets support by promising them they shall be viceroys if the other two 'elect' him duke. When this is settled, Trincalo appears, and, since he escaped on a whole butt of sack, is indisposed to be governed. Rebellion seems imminent but they leave him to cool his heels, and he thereupon discovers Caliban and in him an obvious 'subject' for his rival state. Caliban introduces him, in the second scene, to the monstrous Sycorax, and Trincalo perceives the possibilities of an alliance. If he marries her, he inherits the island by the right of his wife. By this time, the runlet of brandy has run out, and Stephano and the others come to sue for peace. They are offered the choice of submission or starvation, and in the third scene conclude for 'Peace and the Butt'. But Stephano has been making eyes at Sycorax, and seduces that hearty lady from her allegiance to Trincalo, by telling her the latter has spoken ill of her. When Trincalo strikes Stephano, Sycorax flies at him, and at last general war breaks out and they all exit fighting.

The broad tone of this action, which Dryden ascribed to Davenant, by no means obscures the clarity of its argument. All the characters from the ship are governed by their appetites for power and pleasure, and each segment of the plot focuses on a new element by which one or other of them strives to gain control of the others. Their continuous self-interest leads inevitably and hilariously to violence. This is made constantly apparent in the dialogue, and in the physical actions that arise from the conflict. Davenant produces a naive but gestic utterance, the political simplifications of which are extremely effective in presenting ideas of government and self-government through the similitude of the farcical action:

STEPHANO: Trincalo, sleep and be sober; and make no more uproars in my Countrey.

TRINCALO: Why, what are you, Sir, what are you?

STEPHANO: What I am, I am by free Election, and you, Trincalo, are not yourself; but we pardon your first fault, because it is the first day of our Reign.

TRINCALO: Umph, were matters carried so swimmingly against me, whilst I was swimming and saving myself for the people of the Island.

MUSTACHO: Art thou mad, Trincalo? Wilt thou disturb a settled Government, where thou art a meer stranger to the Laws of the Countrey?

TRINCALO: I'll have no Laws.

VENTOSO: Then Civil War begins. (*Vent., Must., draw*)

STEPHANO: Hold, hold, I'll have no Bloudshed, my Subjects are but few: Let him make a Rebellion by himself. (II.i.113–28)

The snide references to recent political events in England create exactly the same dialogue over the characters' heads as was observed in the other part of the play, and are similarly enhanced by the absurd antics of Sycorax, a complement to the travesty role of Hippolito. Her instincts are also similar to his, and create an entertaining counterpoint as Trincalo's complaisance is set against Ferdinand's aggression:

TRINCALO: I found her an hour ago under an Elder-tree on a sweet Bed of Nettles, singing Tory, Rory, and Ranthum, Scantum, with her own Natural Brother.

STEPHANO: O Jew! make Love in her own Tribe?

TRINCALO: But 'tis no matter, to tell thee true, I marri'd her to be a great man and so forth. (IV.ii.77–82)

The cross-references between the plots are continuous and extremely amusing, as are the ironies of the sailor's pretensions to regal behaviour, and the audience was clearly expected to take and applaud such points as they arose. They are following the ideas the characters articulate, not the experiences they are undergoing. The play is addressed to the judgment, not the feelings, and Ariel again provides a suitable caption:

> The Seamen all that cursed wine have spent,
> Which still renew'd their thirst of Government;
> And wanting subjects for the Food of Pow'r,
> Each wou'd to rule alone, the Rest devour. (IV.iii.232–5)

Even though the spirit employs a seditious metaphor, he makes the moral of the 'fable' abundantly clear.

The masque which Pelham Humfrey provided for the first scene with the courtiers does, on the other hand, seek to evoke experience; but even here the splendidly affective qualities of music and dance are not permitted to obscure the design. As Alonso and Antonio wander remorsefully about the island they hear flourishes of strange music 'from under the stage'. Then suddenly the ground opens at their feet – the central stage traps sink, in other words – and Antonio cries:

Lo, the earth opens to devour us quick. (II.iv.45)

Instead, from under the stage, a doleful chorus of Devils sings of how the great meet their punishment in hell. In fact, the episode is a cunning way of 'rationalising' the holes made by the trap doors while they descend to be loaded – always a problem until the invention of a mechanism to slide back the stage floor at the moment the traps rose. The chorus over, the Devils come up through the traps, dressed perhaps like the 'horrid shapes' that appeared in the storm, and singing a mocking chorus. In a series of fierce stanzas, the devils remind the Dukes of their crimes. There is both rhythmic vitality and clarity in Humfrey's word-setting, though it is neither as bold harmonically or as varied rhythmically as Locke's or Purcell's, and the tone is effectively intense. Now fiendish personifications of Pride, Fraud, Rapine and Murder enter, the vices which turned legitimate government to tyranny, and the devils herd the nobles into the middle of the stage to a blandly sinister little chorus and vanish. In a return to dialogue, the conscience stricken rulers beat their breasts in terror, but as they turn to leave another devil rises in their path, and blocking their passage launches into the splendid, declamatory air by Pietro Reggio, calling upon the winds from beneath the earth to rise and torture their guilty minds, and finally to

Drive these Wretches to that part o'the Isle,

Where Nature never yet did smile.

Cause Fogs and Storms, Whirlwinds and Earthquakes there:

There let 'em howl and languish in despair. (142–6)

At his command: '*Two Winds rise, ten more enter and dance. At the end of the Dance, three Winds sink, the rest drive Alon., Anto., Gon., off.*' All the elements of the scene, music, spectacle, and even the whirling confusion of the dance of Winds, have been made by the words to articulate the idea of the passions they evoke and place them in the intellectual context of the rest of the design.[12]

The significance of the original transformation from the disorder of the storm to the cultivated symmetry of the Cypress garden should now be clear. The disruptions of natural instinct, guilt and passion give way to order and civility. In fact, the contrast is the first of a series by which the scenery is made to articulate the idea of the play, giving it, at the same time, an exciting visual rhythm.

There are four other settings required besides the first two: the Cave, the Wild Island, and the two seascapes for the final masque. Of these, the most important is The Wild Island, which is '*compos'd of divers sorts of Trees, and barren Places, with a Prospect of the Sea at a great distance.*' For the action of the play itself, this scene is the echo by land of the disorder of the storm at sea, and forms the background to the scenes with the sailors and the courtiers. For most of the play, it alternates with the Cypress Walks and Caves. The two final scenes are similarly the compliment to the opening storm – the harmony rather than the dissonance of the waters. It is also notable that each of these images, even The Cave which seems to have been taken over from the earlier Lincoln's Inn Fields production, preserve the presence of the sea in the distance. Perhaps the Cypress Walks, which lead simply to 'an open part of the Island', do not do so. Prospero has attempted to shut the troublesome element out of his garden. The iconography of the sea as an image of passion would have been easily taken at the time.

The way in which these scenes were contrived is obviously important to their ultimate rhythmic effect. All six scenes require only two sets of wings, the rocks, and the cypress-trees, since the rocks can be made to serve the storm, the Wild Island, the Cave, and the final scene; thus emphasising the particular importance of the Cypress Walks. Probably, in most scenes, these wings led simply to a pair of painted shutters. Downes tells us that the final vision of the '*rising Sun, and a number of Aeriel Spirits in the Air*' was painted,[13] and so most probably was the Cave, taken over from the earlier production. The Wild Island would have necessarily been on shutters, and they must have been placed in a middle stage groove, since at one point, on a change to the Cypress Walks, Prospero and Miranda are 'discovered' behind them. A position at the second wing would allow sufficient space, and would accommodate two sets of double fly-tracks down stage for Ariel, Milcha, and the two spirits who carry off the table. All four fly-tracks are required in this scene. It is also probable that the chandeliers were up-stage of this groove, out of the way of most of the flying. If so, the garden would be even brighter in effect than the Wild Island. The Garden too was probably a flat scene, painted on the innermost set of shutters, for although the central vista suggests a deep-scene, if it were a divergent perspective, it would have been exceedingly difficult to accomplish in relieve (Figures 13 and 14).

The two great seascapes remain, and it is hardly likely the Dorset Garden used its splendid vista at no point in such a production. The flies and wings masked by clouds into the distance, the vista-scene here would have allowed for the presence of the spectacular wave-machine. A series

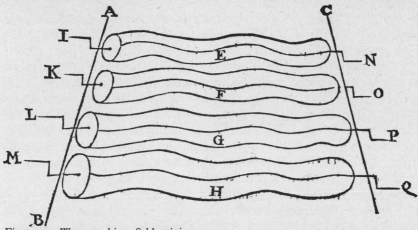

Figure 15 Wave machine. Sabbattini.
The bends in the lateral rollers operate in counterpoint when the handles are turned, giving the effect of rolling breakers. The technique survived into the eighteenth century, and such a machine was discovered at Drottningholm. (*The British Library*)

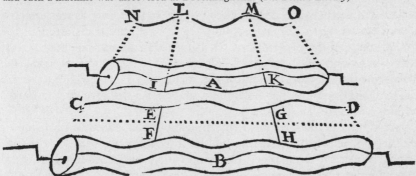

Figure 16 Method for darkening the sea. Sabbattini. The dark profiles CEGD and NLMO are raised from below to dominate the wave machine (*The British Library*)

of ground-rows supported at the sides and carved like sticks of barleysugar were laid across the stage. They were painted blue, highlighted with silver on the crests and darkened in the hollows. When turned gently from handles in the wings, they rotated, effecting a counterpoint of rippling waves (Figure 15). This calm sea could be made to 'Rise, Swell, get Tempestuous and Change Colour.' A piece of wood, profiled like a wave and painted black and silver was set between each of the cylinders with a man beneath the stage to operate it. These dark waves are at first invisible between the ground rows, but as the waves roll faster, the black profiles are raised up and down by their operators, becoming gradually more visible until only the front cylinder is turning, and the heaving black and silver dominates the blue (Figure 16). Such an effect would orchestrate well with the opening tempest on the stage, showing the sea in 'perpetual agitation'. The whole depth of the stage does not return until the revelation of the rolling, glimmering sea for the climax of the entire piece, the masque of Neptune and Amphitrite.

The changing scenes give the action of the whole play a great impetus, and it is worth considering this momentum, and the juxtaposition of images it contrives, in some detail. The quiet of the revelation of Prospero's garden is held for applause and then Prospero and Miranda enter by the two fore-stage doors. They talk on the fore-stage, and there her father inclines her to sleep. He summons Ariel, who enters magically, flying down within the scene. Prospero joins him and their dialogue gains fantasy with distance, and climax with Milcha's entrance. With Caliban's scene, the action returns to the fore-stage, and ends there, with Miranda and Dorinda in intimate conversation with the audience. The Walks remain in sight for the interval, but the second act gets off to a good start with the sudden transformation to the Wild Island, and the entrance of Mustacho and Ventoso for the first of the sailors' scenes.[14] It returns to the garden for the girls' first sight of Hippolito, and an interesting effect is here achieved, as instead of following him to the Cave, as was directed in the earlier version, their peeping scene is simply transferred to the fore-stage, as if the proscenium arch itself formed a cave mouth, against the background of the Cypress Walks. The third scene is again the Wild Island, a suitable setting for the masque of Devils which Shadwell has transferred from the beginning of the act to give it a stronger climax.

Act III is the most complex rhythmically and scenically. It is framed in music. The Wild Island stays for the interval, but instead of a change to give impetus to the new act, Ariel and Milcha enter, leading Ferdinand and singing 'Full Fathom Five' and 'Come Unto these Yellow Sands'. The songs form a prologue to the change to the Walks and Prospero's interrogation of Miranda and Dorinda. This leads to a sequence in the Wild Island. First, the courtiers wander round remorsefully, and Ariel comforts them with Bannister's exquisite song 'Dry those eyes which are o'reflowing', then follows the second scene for the sailors with the first appearance of Sycorax, and when they leave, insulting each other, Ariel and Ferdinand return to sing Bannister's delicate echo-song that Pepys considered the highlight of the earlier performances (7 November 1667, 8 May 1668). The comics would have used the fore-stage, while Ariel, on his track, is of course confined to the scene. The move away from the audience and into song would, as it were, harmonise the disorder of the Wild Island in preparation for a magical return to the Walks, not unlike a cross-fade in a film. As Ferdinand follows Ariel off-stage, the scene changes, 'discovering' Prospero and Miranda in their garden. Ferdinand and Ariel return immediately through the entrance by which they left, creating a charming and bizarre moment of *trompe l'oeil*, a kind of time-slip, to herald the first meeting of Ferdinand and Miranda. The act ends with a change to the Cave, the new scene giving weight and importance to Ferdinand's meeting with Hippolito. Emblematically, the scene sets Hippolito's rebellious desires against the imprisoning rocks and the free seascape outside. The scene could be set in a second groove at either shutter position.[15]

The fourth act returns to the calm of the Cypress Walk, where there is now growing disorder. As Hippolito and Ferdinand prepare to fight, the Wild Island appears, and disorder and violence break out among the mariners. As the farcical battle grows to its climax, the Cypress Walks appear again, but now Ferdinand and Hippolito are striking at each other in the order of Prospero's garden. Hippolito falls, and the act ends with Prospero's condemnation of Ferdinand and Ariel's runic comments, after which it is possible that the symbol of disorder, the Wild Island, returned for the interval. It would certainly seem to begin Act V, though it is not specified, for we find Miranda pleading in vain with Prospero until Ariel returns with the weapon-salve, and they leave to apply it, at which point Hippolito and Dorinda are discovered before the Cave in the Cypress Walks. To find the orderly characters in a scene of disorder would be emblematically appropriate, and the Wild Island was available to make the previous 'discovery' of the Walks, when Ferdinand was following Ariel. Revealed outside his cave, Hippolito requests Dorinda to bring his chair forward 'into the Sun' – in other words towards the audience! – and the scene of the anointing of the sword is then played on the fore-stage. At its conclusion the characters assemble for reconciliation and the finale:

PROSPERO: Now to make amends
For the rough Treatment you have found to Day,
I'll entertain you with my Magick Art:
I'll, by my Pow'r, transform this place, and call
Up those that shall make good my Promise to you.
(V.ii.234–8)

This promise brings the whole show to its harmonious climax.

To a symphony, the '*Scene changes to the Rocks, with the Arch of Rocks, and calm Sea. Musick playing on the Rocks.*' Here at last the full splendour of the stage is revealed. It is a double vista like that of Torelli's finale to *Pélée et Thétis* (Plate 24) though the double arch at the front of the deep-scene is rocks and not clouds – actually very similar shapes are involved. In the 'glory' above the arch, the musicians are painted in the form of sea-creatures playing upon shells and other instruments while the orchestra plays from the pit.[16] In the lower arc of the rocks, Neptune and Amphitrite rise through the waves in their 'Chariot drawn with Sea

Horses' surrounded, from traps to each side of them, by singers and dancers as 'Sea Gods and Goddesses, Tritons and Nereides' in exquisite fantasy costumes that must have resembled those Torelli employed for a similar scene (Plate 22).

The presentation of the harmony of the sea is charming, and a most eloquent emblematic conclusion for the work. Pelham Humfrey surpassed himself in setting it. As the Gods call down Aeolus to calm the sea, Humfrey provides a striking interaction of broad declamation, short and elegant airs, and bouncing choruses during which 'The dancers mingle with the singers.' The scene is divided into three distinct musical and dramatic gestures, separated by dances. First, Amphitrite calls upon Neptune to let her 'celebrate a halcyon day'. The Tritons and Nereides dance. Aeolus now appears in the heavens, probably in the clouds above the Arch of Rocks. He summons the four winds who appear in the air at the corners of the stage. They descend at his command, and vanish into the earth, perhaps through the very traps by which they were released in the earlier masque. (A fourth may now be available – before, we were down-stage of the Wild Island.) The music becomes tranquil, and the Tritons, in charming chorus, 'Sound a Calm', while the dancers *at every repeat of* Sound a Calm, *changing their Figures and Postures, seem to sound their wreath's Trumpets made of Shells.*' Four Tritons then dance to music 'like Trumpets'. Calm is assured and the whole ends with a merry series of short airs and choruses to which the dancers add their movements, now based on the harmonious postures of the *danse noble*, rather than on the false positions which would have dominated the devils' movements in the previous anti-masque.

At the climax, the scene changes again – to the rising sun, spirits in the air, and 'Ariel *flying from the Sun, advances towards the Pit.*' This is a supreme piece of spectacle. All the flying so far has been on lateral tracks: this is from back to front. It had to be last, for, during the final sequence of songs and dances after the descent of the winds, all the wires for the lateral tracks had to be gathered into the wings in order to enable Ariel to fly forwards without fouling them. As the shutters changed, the spirit descended to hang in front of the painted sun, and then, at the moment he flew forwards, the centre of each cloud border was opened like a draw-bridge to let the ropes past. The break in the 'sky' would be unnoticed. All eyes would be on Ariel, 'hovering in the air'. As he sang the charming 'Where the Bee Sucks', the clouds gently closed behind him. Then Prospero spoke his final benediction and the seal of reconciliation was put on it all by an exquisite four-part canon for strings by Matthew Locke, the very musical form symbolising the newly won agreement and harmony.

The Enchanted Island ended magically: but its Epilogue returns its audience firmly to earth:[17]

> When feeble Lovers' appetites decay
> They, to provoke, and keep themselves in play,
> Must, to their cost, make ye young Damsells shine;
> If Beauty can't provoke, they'l do't by being fine.

If this were played in front of the last splendid tableau, the curtain still up as was the custom, the magic of the performance, there in full illusion, was reduced suddenly to poor taste and pounds shillings and pence. The effect of such a transition is only made possible by the detachment with which the performance was viewed, and the dialogue with the audience which was its heart. It began with an act of homage. The spectacle was an event of royal grandeur ordered by the king. It ends by pointing out that this means the people must pay more – charges were doubled on the first nights of new operas.

The combination of irony and insult is characteristic. Of course, nobody takes it as an insult to either Charles's or their own taste. They simply let off steam against the extra prices which they have been willing to pay by barracking and jeering. They have been watching the whole opera with expertise and enthusiasm rather than with feeling, and they now continue, hissing at the charges while they applaud the performance. In an odd way, the Epilogue re-states that interaction of thought and appetite that was at the heart of the play's design, the dialogue of sensuality and reason that is at the soul of the age. The audience was prepared to explore and appreciate this division in their personality, and realistic enough to admit the playhouse as the bawd that can bring them together.

Part Two

Fools and heroes

Poetry and Painting are not only true imitations of Nature, but of the
best Nature, that which is wrought up to a nobler pitch. They present
us with images more perfect than the life in any individual: and we
have the pleasure to see all the scattered beauties of Nature united by
a happy Chymistry, without its Deformities or Faults.

DRYDEN

5 · Building a character

The atmosphere of the Restoration playhouse was that of a sophisticated cabaret. The actor exposed on the fore-stage in a lit auditorium could contact all parts of the house, could speak with the audience as with his friends. This atmosphere required great intimacy of the actor and considerable control. Betterton was the greatest exponent of this art, and Cibber's description of him catches the style perfectly. He 'had a natural Gravity that gave Strength to good sense; a tempered Spirit that gave Life to Wit; and a dry Reserve in his smile that threw Ridicule into its brightest colours.'[1] The actor combines fire and intelligence, but handles both with a 'dry Reserve' that illuminates the mocking ironies of his material. Restoration acting was formal, often rhetorical, but it was neither what is nowadays called 'ham', nor was it necessarily conventional or mechanical. Like the dramatic texts it set out to interpret, its formality was a source of considerable strength. Cibber remarks: 'I never heard a Line in Tragedy come from *Betterton*, wherein my Judgment, my Ear, and my Imagination were not fully satisfy'd.'[2] The Restoration audience appreciated truthful acting as we do today; but the truth of the imagination naturally carried the same stylistic traits as the poetic truth of the texts they presented. It was a style that sought excitement through intelligence.

To show character in action the dramatist designed his scenes so as to make perspicuous the 'movements of the mind'. These movements made manifest man's inner struggle between his will and his desires, his passions and his intellect. Simple passions merely involved acceptance or rejection of the object with which the man was concerned. They were such as admiration, love, hate, desire, sadness, joy. Complex passions showed a mixture of responses, such as fear, hope, boldness, despair, anger. A man's character, his moral essence, was displayed by the sequence of such responses in any given situation.[3] Dryden wrote:[4]

> To express the passions which are seated in the heart by outward signs, is the great precept of the painters, and very difficult to perform. In poetry, the same passions and motions of the mind are

to be expressed; and in this consists the principle difficulty as well as the excellency of that art.

The difficulty was that the poet must use words, where the artist could depict the visual effects of passion itself, for, as John Bulwer put it, in a work he described as being of 'Muscular Philosophie': 'In the semblances of those motions wrought in the parts by the endeavour of the Muscles, we may not only see, but as it were feele and touch the very inward motions of the Minde.'[5] The playwright could share the work of both poet and painter in his choice of words and in his design of the action by separating the passions one from another and presenting them in orderly sequence as language and image: 'He who treats joy and grief together is in a fair way of causing neither of these effects.'[6] Feelings must be isolated in order to be contemplated as movements of the mind.

It was the actor's job to incarnate these ideas for the audience – to physicalise the humours of comedy and the passions of tragedy as conceived and defined by the poet. Bulwer had tried to show that 'Nature assigns to each motion of the Minde its proper *gesture*, *countenance*, and *tone*, whereby it is significantly expressed'[7] and in 1710 we find Gildon giving instructions to actors, derived from no less an authority than Betterton, in much the same terms:[8]

> Every Passion or Emotion of the Mind has from Nature its proper
> and peculiar Countenance, Sound, and Gesture; and the whole body
> of Man, all his looks, and every Sound of his voice, like the strings
> of an instrument, receive their sounds from the various impulse of the
> Passions.

The actor embodied such significant expressions of passion in his looks, his deportment, his voice, and so brought the moral idea visibly to life. In his portrayal of character, he had to place the passions as part of an argument, so that character could take its place within a design which would define new truth about the nature of man.

The chief weapon in the actor's armoury was the tone of his voice. It is in human speech, after all, that idea and action are most closely connected. Since the movements of the mind affect the pronunciation of the thoughts they arouse and articulate, the motivating passion can be defined by the tone in which these thoughts are uttered. Such definitions can seem naïve. 'The Voice, when loud,' wrote Gildon, 'discovers Wrath and Indignation of the Mind, and a small trembling Voice proceeds from fear.'[9] But in fact this is a helpful way of analysing an actor's contribution to the highly artificial structures of Restoration comedies and tragedies. Tone is a formalisation of those various adverbs employed by novelists – icily, sharply, firmly, heartily, and so on. It derives from two fundamental elements of acting – the need to clarify, and the need to project. By analysing speech into its proper tones, the actor could demonstrate a sequence of emotions, and so pinpoint the moral centre of his character. Hughes, writing on stage pronunciation in *The Spectator*, tells us:[10]

ANGER exerts its peculiar Voice in an acute, raised, and hurrying Sound . . . SORROW and Complaint demand a Voice quite different; flexible, slow, interrupted, and modulated in a mournful Tone . . . FEAR expresses itself in a low, hesitating and abject Sound . . . PLEASURE dissolves into a luxurious, mild, tender and joyous Modulation.

It is extremely difficult to describe the qualities of sounds in words; but Hughes captures here clear distinctions in tone, dynamic, speed and rhythm. It is possible to understand very well how the paradoxical 'luxurious, mild, tender and joyous modulation' might colour such lines as those from *Caius Marius*, by Otway, that are quoted in example:[11]

> *Lavinia*! Oh! there's Musick in the Name,
> That softening me to Infant Tenderness,
> Makes my Heart spring like the first Leaps of Life.

There is the same scale of transitions in the lines themselves, and the moral nature of the softening effect of pleasure, which is well placed by Hughes's use of the word 'luxurious', and which is also very characteristic of Otway's writing, would be clearly demonstrated by the flow of sound.

Vocal tone should follow the passions portrayed or the variety of description or narrative to be spoken. To fall into a single tone, to be monotonous in inflection, was to cant. A canting tone could be, of course, suitable to certain kinds of hypocritical character – Harcourt, in *The Country Wife*, is instructed to speak in 'a canting Tone', when he disguises himself as a clergyman – but it was basically a fault, because its monotony was not only dull, but did not distinguish the sequence of feelings that underlay the speech of the character. It was the transition from one passion to another, that, like the transformation from one scene to another, both excited and interested the Restoration audiences.

It is in the light of the need for such a calculated variety of significant vocal tone that one should read Cibber's famous remarks about stage articulation:[12]

In the just Delivery of Poetical Numbers, particularly when the Sentiments are pathetick, it is scarce credible, upon how minute an Article of Sound depends their greatest Beauty or Inaffection. The Voice of a Singer is not more strictly ty'd to Time and Tune, than that of an Actor in Theatrical Elocution: the least Syllable too long, or too slightly dwelt upon, in a Period, depreciates it to nothing; which very Syllable, if rightly touch'd, shall, like the heightening Stroke of Light from a Master's Pencil, give Life and Spirit to the whole.

It has often been thought that Cibber is recommending a kind of chanting delivery for the stage, an idea which gains support from the criticisms of Cibber himself in later life as a chanting actor. But care is needed, in evaluating such criticism. Fashions in vocal expression are constantly changing in everyday speech, and the stage follows such fashions, adapting new inflection and emphasis to its own expressive purposes. From this point of view, actors of a previous generation can often appear to be unnatural, when in their time, it was the naturalness of their delivery for which they were known.[13] Cibber is talking about Betterton, whose restraint he particularly admired, and he is remarking not merely on the musical qualities of a voice and its timbre, but on the importance of delicacy of rhythm, emphasis and inflection. The liveliness is dependent not upon grand gestures but upon a 'minute article' of sound.[14]

If the texts on which Betterton cut his teeth as an actor are considered, one may understand what Cibber meant:[15]

> Swear then by all those powers
> Which the Religious World fears and adores,
> To quit your claim to Empire; Swear you'll make
> Me monarch in that Throne which you'll forsake,
> And with that blood you'll guard that Throne you give;
> If so; your mistress shall have leave to live.

The actor must beware of sounding such words too grandly, or overlaying them with a solemn, swearing tone. Cant is not appropriate. Settle is not the greatest dramatist in the world, but he is very amusing, and his wit depends on the actor articulating it clearly and not clouding the sense with feeling. The cynicism of the atheist Crimalhaz, trapping his enemy through superstitions he does not share, can be very neatly pointed by the correct inflection on the words 'Religious World' and by the nice articulation of the paradoxical verbs that follow, while the accumulation of conditions, round the anaphora on 'Swear', are also very cool and very entertaining in their inversion of his victim's natural inclinations under the circumstances. The tone is not solemn, but polite, and beautifully sets off the pastiche graciousness of the final concession. Betterton was said to have remarked that words were not 'without their Tune or Notes even in common Talk, which together compose that Tune which is proper to every Sentence, and may be pricked down as well as any musical Tune.'[16] The writer, with his reference to common talk, would appear to be referring to the musical subtlety of inflection that irresistibly captures the meaning of a sentence, and the precision of utterance that highlights such inflection by timing and rhythm.

This should also be borne in mind when considering that other crucial aspect of vocal tone at the period – the rant. Gildon remarks that one will find the best actors 'always speaking in the same Tone on the Stage, as they would do in a Room, allowing for the Distance'.[17] There was no need for vocal exaggeration in the Restoration theatre. The actor was close to his public, and the noise they made is better orchestrated by the kind of precision and intelligence I have been discussing than by attempts to shout it down. Of course, actors did shout from time to time, and audiences could appreciate it – carefully calculated vocal excitement in passionate scenes can often, as Addison noted, conceal poverty of thought and win applause;[18] but this should not disguise the fact that rant is essentially a literary term, used often almost as a translation for the French *tirade*, though it has gained a negative inflection. A rant is a climactic, passionate speech which many writers used as an excuse for bombast, and many actors shouted; but this was a fault in both cases.[19] Addison noted: 'We often see the Players pronouncing, in all the Violence of Action, several parts of the Tragedy which the Author writ with great Temper, and designed that they should have been so acted.'[20] He also asked Cibber, at a performance of *Hamlet* by such a player, if Cibber thought Hamlet 'should be in so violent a Passion with the Ghost, which, tho' it may have astonis'd, it had not provok'd him?'[21] Addison liked distinctions of some subtlety in passion, and the Restoration dramatists did also. They usually 'writ with great temper', and are at their best when played with similar restraint.[22]

Rant, cant and tone are all present in the theatre of today. We all know the shouting actor, the whining actor, and the vocalising actor. But to us these terms denote faults, a lack of technique, a lack of variety, and an exaggeration of false feeling. These faults existed in Restoration acting, but the use of such terms does not suggest such an exaggerated style. The Restoration actor employed tone as a form of character analysis.

The same careful interaction of significance and feeling, thought and expression governed an actor's deportment and the gestures of his body. 'Figure and Action', the means by which the actor embodies the movements of the mind, had three distinct elements: the facial expression, the gestures of the arms and hands, and the 'attitude' which can be observed in the whole carriage.[23] Again, much of such gesture is perfectly obvious. As Bulwer says:[24]

After one manner almost we clappe our HANDS in joy, wring them
in sorrow, advance them in prayer or admiration; shake our head
in disdain, wrinkle our forehead in dislike, crispe our nose in anger,
blush in shame, and so for the most part of the more subtle motions.

And Gildon describes similar forms of generally recognisable expression: 'Eyes enflam'd and fiery are the genuine Effect of Choler and Anger; Eyes quiet and calm with a secret kind of Grace and Pleasantness are the offspring of Love and Friendship.'[25] It is natural to suppose that a blush

on the cheeks and the light of love in the eyes had best be left to operate
of themselves. Yet actors have always been conscious of the need to
evolve techniques to stimulate such effects. It was to this purpose that
Stanislavsky devised his 'method of physical actions', believing that if
the actor concentrated on the pursuit of his deed in strongly imagined
circumstances, feeling would follow of itself, and with feeling its natural
physiological effects. The seventeenth-century took a different way, for
a rather different effect. Gildon says:[26]

> The Player . . . ought to form in his mind a very strong Idea of the
> Subject of his Passion, and the Passion itself will not fail to follow,
> rise into the Eyes, and affect both the Sense and Understanding of
> the Spectators with the same *Tenderness*.

Aiming at the mind as well as the emotions, the Restoration actor had to
construct a significant image with his body, and then give that image life
through the strength of his imagination. Gesture, like character, was seen
to be universal in its significance, so that the performer must convey
passion through the proper gestures of face and eyes, while marking the
sense of his lines by delicate movements of his hand, and incarnating the
essential idea of his character in the set of the whole figure.

If such a combination of gesture suggests that the actors must have
behaved like windmills, this is a mistake. The same care and selection
had to be applied here to preserve a natural visual flow, which was based
on the right presentation of the body. As Dryden points out, poetry and
painting present us not only with images of nature, 'but of the best
Nature, that which is wrought up to a nobler pitch'.[27] Actors, as the
sculptors of dramatic poetry, were to present us 'with images more perfect
than the life of any individual'. This perfection began with posture. All
actors were trained in dancing, and the men in fencing also – dancing
and fencing academies were often set up in the upper-rooms of theatres,
and the managers kept dancing-masters in constant attendance. The
heroic actor began from the posture of the heroic dancer. The head and
trunk were severely aligned down the spine, the feet turned out, the
arms, rounded to the wrists and moved cleanly from the shoulder or in
convoluted rotations of the wrists and elbows. This opened the stance
and displayed the figure, which at rest in either the second or fourth
positions, presented itself boldly to the onlooker (Plates 2 and 35, and
Figure 17). This was a point of rest from which more detailed movements
emanated, and was probably neither so stiff nor so limiting as might
appear. The art of theatrical dancing was a heightening of the postures
of social dance, and these were closely related to the evolution of fashionable dress, and therefore to the deportment of ordinary life. Open fourth
positions, a slight curve of the arms, and independent movement of the
hands, are in fact quite natural for the carrying of coats with full backs

Figure 17   Posture for the *danse noble* with opposition of the arms. Rameau. (*The British Library*)

and ruffled sleeves, especially when wearing shoes elevated by wedge heels, and similar dance positions are equally right for women's fashions, with their petticoats and trains and falling lace, – movement from the hip and shoulder, rather than from the body's centre is inevitable when encased in the corsets of the period. Heroic posture is simply an idealisation of the natural posture of the day, and once trained to it the actor could probably accomplish such extension of bearing in a manner that remained relaxed. As Dryden remarks: 'A play . . . to be like Nature, is to be set above it; as statues that are placed on high are made greater than the life, that they may descend to the sight in their just proportion.'[28] The extension is a technical matter like that required of the actor's voice. The heightening is ideal, but not unreal. 'Though a picture to be seen at a distance may be bigger than life, it must not *seem* to be so to the onlooker.'[29] What is aimed at is a heightening which is relaxed enough to appear natural and clear enough to convey its meaning.

The heroic posture of the *danse noble* however does provide a firm support for gesture of the arms and hands, and in its formality a strong focus on the expressions of voice and face. Voice and face express the passion, while gesture articulates the words in which it is made plain. Gildon comments:[30]

> The Movement or Gestures of your Hands must always be agreable to the Nature of the Words that you speak; for when you say, *Come in* or approach, you must not stretch out your hand with a repulsive Gesture, nor on the contrary, when you say, *Stand back*, must your Gesture be inviting.

The gestures meant here are quite natural ones, and are depicted by Bulwer in the second plate of the *Chirologia* as *Invito* and *Dimitto*. The point of them, however, is not that they express a feeling but that they act as a sign of meaning. As such they become not mere reflex actions, but calculated signals to point the meanings of words. One can see how, in the formal context of an actor's posture, they can make more graphic such a speech as that of Cleomenes, when he meditates on his friend's treachery. The light rotation of the dancer's wrist can turn welcome into dismissal, and make rejection palpable (Figures 18 and 19): [31]

> I have been plung'd already twice in Woes,
> And the third time above the Waves I rose.
> Still I have strength to Steer me into Port,
> And shun the Secret Quick-sands of the Court
> But when my Friend, who should expecting stand
> On the bare Beach, to lend his helping Hand;
> When He defends th'Unhospitable shore,
> And drives me thence, I sink for ever more.

The effect is curious. Rhetorical gesture follows the sense of the lines, and adds a satisfying distance to the style. The actor is not imitating the actions of the character, just as the dramatist is not imitating his speech. They are both presenting the idea of the character.

Cleomenes is specifically 'the Spartan Hero'. His character is by definition laconic. In character, he does not succumb to final disaster but shows a stoic control, and Dryden's lines show us '*what* he thought'.[32] Bulwer, perhaps, can suggest how Betterton might have played him at this point: 'In *Cogitation, Admiration, attentive Deliberation*, and *involuntarie Extasies of the Mind*, the Eyes are fixed, and the Eyelids remain unmoved, and the Head let downe, we contemplate the Earth with a set, wist, or musing look.'[33] The hero does not react to the news except to bend his head in contemplation. The small alteration in posture is as significant as a small

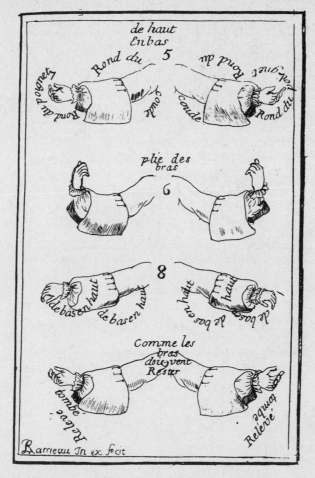

Figure 18   Rotations of the wrist and arms. Rameau. (*The British Library*)

alteration of tone. He thinks his speech through, his hands depicting the rejection he feels and describes. Then he pulls himself together. His head comes up in a decisive resumption of the heroic stance:

But 'tis impossible, his faith is try'd;
The Man who had defam'd him thus, had ly'd.

The defamation, of course, has come from a woman. The sequence of thought and feeling with its crowning irony, is typical of the dry manner of both performer and dramatist, as well as a neat stroke of character.

The focus on the face and carriage of the head is significant. Physiognomy was a matter of much interest and close investigation in the seventeenth century. Bulwer's third book was devoted to the way in which the

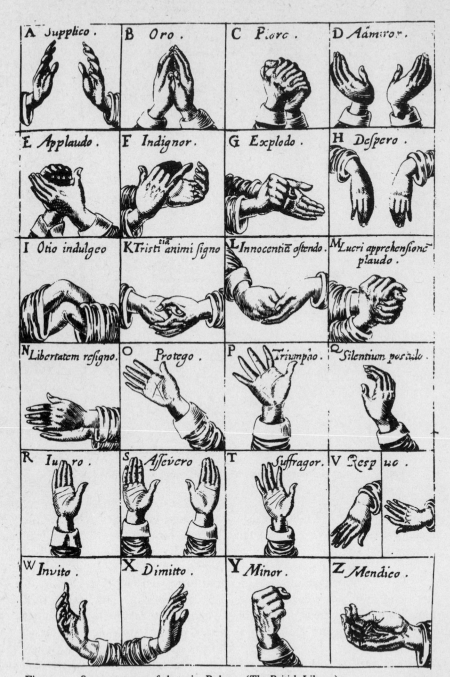

Figure 19 Some gestures of rhetoric. Bulwer. (*The British Library*)

face made visible the 'nods of the soule'[34] and describes and comments on an immense range of facial action, as in the passage on cogitation quoted above. Unfortunately, there are no plates to his book, 'Time', he tells us, 'did not afford it', but in a very valuable work published in Paris at the end of the century, this deficiency is supplied. Lebrun's *Conférence de peinture et sculpture* (1698) is very clearly in the same tradition as Bulwer's work. To take a favourite expression of the period as an example, he analyses Scorn as an admiration at something beneath you. It is shown in the face by[35]

> the Eye-brow frowning and drawn down by the side of the Nose, the other end thereof very much raised; the Eye very open, and the Eyeball in the middle; the Nostrils drawn a little upwards; the Mouth shut, the corners a little drawn down; and the under Lip thrust out beyond the other.

Figure 20 shows the graphic way in which Lebrun executed his conception, and may be compared with Bulwer's even more graphic description: 'They who *Scorn* and *Deride* others are many times seen to wrest their

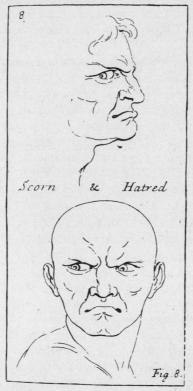

Figure 20   Scorn and Hatred. Lebrun. (*The British Library*)

Mouth by drawing it to one side, like unto the Mouth of a Plaice.'[36] Clearly such expressions, like gestures, must be modified by the actor to his natural looks and bearing; but authors liked to generalise such descriptions in their writing, indicating the visual dimension they required. Thus, Dryden:[37]

> Mark my *Sebastian*, how that sullen Frown,
> Like flashing Lightning, opens angry Heaven;
> And while it kills, delights.

Almeyda is looking scornfully upon the Emperor, and Dryden captures the flashing eye and drawn in brow very neatly. It may also be observed that the actress for whom Almeyda was written, Elizabeth Barry, had her 'mouth opening most on the right side',[38] which may be one of the reasons she was so appreciated in the roles of disdainful women. There was a standard of accuracy. The audience was interested in recognising a particular image as well as feeling its effect, in judging the correctness and originality with which the passion had been drawn, as they heard the author's caption. The actor required to control feeling in the sequence of visual descriptions with which he expressed it.

The juxtapositions of these images had the importance and significance they had in painting. Gildon draws his readers' attention to the value of such effects:[39]

> Thus, *Jordan* of *Antwerp*, in a piece of our Saviour's being taken from the Cross, which is now in his Grace the Duke of Marlborough's hands, the Passion of Grief is express'd with a wonderful Variety; the Grief of the Virgin Mother is in all the Extremity of Agony, that is consistent with Life, nay indeed that leaves scarce any signs of remaining Life in her: that of St. Mary *Magdalene* is an Extreme of Grief, but mingled with Love and Tenderness, which she always express'd after her conversion by our blessed Lord; then the Grief of *St. John* the Evangelist is strong but manly, and mixed with the Tenderness of perfect Friendship; and that of *Joseph of Arimathea* suitable to his years and love for *Christ*, more solemn, more controlled in himself, and yet forcing an appearance in his looks.

It may be that this description was worked up by the writer, Gildon, rather than by the actor, Betterton. It is nevertheless a fine piece of observation, and studying Jordaens's picture (Plate 33), it is possible to see very clearly the kind of truth at which the players aimed in painting the passions. The gestures are exaggerated, as are the expressions on Lebrun's faces, but the effect of melodrama is modulated by the intellect. At first sight the picture may appear extravagant; but if the same kind of attention is paid to it as has been paid by Gildon, if its iconography is considered as the essence rather than the accidents of its composition, it becomes demonstrably a significant structure in which feeling is the

30. *Hamlet*. Frontispiece. Rowe's Shakespeare. The British Library.

31. *Macbeth*. Frontispiece. Rowe's
Shakespeare. The British
Library.

32. *King Henry VIII*. Frontispiece.
Rowe's Shakespeare. The British
Library.

33. 'The Descent from the Cross'. Jordaens. Hamburger Kunsthalle.

34 'The Test of Darius', Lebrun, Réunion des musées nationaux.

35. 'The Conquest of Mexico'. Hogarth. Courtesy of Lady Teresa Agnew.

36. 'Garrick and Mrs Cibber in the characters of Jaffeir and Belvidera', mezzotint by J. McArdell, after Zoffany. Theatre Museum, Harry R. Beard collection.

37. Triple portrait of the actor John Lacy. Reproduced by gracious permission of Her Majesty the Queen.

38. *Trumpets and Drums*. Scene 8, By the banks of the Severn. Brecht's adaptation of *The Recruiting Officer*, given by the Berliner Ensemble. Photo, Percy Paukschta.

39. *Trumpets and Drums*. Scene 9, at Justice Balance's. Photo, Percy Paukschta.

outcome of thought: the postures of John, the Magdalene, and Joseph of Arimathea are projections of their 'characters'. This relationship is crucial to baroque art, and it is important to remember that at the time this was not an abstruse study but a matter of common intellectual interest. It was part of a science of behaviour. Gildon remarks that Lebrun was often said to stop in the street to observe a quarrel and to note the distinct expression of every face concerned in it. Gildon considered the expression of such concernments was part of the painter's genius, as in his splendid 'Tent of Darius' (Plate 34) and that an actor should be similarly scientific in observing and defining truth. A poet like Dryden was fascinated by these ideas, and Dryden after all, like other playwrights, instructed the actors in their parts. It would be very surprising if the nature of the passions to be portrayed and the outward signs that portrayed them had not been common talk in the theatre.

It was certainly central to Cibber's understanding of his own and Betterton's art:[40]

A farther Excellence in *Betterton*, was that he could vary his Spirit to the different Characters he acted. Those wild, impatient Starts, that fierce and flashing Fire he threw into *Hotspur*, never came from the unruffled Temper of his *Brutus* (for I have more than once seen a *Brutus* as warm as Hotspur); when the *Betterton Brutus* was provok'd, in his Dispute with *Cassius*, his Spirit flew only to his Eye; his steady Look alone supply'd that Terror, which he disdain'd an Intemperance in his Voice should rise to. Thus, with a settled Dignity of Contempt, like an unheeding Rock, he repell'd upon himself the Foam of *Cassius*.

This is truly the 'character' of a Stoic, and its clarity is achieved by both study and calculation. Betterton gives to the discoveries of tradition and observation the definitive form of classical art. In *Hamlet*, on his first encounter with the ghost, Betterton again presented a controlled passion, in which the horror of the moment was contained in the love of a son and respect for his father's spirit:[41]

This was the Light into which *Betterton* threw this Scene; which he open'd with a Pause of mute Amazement! then rising slowly to a solemn, trembling Voice, he made the Ghost equally terrible to the Spectator as to himself! and in the descriptive Part of the natural Emotions which the ghastly Vision gave him, the boldness of his Expostulation was still govern'd by decency, manly, but not braving; his voice never rising into that seeming Outrage, or wild Defiance of what he naturally rever'd.

Betterton employs face, voice and posture to throw the scene into a particular 'light'. He raises the audience's emotion as his voice describes the fear he feels, but above all he purposes to move them by showing them the 'character of a son' in Hamlet's horrifying circumstances. If the frontispiece to Rowe's text is taken from his performance, this was with arresting effect as the play went on. On his first encounter with his father's spirit, Hamlet's strength of character enabled him to preserve the outward manners suited to his role as son; but on the second he is either mad or pretending to be so: he is in disarray, his stocking has fallen, he has overturned a chair on which he was sitting, and the dislocation of stance along with the wild posture of the hands, and the staring eyes, indicate a spiritual disarray to complement that of his appearance, which encapsulates the destruction of the self that his unwanted task has brought (Plate 30).

Hamlet looks and is 'unbalanced'. A gesture, like an image, was judged on its ability to render an idea as an object of the mind. How long Betterton held his 'attitude' of terror we do not know; but it is important to realise that it would be long enough for the picture to sink in. It is an image of fear, and is there not simply to express the emotion, but to define it. Cleomenes's attitude of cogitation sustains the speaking of his thoughts; Hamlet's must at least remain until the ghost's beautiful counter-gesture, forswearing harm, sinks into Hamlet's soul. The pictorial holding of gesture, often sustained by applause, is another crucial part of the detached rhythm of performance. Betterton's terror and respect for his father's spirit are original and truthfully observed, but they have been formalised into a vocal and physical attitude, a focal point in the visual texture of the performance, meriting understanding applause. Like the painter, Betterton has caught and defined a new and particular truth out of an old tradition.

The descriptive effect of Restoration acting style was encouraged by methods of staging and rehearsal. The trick was to be able to add your own personal touches to a basically conventional dramatic lay-out. The companies performed a wide repertoire of plays, and changed them frequently. When *The Old Batchelour* ran for fourteen consecutive performances in 1693, it was a record run. Most new plays ran for three or four nights at the most, and were then put back into the programme from time to time when the management felt they might have gained a further appeal. The play to be given next day was only announced at the end of each day's performance, allowing the management great flexibility, but placing considerable strain on the resources of the company. The playhouses were open roughly from October to June, though up to thirty performances are recorded in summer vacations. The actors did not play on Sundays, on 24 December, on 30 January (the anniversary of the execution of King Charles I), on Wednesdays and Fridays in Lent, or in Holy Week. This gave them upwards of two hundred playing days in a year.[42] Under such circumstances proper conventions were essential, and in no way unsuitable to the general style of the dramas.

Rehearsals were important but brisk, and left a great deal to the individual actor. For a revival, it was expected to run through a whole play in a morning before giving it in the afternoon, and for such a method the actor needed to be prepared. A curious interplay must have been demanded between convention and spontaneity. None of the actors possessed copies of the whole text. They had their 'parts' carefully written out by the prompter, with cue-lines only added, apart from some indication of act and scene. The only view they had of the play as a whole was from an initial reading by an author, and from watching the rehearsals. The texts themselves were not printed until the piece was already a success. The prompter also took the cast first through the piece, plotting which doors were to be used for entrances and exits, and which scenes were to be employed. Except for grand tableau there was very little blocking of the stage movement in the modern sense. The actor was therefore required to respond according to his idea of his character within the context of conventions of stage movement.

The eighteenth century provides us with a number of manuals delivering rules for placing yourself on the stage.[43] They may seem forced, and doubtless they differed slightly from country to country, and from time to time, but some such principles were essential. They basically concern stage precedence. An actor alone has the stage to himself and may do as he pleases. As soon as there are two actors, the most important person must take the right-hand side of the stage. If a lady is present this should be she. When three play together, the most important places him or herself in the centre. As larger groups build up, the subsidiary characters form a semi-circle around this person. Such rules of precedence are based on Italian social manners, and it is not necessary to suppose that the English stage was quite so formal; but the best lit area was down on the fore-stage beneath the chandeliers, and this kind of group would therefore have been most appropriate. The precedence itself may have been decided on different principles – who was 'most important' for example may have been decided by dramatic requirements, since the kind of writing we find at the period makes it quite distinct whose 'scene' it is – but the basic idea of the line or the circle confronting the audience and focusing on a protagonist could still obtain, and solve many problems for the actors. The famous picture by Hogarth of the royal children performing Dryden's *The Conquest of Mexico* is late in date, and stiff in execution as suitable with amateurs, but it demonstrates the advantages of the method (Plate 35). The figures stand to face the audience, but when listening, turn their heads towards the speaker, who, however, addresses her words outwards. The emphasis is strongly on the words themselves and the particular attitude of the character speaking them, while that character is able to communicate directly with the audience – to present the character's thoughts rather than imitate her action.

The stances of the children in Hogarth's picture in fact display the opposition of head and trunk that is found in the serpentine formations of the minuet, and this too may be significant. Rules of precedence tell you who should be where, but they do not tell you how to get there. The curved floor-tracks of such a dance could provide the basic means by which the actors could reach the necessary points on the stage gracefully without getting in each other's way. It is interesting to note how, in the long ensemble scenes of many comedies, the actors are directed to 'retire' or 'come forward' or 'converse apart', suggesting that the series of duets and trios of which such scenes usually consist brought the speakers in turn into a row on the fore-stage, while the others circled away to stand in groups behind on the stage itself. The larger *tableaux* were often actually designed by the dancing-master, and the whole effect must have had a pleasing unity, since the modes of social dance were as much a part of the life-style depicted in comedy as they were of the ideals depicted in tragedy. Dryden takes care to remark at the climax of *1 The Conquest of Granada* (Act V) that the King and Almanzor 'stare at each other without saluting' as they pass. The notation of this tremendous breach of manners is interesting. It suggests that the ceremonies of social life in meeting and parting – the bow, the courtesy, the removing of the hat – were practised as an appropriate part of the comings and goings on the stage, adding the formality of ideal manners to the general stylisation of action. Given the verse and prose the actors had to speak, the formality of their society, and the mathematical elegance with which the plays were designed, such behaviour on the stage must have seemed as natural as it was significant.

This formality would also have been most helpful in focusing the individual actor's gestic presentation of character. This was where the life of the play was generated. The authors' instructions on the nature of their characters was the nearest thing to what we now think of as direction that the Restoration actors got. Such coaching must have consisted in the main of the author defining very clearly the character he intended, and the sequence of passions he had designed for the actor to incarnate. He would sometimes go farther than this. Crowne was very proud of having taught the comedian Leigh the precise, toothless lisp he required for the character of Bartoline in *City Politiques*.[44] Certainly the authors were very aware of the possibility of individual actors in the writing and casting of their plays. Dryden tailored many pieces to the talents of Mohun, Hart and Cartwright in the King's Company, and the important actresses there, the formidable Rebecca Marshall, the charming and brilliant Nell Gwyn. Otway conceived his greatest roles for Betterton and Mrs Barry, as did

Congreve for Betterton, Barry and Mrs Bracegirdle. Conversely, the actors themselves were very attached to their roles, and associated with particular types and qualities: Nokes, say, for mild humours and folly, Sandford for misshapen villainy. Once a part had been given out, it stayed with the actor, unless he went on to higher things, so that actors, in a sense, owned their characters, and stayed with them for many years. This could and did lead to anomalies like Betterton playing Romeo at sixty, but it must have also enabled actors on a tight schedule tò grow into their parts and mature their understanding of them. In a fascinating essay, the philosopher Kierkegaard describes how he watched Fru Heiberg as Juliet at eighteen and at thirty, and preferred her at thirty, because, though without the reality of youth, the mature actress was able to present youth more richly.[45] Actors specialised in types; but these types were understood by author, actor and audience as essential aspects of human nature, and as such were susceptible to a great variety of inflection. Against the dangers of repetition were set the delight of recognition and the surprise of new perceptions and observations.

The examples of the acting techniques of the Restoration have so far been drawn mainly from tragedy. This has been intentional. The combination of intimacy and precise stylisation, of psychological observation and physical image are clearest here; but they are also vital to the comic style of the time. There is of course a change of emphasis. As tragedy was to show men 'better than they are', so comedy showed them 'worse than they are'. As tragedy concentrated on the mathematical formulae that brought moral truths into their proper relation, so comedy satirised men's outward behaviour in the interest of moral comment. As tragedy depicted the passions, so comedy depicted the humours and follies of men. Tragedy was deductive, comedy inductive. All this made a difference, but though comedy was more behavioural in its subject matter, it was presented in the same gestic language, with the same concept of character and emphasis on design, and with the same difficulties of rehearsal and conventions of performance. It was probably not so necessary in the *tirades* of comedies to illustrate the movement of the narrative or the sense of the words with the gestures of rhetoric. The sentence structures were simpler anyway. But such gestures would be available if needed, and the same formality of delivery was required in a long speech if the absent ideas were to be made present. The speech may have been more rapid, as the vocabulary is more clipped; but the same precision of inflection or cadence is required to catch the innuendos of Etherege as the ironies of Dryden. This is indeed the music of common speech; for all the calculation of its arrangement:[46]

Methinks, indeed, I have been an age absent, but I intend to redeem the time; and how, and how stand Affairs, prithee now? Is the Wine

good? are the Women kind? Well, faith, a man had better be a
vagabond in this Town, than a Justice of Peace in the Country: I
was e're grown a Sot for want of Gentleman-like recreations; if a man
do but rap out an Oath, the people start as if a Gun went off; and if
one chance but to couple himself with his Neighbour's Daughter,
without the help of the Parson of the Parish, and leave a little
Testimony of his kindness behind him, there is presently such an
uproar, that a poor man is fain to fly his Country.

It is surprising upon 'how minute an article of sound' such a speech
depends for its effect. Sir Oliver Cockwood is not of course articulating
a passion. His is the folly of pretending to potency without the capability
or the presence of mind. His gentlemanly stance is therefore strained and
affected. The whole attitude can be modulated, not simply the eyes and
face; but the accidents of his appearance are carefully selected for their
significance in portraying such a 'character', and must be sustained as an
image through the speech in a similar manner to the cogitations of Cleomenes. Like the scenery itself, each physical image needs time to take,
and the more detailed, the more time it needs. Cibber's remark that
Wilkes could 'never succeed in the loose humours of Palamede'[47] shows
that Dryden's careful differentiation between the two young rakes was
clearly expected to be physicalised 'to the life'. We are not used to such
subtle distinctions of character on the modern stage.

The precision and invention with which such distinctions were made
is finely illustrated by the triple portrait of the comedian John Lacy,
commissioned by Charles II (Plate 37). He is shown as the coarse and
foolish Sawney in Sawney, the Scot, his own adaptation of The Taming of
the Shrew, as the fastidious Scruple in The Cheats, and the snide Galliard
in The Variety. The physical transformation is in each case complete, and
it is notable how the character of the costume is set off by the expression
of face, hands and posture. The detail is remarkable, even down to
Sawney's gesture of picking at his scrofulous wrist. Scrofula was a traditionally Scottish disease (the consequence, it was supposed, of their barba-
rous diet) and much coarse humour is got from this affliction in the course
of the comedy.[48] Similar gestic detail is caught in the business with the
wig in Nell Gwyn's Epilogue to Tyrannick Love (Plate 8), and the dramatists call again and again for such accurate physical gestures from the
actors. When Pepys saw Nell Gwyn as Florimell in The Maiden Queen,
he remarked:

But so great a performance of a comical part was never, I believe, in
the world before as Nell doth this, both as a mad girle and then,
most and best of all, when she comes in like a young gallant; and
hath the motions and carriage of a spark the most that ever I saw
any man have. (2 March 1667)

Dryden had designed for Nell a wonderful, wild, bantering character, and then given her a vivid transformation. Nell's satirical style is clear. In presenting the habits and behaviour of a man, she was still very much a woman. She was presenting a woman's idea of a man, or rather, her attitude to a certain kind of male behaviour to which she was often subjected. It must have been very funny and very winning, similar in effect to that required of the actress playing Hippolito in *The Tempest*. Pepys notes: 'It makes me, I confess, admire her.' Her appeal lay in the wit of her description as well as in the sight of her legs.[49]

Though the heroic postures of the tragic actor were softened in comedy, it remained formal, guided and controlled by an inner idea. Brecht remarked of the Chinese actor that in the process of performance he 'expresses his awareness of being watched'.[50] This is the key to the Restoration style, to the dialogue between the actor and the audience that was its life-blood. Within his specialism, the Restoration actor was called upon sometimes to describe a fool and sometimes a hero. He undertook both tasks with the same sharp eye, and the same precision and intimacy of address. The actor did not live his roles. He shared his author's idea of their nature with his audience. The presentation of Restoration text requires above all accuracy and objectivity. The actor's chief weapon was his judgment. Pepys was delighted when he was told by Killigrew that the actress Mary Knepp, of whom Pepys was fond, was likely to become one of the best players, 'she understanding so well' (2 December 1667). When the prompter Downes wants to praise an actor, he uses words like 'Exactness'. Their parts are 'Accurate', 'Correct', 'nicely [i.e. precisely] performed'.[51] In comedy as in tragedy, the actor's job was to build a proper image of his character, to physicalise it in descriptive gesture that was exciting in its aptness, so that the character was as perspicuous in the visual design of the entertainment as it was in the structure of the text – if necessary, more so. The actors, like the authors, traded in a baroque juxtaposition of images.

It is not helpful in these circumstances to consider whether such acting was naturalistic. Natural acting does not come about simply by a direct comparison of behaviour on and off stage. It comes of the actor's finding the physical consequences of the style of his texts, and adapting them to the space and for the audience of his performance, so as to communicate to them the inner truth of that style. It is of the communication of this truth that any age can say quite honestly it is 'performed to the life'.

6 · *Almanzor and Almahide, or The Conquest of Granada by the Spaniards*

Almanzor and Almahide, or The Conquest of Granada by the Spaniards is probably the most brilliant and paradoxical of those curious and fascinating heroic tragedies that held the stage with such short but such tremendous acclaim in the late 1660s, and early 1670s. It is a play in two parts and ten acts, epic alike in its subject, in its length and in the nature of its themes. Dryden began it with the entrance of Nell Gwyn in a funny hat:[1]

> This jeast was first of th'other house's making,
> And, five times try'd, has never fail'd of taking;
> For 'twere a shame a Poet should be kill'd
> Under the shelter of so broad a shield. (I, Prologue, 1–4)

The favourite actress was wearing a 'broad-brimmed hat and waist-belt'. The hat itself, reputedly as round as a cartwheel, had been worn by Nokes, the much-loved clown of the Duke's Company, in parody of the exaggerations of French fashion, for a performance before Henrietta Maria in May 1670, and also in Crowne's comedy *The English Monsieur*, in which Nokes had added to his costume the Duke of Marmontel's enormously long French sword.[2]

> This is that hat whose very sight did win yee
> To laugh and clap, as though the Devil were in yee.
> As then for *Noakes*, so now, I hope, you'l be
> So dull, to laugh, once more, for love of me. (ll. 4–8)

In the later months of 1670, when *The Conquest of Granada* was first presented by the King's Company at the Theatre Royal, Bridges Street, the joke was obviously still sufficiently popular for Dryden to pinch it for his new work, setting the performance of his play firmly in the context of that 'war of the theatres' which was still providing material for satire and humour when the operatic *Tempest* was given at the Dorset Garden three years later. He is also using it very skilfully for both thematic and dramatic purposes.

Nellie is bantering her audience with the now familiar combination of flattery and insult:

> I'll write a Play, sayes one, for I have got
> A broad-brimm'd hat, and wastbelt to-w'rds a Plot.
> Sayes t'other, I have one more large than that.
> Thus they out-write each other with a hat. (ll. 8–12)

As usual, the rhetoric is hardly fair: *Granada* is out-writing its rivals in almost every way; but after the initial gibe at 'dull' audiences, Dryden is using the charm of the actress and his own meticulous utterance to build an intimacy with his public, an atmosphere of interest and agreement, at the expense of the rival company:

> They bring old Ir'n, and glass upon the Stage,
> To barter with the *Indians* of our Age.
> Still they write on; and like great Authors show;
> But 'tis as Rowlers in wet gardens grow;
> Heavy with dirt and gath'ring as they goe. (ll. 27–31)

Dryden is tilting at the other theatre's introduction of French farces which had hit the public taste; but he is also chatting the audience into a more sophisticated mood, weaning them away from his opening belly-laugh into a relaxed critical attention. By the end of the speech, a sense of togetherness and mutual understanding has been achieved. The audience is no longer 'dull'; it has become discerning. It prefers the edge of thought and wit to vulgar and farcical jests:

> For these, in Playes, are as unlawful Arms,
> As in a Combat, coats of Mayle, and Charms. (ll. 45–6)

The applause that greets the final military image is the result of a new kind of attention. Dryden has set his audience apart from his play, alert, in expectation of intellectual and imaginative nuance. He has also introduced a subtle distinction between contemplation and direct and uninhibited response which is the basis of his dramatic strategy throughout the long drama.

The dramatist immediately and brilliantly capitalises on this. The play opens with an epic narrative which substitutes for the scenic spectacle of the opening of *The Tempest* a verbal spectacle that is scarcely less astonishing. The curtain flies up on the palace of Granada. Here is Boabdelin, the Moorish king, with two of his high courtiers and his guards. The king was probably costumed with some Moorish accoutrements. A scimitar, an imposing turban and crown. The courtiers are venerable Restoration noblemen. The opening picture provides just that juxtaposition of the contemporary and the exotic we have found so characteristic. The three actors advance on to the fore-stage, the king in the centre, the courtiers to the left and right and respectfully behind. Boabdelin speaks:

> Thus, in the Triumphs of soft Peace I reign;
> And, from my Walls, defy the Pow'rs of *Spain*;
> With pomp and Sports, my Love I celebrate,
> While they keep distance; and attend my State (1,I.i.1–4)

At once the epic tone of Ariosto is established:[3]

> Of Dames, of Knights, of Arms, of loves delight,
> Of courtesies, of high attempts I speake.

It picks up the end of the prologue neatly, and is reflected in and sustained by the heroic posture of the three actors, who now evoke the wonders of a Moorish bull-fight with all the brilliance of language the poet can muster:

> *Castile* could never boast, in all its pride,
> A pomp so splendid; when the lists set wide,
> Gave room to the fierce Bulls, which wildly ran
> In *Sierra Ronda*, ere the War began:
> Who, with high Nostrils, Snuffing up the Wind,
> Now stood, the Champions of the Salvage kind.
> (1,I.i.20–5)

It is, in a way, as direct a verbal challenge of the other theatre as the prologue was. It is a demonstration of a poet's virtuosity, his ability to make absent objects present to the mind's eye.

It may at first seem a rather static opening; but the stasis conceals its own art. The stance of the actors is reminiscent of soloists in an oratorio, and such artificiality is quite in accordance with the manner in which their conversation is contrived. Their words begin addressed to their companions on the stage, but as the speeches develop, a turn of the head directs the description straight to the audience in the theatre. The very stillness of the actors serves to focus attention on the delicate nuances of the words and these give the play its forward movement through the brilliant juxtapositions of idea and image. The characters are physically and psychologically static, but the action moves forwards in an intellectual dance, the coolness of which can incorporate dry humour into the excitement of the narrative. An unknown knight eventually beheads the fearsome bull.

> Not heads of Poppies, (when they reap the grain)
> Fall with more ease before the lab'ring Swayn,
> Then fell his head:–
> It fell so quick, it did even death prevent:
> And made imperfect bellowings as it went. (ll. 92–6)

The final couplet, with its apposite reminiscence of the dying bull in Virgil's *Aeneid* (II, 222–4), invites both laughter and delighted applause from an informed audience. The cool delivery and epic style play with the mind, pitting imagination and tradition against each other. It is a style to be savoured, in which idea and allusion are an important part of the pleasure, and it is not undramatic; the subtleties of tone were in good hands: Dryden orchestrated his description for three of the leading actors of the company, all experienced men and favourites of the audience – Edward Kynaston as Boabdelin, William Cartwright as Abenamar, and Michael Mohun as Abdelmelech.

After the pathetically humorous slaughter of the bull, the play erupts into action. Dryden had given the bulk of the narrative to Major Mohun, a favourite of the king's, and he gives him a final couplet, to still his applause and act as an up-beat to the new scene:

ABDELMELECH: Then all the Trumpets Victory did sound,
And yet their clangors in our shouts were drown'd.
(*A confus'd noise within*)

BOABDELIN: Th'Alarm-bell rings from our *Alhambra* walls,
And, from the Streets, sound Drums and Ataballes.
(*Within, a Bell, Drumms and Trumpets*) (ll. 97–100)

The contrast is brilliantly placed. The narrative action has lasted long enough and a change of attention is needed. A mode of contemplation is changed suddenly to a mode of action, as, to create a new impulse to our interest Dryden carries the epic out of words into picaresque event. This interchange between action and description is the basic technique of the play, and reflects the movement from farce to critical attention generated by the prologue. The rest of the first act establishes it fully.

There now enter the leaders of two factions, the Zegries and the Abencerrages, two noble families of the Moorish kingdom presently at feud. Abenamar and Abdelmelech join the Abencerrages, and the parties confront each other with drawn swords, four on one side and three on the other. At this point Almanzor appears. He is the stranger who slew the bull, and with a hero's generosity, he joins the weaker side.

I cannot stay to ask which cause is best;
But this is so to me, because opprest. (ll. 128–9)

As his gesture is applauded, the king's guards enter, and come between the parties. The flurry of physical action leads into a rapid dialogue of abuse, which Boabdelin fails to subdue. It culminates in a swift fight between Almanzor and one of the Zegries, who is killed as Almanzor is seized by Boabdelin's guards. The direction changes again. There is now a sharp, intellectual confrontation between the king and the knight, which substitutes exciting dialectic for sword-play. By duelling in the king's presence Almanzor has forfeited his life:

BOABDELIN: The word which I have giv'n I'l not revoke;
If he be brave he's ready for the stroke.

ALMANZOR: No man has more contempt than I, of breath;
But whence hast thou the right to give me death?

> Obey'd as Soveraign by thy Subjects be,
> But know, that I alone am King of me.
> I am as free as Nature first made man
> 'Ere the base Laws of Servitude began,
> When wild in woods the noble Savage ran.

BOABDELIN: Since, then, no pow'r above your own you know,
> Mankind sho'd use you like a common foe,
> You should be hunted like a Beast of Prey;
> By your own Law, I take your life away. (ll. 201–13)

Hobbes has been substituted for Virgil, and there is personal conflict instead of narrative, but the same detached play of idea and allusion are manifest.[4] The mode of contemplation returns as the clash of swords is replaced by the clash of ideas, and the 'salvage' Knight takes his place in the arena, following the 'salvage' bull.

Dryden has laid the foundations of his great play with a care for both its intellectual content and its general ambiguity of tone. He has demonstrated his own precept that 'as in a perspective, so in tragedy, there must be a point of sight in which all lines terminate; otherwise the eye wanders and the work is false.'[5] The moral is the 'point of sight' of a drama, and that of *The Conquest of Granada*, Dryden tells us, is the same as that of the *Iliad* – 'that union preserves a commonwealth and discord destroys it'.[6] The appearance of the factions is the physical manifestation of this discord in Granada, and has been graphically portrayed as they burst in to drums and alarums. It has also been held as an exciting image through all the dialectic of the scenes with Almanzor, for the unreconciled enemies stand throughout their swords drawn though in the king's presence. As part of the argument, indeed, Almanzor himself actually articulates the moral, warning Boabdelin:

> Divided inter'sts, while thou thinkst to sway,
> Draw like two brooks thy middle stream away:
> For though they band, and jar, they both combine
> To make their greatness, by the fall of thine (1,I.i.226–9)

And this is echoed in Part 2, when Ferdinand of Arragon supports Abdalla, whom the Zegries have set up as a rival to his brother. Ferdinand succinctly remarks:

> He brings a specious title to our side;
> Those who would conquer, must their Foes divide.
> (2,I.i.39–40)

The plan works, and the framework of the elaborate plot is the means whereby Ferdinand and Isabella are enabled, by the dissensions within the city, to subdue it.

But the ideas sleeping within this moral concept are far more complex, and some of these ramifications have also been hinted at and graphically presented on the stage. Although dissension is a catalyst to the action, it is really ideas of power and authority that the play sets out to analyse and embody. Ferdinand and Isabella, as Christian rulers, have a legitimate right to Granada. They are its true rulers, and the machinations of the plot establish their authority.[7] But this 'fable' is really symbolic. It is the outer shell of right and wrong, law and order, within which the nature of right and authority is examined in far greater detail through analogous relationships – of king and subject, of lover and mistress, of father and child. The problem of king and subject lies at the centre of this first act. Boabdelin fails to reconcile or subdue the rival factions. He also fails to obtain the death of Almanzor, though he orders it. Though Boabdelin is king, Almanzor is more kingly. The former is rash and unstable, unable to carry through his designs. The latter, though rash enough, is secure in his own personality and strength. Where the one has official dominance, the other commands by personal power.

Dryden has employed the personalities of his actors to embody this paradox. Kynaston had originally played women's parts on the stage, and Pepys had remarked that as Epicoene in *The Silent Woman* he had at first appeared as the prettiest woman, and then as the handsomest man on the stage (8 January 1661). With the advent of actresses, he began to specialise in the more temperamental kinds of male character, and Cibber noted: 'He had a piercing Eye, and in characters of heroick Life, a quick, imperious Vivacity, in his Tone of Voice, that painted the Tyrant truly terrible.' (p. 73) This is perfect for the changeable yet vicious Boabdelin, and it is important to note that the violence he gives the character is a youthful violence. This is present in his figure, and frequently noted by others. His is an arbitrary power like that of the young as Horace describes them:[8]

> A Youth that first casts off his Tutors yoke,
> Loves Horses, Hounds, and Sports and Exercise,
> Prone to all Vice, impatient of Reproof,
> Proud, careless, fond, inconstant, and profuse.

He is opposed by a very different young man, whose temptations toward similar behaviour are ruled by a stronger will and deeper understanding. Almanzor is an astonishing part, and designed very carefully for Charles Hart, the most glamorous of the Restoration actors. Rymer has left this description of him: 'The audience are prepossessed and charmed by his action, before aught of the poet can approach their ears; and to the most wretched character he gives a luster that so dazzles the sight, that the deformities of the poet cannot be perceived.'[9] In this passage Rymer is remarking that many bad poets owe their success solely to such an actor. Dryden is not a bad poet, but he is using precisely this 'lustre' of personality to very particular effect. Boabdelin is violent and

sinister; Almanzor is unruly, charming and absurd. His heroic gestures
are those of an innocent, and fine play is made with the way those gestures
cut across accepted behaviour and patterns of thought. Faced with the
desertion of an army, he remarks:

> What are ten thousand subjects such as they?
>
> If I am scorn'd – I'le take my self away. (1,III.i.497–8)

When his mistress has consented to marry the king in order to save her
lover from execution, he cries out:

> Would you to save my Life, my love betray?
>
> Here; take me; bind me; carry me away;
>
> Kill me: I'll kill you if you disobey. (1,V.i.405–7)

and again, when she is accused of adultery:

> 'Tis false; she is not ill, nor can she be;
>
> She must be Chaste, because she's lov'd by me.
>
> (2,IV.iii.396–7)

His responses contain a wild logic which would be intolerable were it not
funny and not so accurately observed. Hart's personality at once softens
the absurdity and lends conviction to the act. He and Kynaston embody
positive and negative aspects of the same elements of youthful wilfulness.

The significance of this for the main idea of the play is demonstrated
at the climax of the first act. Boabdelin, reconciled to Almanzor through
Abdalla's intercession, again fails to reconcile the rival factions. Almanzor
takes over:

> What Subjects will precarious Kings regard?
>
> A Beggar speaks too softly to be heard.
>
> Lay down your Armes; 'tis I command you now.
>
> Do it – or by our Prophets soul I vow,
>
> My hands shall right your King on him I seize.
>
> Now, let me see whose look but disobeys. (1,I.i.275–9)

The hero prowls around the ring of figures on the stage, quelling them
with his eyes. He finishes, and they shout with one accord:

> Long live King Mahomet Boabdelin!

It is outrageous, but brilliant. Given the hypothesis of the hero, Dryden
devises a dramatic gesture which by its absolute rightness must induce the
'laughter of approbation'. He then capitalises on it. Abruptly, Almanzor
silences the shouts:

> No more; but hush'd as midnight silence go:
>
> He will not have your Acclamations now.
>
> Hence you unthinking crowd
>
> (*The common people go off on both parties*)
>
> Empire, thou poor and despicable thing,
>
> When such as these unmake or make a King. (ll. 282–6)

The moral sentence gets its applause for actor, dramatist and image, and finally Abdalla neatly verbalises the whole concept for the audience:

> How much of virtue lies in one great soul,
> (*embracing him*)
> Whose single force can multitudes control. (ll. 287–8)

The little scene has posed a central question about the nature of greatness and legitimate authority with an ironical, serio-comic tone that beautifully combines excitement and detachment.

Dryden can now carry his audience with him into the various vistas he has planned. These have the labyrinthine complexity of Ariosto rather than the uncompromising solidity of Homer. The play is a baroque not a classical structure; and it probably helps to understand the quality of the experience it presents if this tension between epic and romance is allowed to colour, in the imagination, that between the rational tone of the play and the passionate material it explores. Dryden works out these tensions through nine acts of accelerating action, achieving the increasing pace both through the visual presentation and the plotting of his epic. His central theme is wittily echoed by the winding actions of three separate love-stories, to which, despite the rigorous abstractions behind their arrangement, Dryden gives a powerful theatrical excitement. He employs the temperamental characteristics of his actors, whom he knew well, to build a complex texture of responses in the audience. Their emotional talents are rigidly controlled by the formal techniques of the period. Attitude, tone and character are clearly indicated and sharply focused. But Dryden's invention of visual emblems is highly original, setting novelty side by side with convention and enabling the actors to break out of formality from time to time in startling moments of intense expressiveness. The presences of the actors play on our feelings, while the formality of the action with its subtle juxtapositions of character and idea, makes the experience an object for the mind.

In the first of the love-stories, Almanzor and Boabdelin are brought into conflict by their love for Abenamar's daughter, Almahide. Sexual rivalry now augments the natural rivalry of the two men for personal authority. In Boabdelin this produces an erratic jealousy born of his need for Almanzor's support in his wars, and his intolerence of his presence. In Almanzor, whose previous thoughts have been only for war and honour, however, love provides a civilising force, as in the savage Cymon of Dryden's later fable:[10]

> So Reason in this Brutal Soul began:
> Love made him first suspect he was a Man . . .
> Love taught him Shame, and Shame with Love at Strife
> Soon taught the sweet Civilities of Life.

Almanzor has a natural authority over others. Love teaches authority over himself. In Boabdelin, who has no such authority, it destroys even his self-possession.

The first encounter of the lovers is touching, comical, and outrageous by turns. Almanzor has ousted Boabdelin from his palace, and Almahide is at his mercy. She determines to throw herself upon his pity, and, as the woman-hating hero returns in triumph, '*falls at his feet, being veyl'd*',

ALMAHIDE: Turn, mighty Conqu'ror, turn your Face this way,
        Do not refuse to hear the wretched pray. (1,III.i.308–9)

The pretty, drooping attitudes of the woman and her female attendant is a nicely ironical opening, contrasted with the glamorous Hart's firm question to the expectant audience:

ALMANZOR: What business can this Woman have with me?

ALMAHIDE: That of th'afflicted to the Deity. (ll.310–11)

It is really very naughty. The drooping hands (Figure 19) are lifted with the veiled head into an attitude of worship. It is the Magdalen at the feet of Christ.

ALMAHIDE: So may your Arms success in battels find;
        So may the Mistris of your vows be kind,
        If you have any; or if you have none,
        So may your Liberty be still your own. (ll. 312–15)

Almanzor is touched; but he knows his duty:

ALMANZOR: Yes, I will turn my face; but not my mind:
        You bane and soft destruction of mankind,
        What would you have with me? (ll. 316–18)

Now she unveils, and the hero's eyes are riveted on hers, turned upward in holy veneration (Figure 21) as in the portrait of the queen as St Catherine (Plate 1).

ALMAHIDE: I beg the Grace
        You would lay by those terrours of your face.
        Till calmness to your eyes you first restore
        I am afraid, and I can beg no more. (ll. 318–21)

Her eyes now meet his, with the openness of 'esteem' (Figure 22); but the hero is caught fast.

ALMANZOR: I'me pleas'd and pain'd since first her eyes I saw,
        As I were stung by some *Tarantula*.
        Armes, and the dusty field I less admire;
        And soften strangely in some new desire . . . (ll. 329–31)

A happier commentary on the delicate effect of formalised expression could not be found. Almanzor is overcome by what he calls the 'lethargy of love', and as he describes its effects, his normally aggressive attitude softens into tenderness before our eyes:

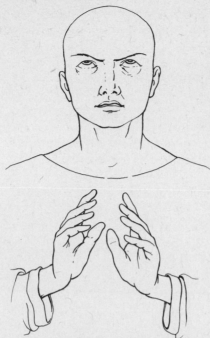

Figure 21   Supplication and Veneration. Cf. Figure 19 (*Composite drawing by Lesley Skeates after Bulwer and Lebrun*)

> 'Tis he; I feel him now in every part:
> Like a new Lord he vaunts about my Heart;
> Surveys in state each corner of my Brest,
> While poor fierce I, that was, am dispossest. (ll. 338–41)

The mocking laugh that greets the reference to the parts in which the effects of love are manifest is softened by amusement and sympathy. The audience's awareness of the accuracy of the description makes them share the experience and the moral.

But there is, of course, another dimension to the scene. The glamorous Hart was matched by the yet more glamorous Nell Gwyn. Nell was chiefly known as a comic actress of wit and verve. She had soft brown hair, a slightly chubby face and dimples.[11] Pepys disliked her in tragic parts, but Dryden here seems to be making specific use of her personality, firstly to give an ironical charm to the play and secondly, perhaps, to add malice to the irony by contemporary allusion.[12] Nell had been Hart's mistress, and had recently been taken up by the king. The actor was known to have taken this badly, which must have added a curious undercurrent to his heroic restraint upon the stage. The scenes between Almanzor and Almahide turn on the same, reiterative gesture. Her sweetness comes up

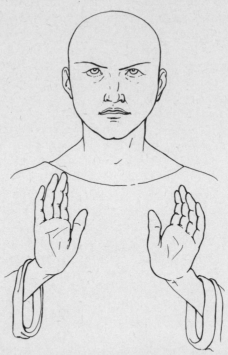

Figure 22   Admiration and Esteem. Cf. Figure 19 (*Composite drawing by Lesley Skeates after Bulwer and Lebrun*)

against the jagged corners of his delightfully *farouche* personality and makes them smooth. The actions are elegant and symbolic. At the end of their first encounter he finds he cannot have her because she is betrothed to another, and after an onset of fury he controls himself:

> Retire, fair Creature, to your needful rest;
> There's something noble labouring in my Brest:
> This raging fire which through the Mass does move,
> Shall purge my dross, and shall refine my Love. (ll. 421–4)

The formality of the gesture is precisely what makes it moving in its ironical context. Addison noted:[13]

> The ladies are wonderfully pleased to see a man insulting Kings and affronting the Gods in one scene, and throwing himself at the feet of his mistress in another. Let him behave insolently towards the men, and abjectly towards the fair one, and it is ten to one he proves a favourite with the boxes.

He was quite right that Dryden exploited this pattern; but its implications are at once more subtle and more truly observed. The conventional opposition describes a series of movements of the mind. It enacts another series of puns on the nature of possession and self-possession.

The ironies of this conception gain a telling variation in the second of Dryden's plots. Lyndaraxa, the sister of the Zegry leader, has two lovers – the king's brother, Abdalla, and his minister, Abdelmelech – and she rules them both with a rod of iron. This is an unnatural state of affairs. Man is the rightful ruler of woman, as are Ferdinand and Isabella of Spain; but the two men allow their actions to be dominated by their desires. Abdalla is coaxed by Lyndaraxa into trying to depose his brother: she will marry him if he becomes king. Abdelmelech tries to woo her from the oath of treachery, but is always deceived by his love for her. This echoes the previous concept of men's authority over himself, the perennial conflict of desire with duty and self-government. Lyndaraxa has the personal authority of Almanzor, and like him has no right to authority over others. Like him also, there is an anti-social centre to her strength:

> Yes! I avowe th' ambition of my soul,
> To be that one, to live without controul:
> And that's another happiness to me
> To be so happy as but one can be. (1,II.i.147–9)

But love does not civilise her, and she remains alone to the end, using it as a weapon, while her lovers, like the city, stand divided against themselves.

The contrast between Mrs Marshall as Lyndaraxa and Nell Gwyn as Almahide provides a vital clue to the dynamics of the play. Mrs Marshall was the tragedienne of the company, a woman of dark and passionate intelligence.[14] The contrasted hardness and softness of their personalities is brought to together at a vital moment in Part I. Almahide's Zambra dance is interrupted by a surprise attack, and the two women are left together:

> (*An Alarum within*)
> ALMAHIDE: What dismal Planet did my Triumphs light?
> Discord the Day, and Death does rule the Night:
> The noise, my Soul does through my Senses wound.
> LYNDARAXA: Me thinks it is a noble, sprightly Sound,
> The Trumpet's clangor, and the clash of arms?
> This noyse may chill your blood, but mine it warms.
> (1,III.i.249–54)

The two characters are boldly juxtaposed by the shared couplet. The impression of warmth and violence is sharply presented in a contrast that is also not without humour.

Lyndaraxa is one of Dryden's most brilliant creations. She is a figure of high comedy endowed with the passions of tragedy, and Dryden builds a splendidly ambiguous response in his audience by devising dramatic gestures that demand the 'laughter of approbation' (for author and

performer) at actions of sinister moral purpose. By making Lyndaraxa a
character of great wit, Dryden allows the actress to make the audience
accomplices in her plans. She is given the opportunity to use all her
charms (and the proximity to the audience the stage affords) in asides or
part-asides that clarify, amuse and astonish:

> I will be constant yet, if Fortune can;
> I love the King: let her but name the Man. (1,IV.ii.7–8)

The 'character' of ambition is captured in two lines with irresistible
frankness, and she can be as frank with her lovers:

> Either confess your fault or hold your tongue;
> For I am sure I'm never in the wrong. (1,IV.ii.199–200)

So she keeps the Prince Abdalla in his place until he has murdered his
brother for her and made himself king. After all, as she tells him:

> Princes are Subjects still:–
> Subject and Subject can small diff'rence bring:
> The diff'rence is twixt Subjects and a King.
> And since, Sir, you are none, your hopes remove;
> For less than Empire, I'le not change my love.
> (1,II.i.118–22)

Sir Walter Scott rather unfairly remarked that Lyndaraxa's success could
only be justified 'by the extreme imbecility of her lovers.'[15] This is surely
to miss the point. A good many men are finely taken in by women of wit
and charm, and Dryden's psychology is expertly observed. It is rather
the clarity of the process by which they are manipulated that makes these
men seem fools to the modern reader. Yet it is precisely this clarity that
the Restoration audience demanded. The succession of scenes in which
Lyndaraxa deceives the two men may seem at first sight repititious or
banal, but in fact each scene depicts a quite different technique of deception on the lady's part as she adapts to each new attempt to gain control
of her mind and person. The scenes articulate a magnificent vocabulary
of the weaknesses, self-deceptions, greed and aggression of love.

The snide irony may not be sympathetic, but it can be profound. By
opposing Mrs Marshall with Mohun as Abdelmelech, Dryden was able
to deepen the audience's response to his comic presentation in a highly
original way. Mohun had fought on the king's side in the civil war, and,
from the roles Dryden wrote for him clearly combined a blunt, military
presence with dignity and feeling. Indeed, he seems to have been an actor
who could actually cry on stage. In their first scene together, Lyndaraxa,
by a studied alternation of kindness and asperity, reduces Abdelmelech,
who has had the temerity to reprimand her, to a state in which he is 'half
crying'. In their second scene, the turning point is a gesture which is
posed with a rigorous formality; but one character's tears are real, the
other's feigned. This is very bold, and the artificial manner of the time

must have been extremely sophisticated to do justice to such a contrast. Lyndaraxa has followed Abdallah to the rebel camp. Abdelmelech, in his turn, follows her, and demands her return as a proof of love and loyalty. She has no intention of losing the opportunity of the crown presented by Abdallah's present success but does not wish to burn her boats with the other man. Predictably, she has recourse to tears. She weeps. She wrings her hands. It has its effect.

LYNDARAXA: Leave me alone to mourn my Misery;
               I cannot cease to love you, but I'le die.
               (*Leans her Head on his Arm*)
ABDELMELECH: What Man but I so long unmov'd could hear
               (*Weeping*)
               Such tender passion, and refuse a Tear?
               But do not talk of dying any more,
               Unless you mean that I should die before.
               (1,IV.ii.82–7)

The lady knows she has won, and plays out the line:

LYNDARAXA: I fear your feign'd Repentance comes too late;
               I dye to see you still thus obstinate:
               But yet, in Death, my truth of love to show,
               Lead me; if I have strength enough I'le go.
ABDELMELECH: By, Heav'n, you shall not goe: I will not be
               O'recome in Love or Generosity. (88–91)

Abdelmelech's firmness of purpose is undermined by his feelings. His natural honesty and desire to believe in the truth of her beauty ensures his downfall. The scene demonstrates the way a man is unmanned by love, and it is both true and funny. But it is also tragicomedy of a most complex kind. The man knows he is being cheated and violence and frustration are made explicit beneath the lack of will:

               Now I too late perceive I am undone:
               Living and seeing to my Death I run.
               I know you false; yet in your Snares I fall;
               You grant me nothing; and I grant you all. (ll. 102–5)

The very clarity of the statement enables the audience to feel the pain of the experience while laughing and applauding the wit of the observation. The style is grandiloquent and the action heroic, but the formal gestures of the actors and the balanced precision of the couplets combine with the passion of the actor to create a dialectic which, like Witwoud's enquiry to a lady about her husband, is at once foreign and domestic, placing human reality and heroic ideal in mocking conjunction. The everyday relations of men and women are magnified by a royal and exotic action, and the resulting irony becomes the means of communicating feeling within a formal style.[16]

The undercurrent of emotion and violence in the character of Abdelme-lech, and its almost wanton provocation by Lyndaraxa move *The Conquest of Granada* towards a genuinely tragic intensity. This intensity is further supported by the third plot. The story of Ozmyn and Benzayda first appears in the fourth act of Part 1, and brings a new note into the pattern of responses. It carries over to the fourth act of Part 2, and in its almost continuous seriousness of tone binds the varying moods of the long play together. Ozmyn is an Abencerrago, the son of Abenamar; Benzayda is a Zegry, the daughter of Selin. They are in love, but their parents are at war. Far from concentrating on the emotional tensions of the children, as Shakespeare does in *Romeo and Juliet*, Dryden presents us with a series of clearly articulated dilemmas, which underlie the whole action and call into question the nature of our concepts of right and wrong, authority and obedience. As Benzayda puts it:

> When parents their commands unjustly lay
> Children are privileg'd to disobey. (1,IV.ii.283–4)

Dryden is creating a dialectical manner similar to that of Corneille, and building a plot which is in fact a symphony of ideas.

Benzayda was played by Mrs Boutell. Young, and a favourite of the town, she had chestnut hair and bright blue eyes. Curll tells us that she was a considerable actress: 'She was low of Stature, had a very agreable Features, a good complexion, but a Childish look. Her voice was weak, tho' very mellow; she generally acted the young, Innocent Lady Whom all the heroes are mad in love with.'[17] Dryden uses these attributes with some skill. The light-weight, mellow voice, and the innocent, rather childish beauty are perfect for Benzayda, and act as a foil to the absolute-ness of the character, and to the passionate severity of the two older men who oppose her. When Abenamar rejects Benzayda although she has saved Ozmyn's life; he remarks:

> What constancy canst thou 'ere hope to finde.
> In that unstable, and soon conquer'd mind?
> What piety canst thou expect from her,
> Who could forgive a Brothers Murderer?
> (1,V.i.116–19)

Her change of allegiance, guided by love, is morally right, whereas his unbending anger proves a parody of virtue. In fact Selin and Abenamar complement Almanzor and Boabdelin; they are two types of the wilfulness of age. Of these Selin, played by Wintershall,[18] specialist in such fierce roles, is the more spontaneously emotional and Dryden contrives to explore his temperament in a series of formal gestures, which are thus contrasted to the arrogant implacability of his opposite, Abenamar, played by the veteran Cartwright, then rising seventy, a great age indeed at that period.

Throughout these scenes, Dryden meets the challenge of formalising overpowering emotions with great brilliance. Sometimes he used conventional gestures to incarnate the feeling, and sometimes gestures of surprising originality, always keeping distinct the 'character' of the two old men. The climatic gestures demonstrate the shameful realisation of the inadequacy of their conventional virtue. Selin is the first to be reconciled and Dryden contrives a wonderful breakdown of rhythm in the formal couplets, indicating a melting of his heart into tears. The static actor is enabled to present his breakdown by means of a vocal gesture. Abenamar's fall is greater and rises to a full stage gesture in which all formality is abandoned. Cartwright was one of Dryden's favourite actors and the poet clearly admired his combination of age and passion, and uses it to give life to a character of absolute and ferocious will. When Ozmyn confronts him, in his father-in-law's defence, he says:[19]

> In armes too? fighting for my enemy?
> I'le do a *Roman* justice; thou shalt dy. (2,II.i.34–5)

When he hears that Benzayda has saved his son's life and learns who she is, he comments:

> Know that as *Selin* was not won by thee,
> Neither will I by *Selin's* daughter be.
> Leave her, or cease henceforth to be my Son:
> This is my will: and this I will have done. (1,V.i.128–31)

Given the strength and age of the actor, such absoluteness is both exciting and convincing. It enables Dryden to produce his final and most extreme Corneillean hypothesis.

Abenamar captures Selin, and announces that he will release him only if Ozmyn comes to take his place. Both Ozmyn and Benzayda come to offer their lives instead. Selin would die for them both. As the scene unfolds Abenamar falls silent. At each new proposal he is more overcome. The gradual change of his facial expression is completed as usual in the dialogue:

> SELIN: This virtue wou'd even Savages subdue;
> And shall it want the pow'r to vanquish you?
> OZMYN: It has, it has: I read it in his eyes;
> 'Tis now not anger, 'tis but shame denyes;
> A shame of errour, which great spirits find,
> Which keeps down vertue strugling in the mind.
> (2,IV.i.122–7)

The actor's task is wonderfully simplified by the combined clarity and complexity of the verbal description. Feeling is now allowed to break out:

> ABENAMAR: Yes; I am vanquished! the fierce conflict's past:
> And shame itself is now ore'come at last. (ll. 128–9)

The man's hesitant acceptance of his own misconduct is finely articulated:

> 'Twas long before my stubborn Mind was won;
> But, melting once, I on the suddain run;
> Nor can I hold my headlong kindness, more
> Than I could curb my cruel Rage before. (ll. 130–33)

The image of the melting river proves to be a curious and brilliant pun, giving the actor a verbal foundation from which to break out into 'headlong' and unexpected movement.

> (*Runs to* Benzayda *and embraces her*)
> *Benzayda*, 'twas your Vertue vanquish'd me:
> That, could alone surmount my Cruelty.
> (*Runs to* Selin *and unbinds him*)
> Forgive me, *Selin*, my neglect of you!
> But men just waking scarce know what they do. (ll. 134–7)

The contrasted depiction of the passions of shame in two different natures is beautifully captured: Selin's voice, choked with tears; Abenamar's silence bursting into action – the character of wrath and that of pride. In fact Abenamar's gesture is basically a conventional one. Gildon tells us: 'The constant and direct Foot is the Index of steady, certain constancy, and right Study and Aim of our Designs. But on the contrary, Feet full of Motion are the Habit of the inconstant and fluctuating in their Counsels and Resolves.'[20] The melting of the silent, stubborn attitude into the strange confusion of actually running about the stage is splendidly emblematic in its breach of all decorum. But Dryden can cap it. He still has one climactic gesture in store:

> OZMYN: O Father!
> BENZAYDA: Father!_____
> ABENAMAR: Dare I own the name!_____
> Speak; speak it often, to remove my shame.
> (*They all embrace him*) (ll. 138–9)

It seems in this last embrace as if harmony is restored; but marvellously, Abenamar cannot bear it: he fights them off:

> O Selin; O my Children, let me goe!
> I have more kindness than I yet can show.
> For my recov'ry, I must shun your sight;
> Eyes, us'd to darkness, cannot bear the light.
> (*He runs in, they following him*) (ll. 140–3)

The *volte-face* is a magnificent piece of psychological observation, while the return of his confusion of step and gesture, and the brilliant final couplet encapsulate the observed truth in language and in action.

The Restoration style of acting and presentation is the key to Dryden's dramaturgy in *The Conquest of Granada*. The 'brilliance of event' upon which Scott commented is a highly complex theatrical phenomenon.[21]

Although it is an epic action, it is a fore-stage play. The baroque convolutions of the plot are offset by an intimate and steely presentation of ideas. In the notorious Epilogue to Part 2, the poet claimed the superiority of his time to that of Shakespeare and Jonson, and he claimed it on the grounds of delicacy and subtlety of language, form and manners. The arrogance of the claim outraged many; but it is true. The real difficulty is that such refinement does not fit easily into drama, as it does not fit easily into life.

Dryden unfolds the first part of his epic in what appears to be a *palais à volonté*. The place is formally the same, the action apparently unbroken, the *liasion des scènes* usually observed. But this neo-classical elegance is no more than a clever cheat. In the very first act the scene changes from Boabdelin's palace to the Vivarambla place, without the characters leaving the stage. The change is solely in the dialogue. Act IV begins with Boabdelin and Abenamar ousted from the palace, yet there is no indication of a change of scene. The fifth act begins with Abdalla '*under the walls of the Albayzin*', and then changes to Abenamar's appartments and then to the palace again. It could appear that the text merely lacks scenic directions; but this is not so in Part 2, and their absence in Part 1 is clearly intentional. The changes of place are slight, and are indicated by a clever use of the fore-stage. So, the opening descriptions are played on the fore-stage, but when the factions enter, and the scene should alter, the action simply employs the full stage area for additional guards and rabble, extending the image and so redefining the space. For the central acts, transition from intimate to epic actions is handled in a similar manner. In Act IV there is a crucial change of place, but the presence of characters inside or outside the Alhambra is merely suggested by entries from left or right fore-stage doors. When Lyndaraxa goes into the fortress of the Albayzyn, she uses one of the down-stage doors. When Abdalla wishes to return there, he knocks at the same door. She appears in the fore-stage balcony, and repulses him. The new place is again indicated without a scene change. The same setting transfers its location through the presence of different groups of characters, and it is only occasionally that an empty stage occurs, usually to allow a transition from one plot to another, and so to mask the awkwardness implicit in the spurious unity of place.[22]

The point becomes clear as we study Part 2. The intricate dialogues of Part 1 demand stillness and direct communication with the audience to put over their detail and design, to hold the audience's attention to the words; but for the second play something more must be added. The first act begins in 'A Camp', with the first appearance of the Spanish army; the second, in 'A Grove'. For most of the fourth, we have 'A Gallery in the Alhambra', and in between we alternate 'The Alhambra' and 'The Albayzyn', and reach a fine climax in 'The Vivarambla'. These changes are now all mentioned explicitly in the stage directions. For the second part of his play, Dryden has quickened his visual rhythm by beginning to change location before the eyes of the audience, and so increase the excitement of the spectacle and give an added sense of movement. Actually, he has been very economical about it. 'A Camp' and 'A Wood' clearly come from the theatre's stock, as can 'The Gallery', though as a 'night scene' the latter might have had to be got up specially. 'The Alhambra' may well have been the main setting presented for Part 1 (since this scene is only clearly 'The Alhambra' at the beginning of Act IV, it emphasises the general ambiguity of place in Part 1 – the 'general' location of this play is never needed in Part 2). 'The Albayzyn', being a fortress, could have employed the elements of a stock castle, in contrast to the Moorish grace of the main palace. The climax is 'The Vivarambla', a new scene probably only here employing the full depth of the stage, and allowing a space in the deep scene for the setting of the necessary scaffold and throne, and for the spectators that are said to fill the stage. Since the scene remains for most of the rest of the play, which contains much private action (on the fore-stage for intimacy) and a battle for the city, crowds painted in the stands would seem out of place even on the Restoration stage. Both visually and dramatically, action takes over from contemplation in Part 2.

Dryden is already aware that the intense accuracy and intellectual precision of his approach is caviar to the general. In the beautiful Epilogue to Part 1, he wrote:

> Success, which can no more than beauty last,
> Makes our sad Poet mourn your favours past:
> For, since without desert he got a name,
> He fears to lose it now with greater shame.
> Fame, like a little Mistriss of the Town,
> Is gaind with ease; but then she's lost as soon:
> For as those taudry Misses soon or late,
> Jilt such as keep 'em at the highest rate:
> (And oft the Laquey, or the Brawny Clown,
> Gets what is hid in the loose body'd gown;)
> So Fame is false to all that keep her long,
> And turns up to the Fop that's brisk and young.
> (p. 99, ll. 1–12)

The image is a subtle and significant one. At the play's opening, Nell Gwyn satirised the public's pleasure in farce and show – the lackey and the brawny clown of popular taste and favour; now the old man laments the victory of vigour over subtlety (which actor delivered these lines? Cartwright, perhaps, or Mohun?). And subtlety, after all, is the poet's real love. The point is, that in his epic, Dryden has striven to combine the two. With the mode of action, the turns of plot, the sword play, the brilliant clashes of dramatic temperament, the carefully placed spectacular scenes, he has tried to stimulate the excitement of popular melodrama; and then he has endeavoured to glean from that excitement moments in a mode of contemplation in which the mind can observe the ironies of human endeavour. By juxtaposing the picaresque and the philosophical in this way, he has of course, accomplished a further irony.

The real strength of *The Conquest of Granada* lies in the way it takes the popular ideals of its audience and through the medium of ironical dialogue with the spectators plays upon their awareness of the gap between those ideals and actual human behaviour. Dr Johnson remarked that the scenes 'exhibit a kind of illustrious depravity, and majestic madness: such as, if it is sometimes despised, is often reverenced, and in which the ridiculous is mingled with the astonishing.'[23] Dryden himself said that the purpose of his play was to raise wonder and admiration, but this exemplary intention is contradicted by his dramatic strategy. His studied ironies do precisely mix the ridiculous with the astonishing, if not in exactly the way Dr Johnson meant. Dryden is writing about the ways in which the idealised and the observed, the hypothetical and the actual, build incompatible versions of the same truth. He provides an hilariously cynical view, not of heroism itself, but of the ideal of the heroic, and at the same time manages to suggest the touching beauty of the ideal itself.

At the climax of the last act, Lyndaraxa, after betraying the city, is at last proclaimed Queen of Granada by Ferdinand and Isabella. Triumphant, she turns on Abdelmelech and promises that her new power will at last enforce his abject obedience to her will. It is an action that is a moral simile: the woman's sexual tyranny is now assimilated into political tyranny. It is too much for the man, who finally revenges his shame by stabbing her to death. It is a powerful moment. The Restoration liked their deaths bloody, and the physical realities would not have been spared.[24] The good manners and wit of their earlier dialogue suddenly sprawls with uncontrolled fury.

KING: Look to the Lady! – Sieze the Murderer!
ABDELMELECH: I'le do myself that Justice I did her. (*Stabbing himself*)
                  (2,V.iii.246–7)

And yet even in the execution of the bloody deed there is order and objectivity. The private moment is a violent parody of the sexual act, but it is played on a crowded stage. Ferdinand and Isabella are there, perhaps in emblematic Renaissance clothes along with their soldiers; around are Moorish gentlemen in their seventeenth-century coats, with turbans; the dying pair wear contemporary dress. The heart of the fable lies in Dryden's perception of the close connection between the stupendous and the familiar in the workings of the human imagination. The action comes to rest in a picture with a caption:

ABDELMELECH: Thy blood I to thy ruin'd Country give,
But love too well thy murther to outlive.
Forgive a love, excus'd by its excess,
Which, had it not been cruel, had been less.
Condemn my Passion then, but pardon me;
And think I murdered him who murder'd thee.
(*Dies*) (ll. 248–53)

It is notable that far from losing the energy of the action by these means Dryden focuses it and brings it to a head as the ordinary woman dies aping an empress, with a gesture of passionate parody:

LYNDARAXA: Sure Destiny mistakes; this Death's not mine;
She dotes, and meant to cut another Line.
Tell her I am a Queen; – but 'tis too late;
Dying, I charge Rebellion on my Fate:
Bow down, ye Slaves . . . (*to the Moors*)
Bow quickly down, and your Submission show.

The Moors prostrate themselves before her, and the actress struggles for a long moment to sustain her attitude of triumph against the reality of death.

I'm pleas'd . . .

Lyndaraxa cries at last, combining, in a little verb, gracious consent and agonised achievement,

to taste an Empire . . .

however small the sip, as at a wine-tasting, or perhaps, even more ironically, as to the page who tests to see that the royal cup contains no poison,

ere I go . . .

She collapses and dies, and by precision of word, image and allusion – the whole scene has echoes of Marlowe's *Tamburlaine* – Dryden encapsulates the ironies of her mind. However exaggerated such gestures may seem today, I am not sure that any stage has been able to embody so tellingly the distance between man's actual behaviour and his image of himself.

7 · *The Country Wife*

It is an arresting device to open a play with an aside. Wycherley does so in *The Country Wife*:[1]

> (*Enter* Horner, *and* Quack *following him at a distance*)
>
> HORNER: A Quack is as fit for a Pimp, as a Midwife for a Bawd; they
> are still but in their way, both helpers of Nature. – Well,
> my dear Doctor, hast thou done what I desired? (I.i.1–4)

It is one of the most direct openings in drama. The leading actor, as the curtain rises, walks forward to the front of the fore-stage and addresses the audience, at once taking them into his confidence with an apposite comment on the seedy character lurking behind him on the stage. Then he turns, and begins the action. The effect is simple, but it has at once set the audience up as observers to the fiction. They have become involved intellectually with the implications of Horner's witty 'character' of a doctor, and have his words against an actual presence on the stage. They should also be aware of a further irony. Horner is describing a pimp; but the actor of Horner, Charles Hart, has just given a prologue in which he himself acts as pimp for the play, ingratiating himself as an actor, condemning the author's arrogance, submitting to the judgment and the desires of the audience:

> Well, let the vain, rash Fop, by huffing so,
> Think to obtain the better terms of you;
> But we the Actors humbly will submit,
> Now, and at any time, to a full Pit;
> Nay, often we anticipate your rage,
> And murder Poets for you, on our Stage:
> We set no Guards upon our Tyring-Room,
> But when with flying Colours, there you come,
> We patiently you see, give up to you,
> Our Poets, Virgins, nay our Matrons too.
> (pp. 245–6, ll. 19–28)

It is snide, salacious and suggestive – a deceptively flattering opening for what is to be a very acid comedy, but it has a subtle and important effect: by gently prodding the audience into laughter against the poet and applause for the actors, it establishes them, as did Dryden's *Granada* prologue, as accomplices to the action. Hart's opening aside transfers their complicity from himself to his character, and establishes a relationship which is fundamental to the satirical force and emotional depth of the play.

The whole comedy is written in this direct, presentational style. It allows the characters to comment continually to the audience, to provide their own captions to the action as it proceeds. It is crucial to realise that the asides in Restoration drama are not merely surreptitious means of slipping the audience extra information, and to be got through as quickly as possible. They are not a crude technique of a primitive playwright, but a smooth and witty way of manipulating an audience to astonishingly sophisticated effect. They are spoken 'aside' from the play, but out to the house, so that while they continually objectify the action they demand collusion and agreement in the comments made upon it. The technique changes the rhythm of the play in a vital way, and creates a theatrical ambiance of great significance. The success of the play, the whole tone of its humour, is as dependent on the theatrical context of its time as *The Conquest of Granada* and *The Tempest*, although at first sight it may seem a straightforward comedy of manners, easily transportable onto the modern stage.

The Country Wife was also written for the King's Company, and given in the Theatre Royal, Drury Lane, in January 1675. Wycherley really used his theatre – the intimacy of the fore-stage, the pictorial effect of the scene, and above all the qualities of his actors. It was the second play he had written for the company, the first being *Love in a Wood* which he had composed in 1671 when they were still playing in the Bridges Street theatre. In between, he seems to have defected to the Duke's, and *The Gentleman Dancing-Master* was presented at the Dorset Garden in 1672. For *The Country Wife* he secured the services of all the major actors of the company. Major Mohun created Pinchwife, with the virginal Mrs Boutell ironically cast as Mrs Pinchwife. Hart was Horner, Kynaston Harcourt, and Cartwright Sir Jaspar Fidget. To them were added two of the great comedians of the company – Jo Haines was Sparkish, and Pepys's friend Mary Knepp, whose 'understanding' had been so praised by Killigrew, undertook the brilliant role of Lady Fidget. Haines's French training, he had danced in *Le Bourgeois gentilhomme* for Molière and Lully, must have stood him in good stead with Sparkish's foppish manners, and Mrs Knepp's physical beauty and singing talents – her husband described her rather more coarsely than Killigrew as 'That delicate compound of Spirit and Rump'[2] – were put to spectacular effect in a *coup de théâtre* in

Act V; but Wycherley seems to have been most interested in the exploitation of important dramatic actors in comic roles. Mrs Boutell's heroic innocence and dulcet tones, applied here to the country wife's 'simplicity', must have given the part another and delightful dimension to ears and eyes that had lately been enjoying her as the virtuous Benzayda, just as Hart's glamour and gallantry must have given Horner a curious mock-heroic subtext. Almanzor and he are both heroes and both valiant men, though in rather different meanings for the words. The role of Pinchwife, almost the opposite to that of Abdelmelech both physically and morally, gives Mohun a series of fascinating opportunities to suggest emotional depths in ironical contexts in a very similar way to that contrived by Dryden in the earlier epic. As tragedy and comedy, indeed, the two pieces are in admirable contrast as examples of Restoration style. They both have the verbal centre, formal structure, and moral design that we expect of the period; but where Dryden employs wit and the devices of comedy of manners to enliven his heroic abstractions, Wycherley seems to play with the presentation of the passions to offset the follies of traditional comic form, creating a bold juxtaposition of styles and responses that has almost the effect of collage.

The design of *The Country Wife* is as subtle as it is intricate. It is certainly the best organised of Wycherley's comedies. The fable is taken from Molière's *L'École des femmes* – a middle-aged man, desiring to marry but not wishing to be made a cuckold, brings up a girl in the seclusion of a convent in order to ensure her innocence before bringing her to town to become his wife. Her innocence proves a two-edged weapon. Since it is based on ignorance, the girl lacks a conventional moral sense without in any way lacking conventional physical desires. Molière's play is extremely elegant. In a series of simple scenes, he exposes the central character to continuous ridicule, as Arnolphe's obsession with his own honour turns continually against himself and his plans. The moral centre of the play is his attempt to stultify another human being to achieve his own personal security. It is self-opinion rather than personal jealousy that is at the root of his obsession. Wycherley takes over two central ideas – that of the young girl who is innocent of the ways of the world but not of the desires of the flesh, and of the older man who is both possessive and insecure; but he abandons Molière's convent in favour simply of a country education, and the betrothed ward in favour of an innocent already trapped in marriage, building up around these characters an elaborate series of counter-points that explore the oppositions of town and country, jealousy and complacency, love and lust. In doing so he changes the emphasis of the play from character to behaviour, giving as much play to the presentation of social *mores* as to moral ideas.

Around the central plot of Pinchwife's obsessive jealousy, which is here almost more physical than moral, two contrasted stories are laid out – that of Sparkish, Harcourt and Pinchwife's sister Alithea, and that of Sir Jaspar Fidget and his wife and Horner. The point of Sparkish's behaviour is that where Pinchwife is jealous, he is complacent, and his complacency is seen not as trust in his future wife, or care for her independence, but as personal self-satisfaction which amounts to impertinent neglect of her and is as extreme in its carelessness as Pinchwife's jealousy in its carefulness. Sir Jaspar is easy in another way again. He is a busy and self-important man, who gives his wife her freedom so that he can be occupied with more vital matters in the Court or City, and who sees in Horner a fool he can use to get his wife safely off his hands. The three men are set against three suitably contrasted women: Margery innocently and Lady Fidget sophisticatedly lusty, Alithea tried and virtuous. Horner's trick of giving himself out a eunuch acts as the catalyst to all these designs, setting off a series of chemical reactions in the relationships of each group of characters.

Wycherley sets his design moving with a series of presentational scenes that show up the characters to the audience and establish an almost dialectical relationship of stage and fore-stage. The first act comprises three major sections each devoted to a new 'character' and interspersed with a kind of choric commentary which has the same effect in demonstrating clear ideas as do the opening narratives of *The Conquest of Granada*. These sections are also devised as visual and verbal character gestures so that the characters are demonstrated in words and in action. In the first, we see Sir Jaspar with his wife and sister. Knowing about Horner's impotence Sir Jaspar is happy for the ladies to remain in his company while they, thinking they can get nothing by staying, are anxious to leave the house. Then comes Sparkish, and Horner and his friends end by '*thrusting him out*' for his impertinence. Then comes Pinchwife, and contrastingly, they have to hold him back from continually leaving to return to his wife. The physical theme of staying or going links the episodes and is employed as a touchstone for the character-studies whose significance is continually pointed by the presence of commentating characters.

At the opening, Horner comments on Quack as the latter is framed in the proscenium arch. Quack then challenges Horner's plan and is asked to observe its effects. Sir Jaspar and the ladies appear, now framed on the stage as Quack was before, and given the same opportunity, as they make their reverences, to present their 'characters' in physical attitudes at once formalised and carefully observed. A kind of genre picture is created within the scene of 'this formal fool and women!', and Quack neatly adds to the caption 'His Wife and Sister'. When Quack leaves, his role as commentator and observer is taken over by newcomers. Harcourt and Dorilant are gentlemen of the town, but they are not in the plot and so see the situation differently.

HARCOURT: Come, your appearance at the Play yesterday, has I hope hardened you for the future against the Women's contempt, and the Mens raillery; and now you'l abroad as you were wont.

HORNER: Did I not bear it bravely?

DORILANT: With a most Theatrical impudence; nay more than the Orange-wenches show there, or a drunken vizard Mask, or a great belly'd Actress; nay, or the most impudent of Creatures, an ill Poet; or what is yet more impudent, a second-hand Critick. (I.i.166–73)

The dialogue is in a choric style that is emphasised both by its aphoristic language and the way in which it is divided artificially between the two gentlemen. The conventional grouping (with the three in a line on the fore-stage, Horner in the centre) and the manner in which the dialogue is directed to the audience for them to catch its nuances rather than to the other characters, would complement the verbal brilliance. The tension between audience and action is further thrown into relief by the theatrical reference. The gentlemen doubtless addressed their remarks to the parts of the house to which they refer, so that in a remarkable way the fictional description becomes actually present as Horner stands exposed in the theatre to the witty comments of his friends:

HARCOURT: But what say the Ladies, have they no pitty?

HARCOURT: What Ladies? the vizard Masques you know never pitty a Man when all's gone in their Service.

DORILANT: And for the Women in the boxes, you'd never pitty them, when 'twas in your power.

HARCOURT: They say 'tis pitty, but all that deal with common Women shou'd be serv'd so. (ll. 174–80)

The style of the scene keeps up the complicity of actors and audience, and while essentially abstract in its substitution of word for action none the less captures the outward, physical aspects of observed social behaviour with clarity and verve, increased, no doubt, by the idea of Hart, the ladies' favourite, playing a eunuch. Wycherley uses structured gesture and the actors' skill in creating physical 'attitudes' to capture the moral character of the society in which his fictions live.

The character studies of Act I provide, in fact, a series of star-turns with a distinctive visual rhythm. Each character first appears framed in the scene, and then moves forward onto the fore-stage and into the action.[3] The exit of the previous character is taken through the fore-stage doors – he 'fades' as it were, as the audience's attention is thrown on to the newcomer up stage. It is a vivid technique, which gives an actor an excellent opportunity to create a physical image on which to build a scene, or indeed a whole performance, and it is frequently used elsewhere in the play as well – Sparkish's entrance in the New Exchange, for example, 'looking about him', or Lady Fidget's similar appearance in Horner's lodgings in Act IV. They are beautifully calculated moments where the player can create by his gesture and attitude the essence of a new situation. In Act I, the juxtaposition of such cameos creates almost the effect of montage. The transitions are extremely coarse technically, as so often on the Restoration stage, but provide a carefully orchestrated clash of images:

SPARKISH: Pshaw, with your fooling we shall lose the new Play; and I wou'd no more miss a new Play the first day, than I wou'd miss setting in the wits Row; therefore I'll go fetch my Mistris and away.
(*Exit* Sparkish; *Manent* Horner, Harcourt, Dorilant; *Enter to them* Mr. Pinchwife)
HORNER: Who have we here, *Pinchwife?*
PINCHWIFE: Gentlemen, your humble Servant.
HORNER: Well, Jack, by thy long absence from the Town, the grumness of thy countenance, and the slovenlyness of thy habit; I shou'd give thee joy, shou'd I not, of Marriage? (ll. 322–30)

Haines, as Sparkish, whips out to applause, doubtless all the louder for his pointed simper at Fops corner. Mohun, as Pinchwife, appears up stage and stays focused there, in his shabby clothes, making his bow, while Horner points the 'character' of a married man. Pinchwife, it should be noted, is addressed as Jack. We see a transformed man about town, only a little senior to the young gentlemen, and one with whom they are on familiar terms. Such a character is apposite for Major Mohun, and has little to do with the doddering cuckolds that seem to have become conventional in twentieth-century productions. The reverence completed, he comes sharply forward, and before beginning the action gives his own view of the matter straight to the audience, centre front:

PINCHWIFE: (Death does he know I'm married too? I thought to have conceal'd it from him at least.) (*Aside*) (ll. 331–2)

The contrasted appearance of the two actors, Haines soft and foppish, Mohun hard and aggressive, allied with the expectations aroused by their well-known qualities as artists, sets off a dialogue with the audience whose laughter and applause easily cover the apparent gap in the text, while the opening aside serves brilliantly to initiate a new dialogue with a new character, and gets the scene off to a flying start.

Like *The Conquest of Granada*, *The Country Wife* is provided with a distinctive visual rhythm that articulates the whole play through the pictorial structure of its scenes. Act I takes place in Horner's lodging, Act II in Pinchwife's House, the change of scene after the first interval pushing the play forward. These two settings were probably taken from stock, though contrasted in tone as were the characters of their proprietors. Shadwell, in *Bury Fair*, calls for 'the rich lodgings', and such a setting might well do for Horner's wealthy but impotent image – the 'Bury Fair' setting is from a later play, of course, but it indicates the kind of contrast that conventional settings might make. Pinchwife would presumably require a gloomier, shabbier dwelling to match his clothes. The contrast also provides a neat emblem of Horner's sexual prodigality and Pinchwife's sexual meanness. The various elements of the play's design are sharpened in this way by the visual backing, and in Act III a climactic transformation is contrived with a scene that may well have been got up for the occasion. Pinchwife's House rests through the second break, and continues into Act III. Margery demands to be taken to the New Exchange, and the old stock scene slides away as wings and shutters change either to a deep perspective of a covered arcade, or perhaps a view of the open courtyard and lower walks of the favourite shopping centre. This may well have been thronged with painted people, emphasising the freedom granted by the move from the closed house to the outside world (Plate 4). The scene was a witty blend of fantasy and reality. The style of the place was preserved, but we learn from the text that the shops' signs are all of horned beasts. Though the New Exchange contained Bull's heads and Ram's heads enough, it makes one wonder if Clasp's bookshop had not the publisher Cademon's sign of the Pope's Head, with horns on. The obvious symbolism makes a nice comment on a popular meeting-place as well as upon Pinchwife's fears.

The visual development through two kinds of private world to the public world has an almost classical precision, despite its use of different locations, and within this simple movement a series of gestic actions are devised whose formality of manner makes for clear articulation against the progression of scenic images and throws the complexity of the dialogue into relief. Wycherley contrives out of the dialectic of stage and fore-stage, comment and presentation, another dialectic of observation and involvement. This is obviously a function of his own response to life and art; but it creates an emotional texture that is important to a satirist. If the characters or situations are completely objectified or distanced, the audience loses the crucial experience of feeling a part of themselves involved in the action they are criticising. Objectivity of comic style seems simply to ensure that the audience associate the vices and follies they see with others rather than with themselves. Wycherley's technique arouses a deeper level of response. By associating the audience in the feelings underlying the behaviour observed, he makes them not only analysts, but also the subjects of analysis. This sets up a fascinating tension between thought and feeling.

The technical devices employed to create this effect are simple but striking. In the first place, the dramatist gives each of the characters their moments with the audience. Pinchwife and Alithea both comment on the simplicities of Margery, but Alithea also comments on the follies of Pinchwife. When Sparkish or Sir Jaspar are there, Pinchwife gets his turn to comment on the absurdities of their behaviour. In his first-act scene, Sparkish was given a story about a joke he made at the expense of Horner's impotence. He tells his tale in front of Horner, and it becomes a marvellous gesture of thoughtless self-display. He is similarly thought-less with Alithea, but now Wycherley presents a more complex demon-stration. Sparkish is so busy using Alithea to show off his 'parts' that he refuses to see the way in which his friend Harcourt is openly trying to seduce her. Pinchwife stands aside during the scene, exclaiming 'Monstrous!', 'Wonderful!', etc., out to the audience. His presence as commentator here objectifies Sparkish, and also demonstrates Pinchwife as a reasonable being. The real emotion of the scene is thrown into relief. Alithea becomes genuinely distressed at Sparkish's insensitivity. She tries to show him what Harcourt is doing, but he constantly turns its signific-ance in a positive ecstasy of vanity. Finally her distress turns to anger and malice. 'He said you were . . . a senseless drivelling Idiot,' she tells him. This is in fact not true. There was no 'drivelling' in the speech she was reporting. It is her own reaction to the whole event that is expressed in the word, demanding a new timbre in the voice of the actress. Because of the texture of observers and observed, this slight but crucial moment catches and grips the imagination.

These moments of feeling are embedded in the rigorous artificiality and formality of the style. The choric dialogues continue, in repartee with the audience, not between the characters:

SQUEAMISH: That Men of parts, great acquaintance, and quality shou'd take up with, and spend themselves and fortunes in keeping little Play-house Creatures, foh.

LADY FIDGET: Nay that Women of understanding, great acquaintance and good quality shou'd fall a keeping too of little Creatures, foh.

SQUEAMISH: Why, 'tis the Men of qualities fault, they never visit Women of honour and reputation, as they us'd to do; and have not so much common civility, for Ladies of our rank, but use us with same indifferency, and ill breeding, as if we were all marry'd to 'em.

LADY FIDGET: She says true, 'tis an errant shame Women of quality

shou'd be so slighted; methinks birth, birth shou'd
go for something; I have known Men admired, courted,
and followed for their titles only.

SQUEAMISH: Ay, one wou'd think Men of honour shou'd not love
no more than marry out of their own rank.

DAINTY: Fye, fye upon 'em, they are come to think cross-
breeding for themselves best, as well as for their Dogs
and Horses.

LADY FIDGET: They are Dogs and Horses for't. (II.i.341–59)

The ambiguity of such a passage on the Restoration stage is brilliant. The
actresses are playing ladies who despise the relationships men of their
own class have with actresses. They are doing so in front of the very
ladies and gentlemen they describe, and they are able in the light of the
auditorium and fore-stage to address their comments personally to the pit
and boxes. Lady Fidget's 'She says true' is not to the other ladies on the
stage, but to the ladies in the audience, and her comment on women-
keepers rather bold since the audience would know that the author of her
words had himself been kept by Lady Castlemaine. The real situation in
the playhouse forms a piquant dimension to the fictional double-think
that is displayed by the 'ladies' as they use moral stricture in order to
complain of sexual neglect. The passionate vulgarity of the final image is
extremely telling, hurled in insult at the laughing gentlemen in the pit.

Such verbal iconography is complimented with a suitable visual iconography developed out of the changing relationships of the plot. Wycherley
continues to provide 'entrance moments' for the actors; but he also follows
these up with an even greater precision of physical *gestus* as the play
proceeds. He often marks the climax of his scenes with formal pictures
significant to the design. In Act II, when Sparkish has loosed Harcourt
on Alithea and Pinchwife objects, 'Sparkish *struggles with* Pinchwife *to
keep him from* Alithea'. This must be formalised and pictorial. It is directly
related in style to such gestic groupings as Abenamar's embrace in
Granada. Any kind of naturalistic scrap would be clumsy and detract
from the main dialogue of Alithea and Harcourt. The struggle must be
phrased to move from picture to picture as provoked by the increasing
intimacy of Harcourt's gestures to Alithea. In between the picture is held
– not frozen, but sustained in a breathing, listening 'attitude'. The actors
would phrase their actions to incarnate the designed contrast between the
characters of the jealous husband and the complacent lover.

The dialogue between the ladies in Act II cries out for the same kind
of physicalisation, and its interaction of conversation and direct address
might have been written for the accompaniment of Addison's famous
'language of the fan':[4]

When my female Regiment is drawn up in Array, with every one her

Weapon in her Hand, upon my giving the word to *Handle their Fans*, each of them shakes her Fan at me with a Smile, then gives her Right-hand Woman a Tap upon the Shoulder, then presses her Lips with the Extremity of her Fan, then lets her Arms fall in an easy Motion, and stands in a Readiness to receive the next word of Command. All this is done with a close Fan, and is generally learned in the first Week.

Such manoeuvres can add a great deal to the rhythm of a scene, and they need not always be affected as they so often are when we see them employed today. They are flirtatious gestures, and could be affected even in the seventeenth century; but the actresses calculate the affectation, and, following the 'understanding' Knepp, use the gestures as a commentary on their lines. The effectiveness of the operation lies in the emphasis it gives to the sense of what is said: manner is at the service of meaning:

LADY FIDGET: To report a Man has had a Person, when he has not
had a Person, is the greatest wrong in the whole
World, that can be done to a person.

SQUEAMISH: Well, 'tis an errant shame, Noble Persons shou'd be so
wrong'd and neglected.

LADY FIDGET: But still 'tis an erranter shame for a Noble Person, to
neglect her own Honour, and defame her own Noble
Person with little inconsiderable fellows, foh! –

DAINTY: I suppose the crime against our honour, is the same
with a Man of quality as with another.

LADY FIDGET: How! no sure the Man of quality is likest one's
Husband, and therefore the fault shou'd be the less.

DAINTY: But then the pleasure shou'd be the less. (II.i.364–76)

The fans flutter at the audience and at each other. Lady Fidget accuses the audience, taps Mrs Squeamish, spreads her fan and hides behind it at the thought of 'the little inconsiderable fellow'. Dainty quizzes the audience, her fan to her lips, with hopeful, wondering eyes. Lady Fidget's eyes roam the pit and boxes for men of quality. A climax is reached at the entry of the dreaded word 'pleasure':

LADY FIDGET: Fye, fye, fye, for shame Sister, whither shall we
ramble? be continent in your discourse or I shall hate
you. (ll. 377–8)

As Addison notes:[5]

Upon my giving the word to *Discharge their Fans*, they give one
general *Crack* that may be heard at a considerable Distance, when the
Wind sits fair. This is one of the most difficult parts of the Exercise,
but I have several Ladies with me who [at first] could not give a
Pop loud enough to be heard at the further End of a Room, who can

now *discharge a Fan* in such a manner, that it shall make a report like a Pocket-Pistol.

The fans of Wycherley's time were longer and clumsier than those of Addison's. It is a more stately, but equally vigorous effect that would be obtained, especially in conjunction with the forceful prose rhythms. The energy and action of the scene necessarily arise from the intellectual movement of the language, punctuated by the physical emphasis of attitude and gesture.

The whole inter-relationship of actors and audience, words and gestures comes into its own in the famous china scene in Act IV. At its opening we seem to be returned to the very beginning of the play with Horner and Quack discovered: there is an almost musical sense of homecoming created by their appearance and the return to the opening set which has not been seen since Act I. We have arrived, as it were, at the moment promised by the opening of the play. Again, too, Quack is to be a witness to the action, this time concealed behind a screen. This was certainly no practical property in the manner of *The School for Scandal*. Perhaps it was painted on a downstage wing, through which Quack would simply exit, or the upper door of one side of the fore-stage may have been used, and the screen itself merely mentioned. The latter location is certainly most convenient for the progress of the scene, though the directions in the text say 'behind'. He is stowed away on just such a 'framed' entrance as we had in Act I. Quack and Horner are talking on the fore-stage:

(*Enter* Lady Fidget. *Looking about her*)

HORNER:　Now we talk of women of Honour, here comes one, step behind the Screen there, and but observe if I have not particular privileges with the women of reputation already, Doctor, already.

LADY FIDGET:　Well, *Horner*, am I not a woman of Honour? You see I'm as good as my word. (IV.iii.30–4)

She sees him, reverences, and comes down on to the fore-stage.

Their love-scene proceeds on the fore-stage, and in the full light of the Restoration auditorium takes on a curious ambivalence – all that talk of secrecy and the 'wicked censorious world', when in fact totally exposed to it, and getting it to agree with your points about it!

LADY FIDGET:　A secret is better kept I hope, by a single person than a multitude; therefore pray do not trust any body else with it, dear, dear Mr. *Horner*.

(*Embracing him.*

Enter Sir Jaspar Fidget)

SIR JASPAR:　How now! (ll. 68–71)

Sir Jaspar enters behind, and as he speaks the *tableau* freezes. Lady

Fidget turns her head to the audience and deliberately, with no sense of hurry communicates her idea of the situation:

LADY FIDGET: (aside): O, my Husband – prevented – and what's almost as bad, found with my arms about another man – that will appear too much – what shall I say? (ll. 72–4)

The lines have a splendid richness of implication that must not be rushed. Each utterance encapsulates a new aspect of the situation. The 'freeze' is easily sustained by the stage picture, Lady Fidget need not go into her tickling act until she is good and ready. In the brusque improvisation that follows, Wycherley allows both Horner and Sir Jaspar their own moments of direct communication with the audience.

Lady Fidget runs off through one of the lower fore-stage doors, and the scene now builds gradually around the nice baroque wit of the truly locked door, and the fictional action.[6] The locked door itself, in fact, contains a neat cross-reference. Pinchwife uses one of the doors – probably that on the opposite side of the stage, since such an action concludes the preceding scene – to lock Margery away whenever he goes out of his house. The husband who locks up his wife is opposed to the wife locking herself in with her lover. The joke is elaborated again in Act V, when Horner locks Margery behind the door behind which Lady Fidget is here locking herself. If poor Margery is not being locked away on one side, she is on the other! The symmetry of the stage arrangements would make these felicities of design immediately apparent.[7] Horner goes out to Lady Fidget by the upstage door on her side, and Quack rounds off the section by a comment from his hiding-place which emphasises the designed artificiality of the sequence: 'This indeed, I cou'd not have believ'd from him, nor any but my own eyes.' (ll. 131–2)

With Act IV, however, the play seems to get structurally and emotionally out of control. The last two acts are almost as long again as the first three, and packed with action in a way that makes them seem cramped in the reading. As in so many plays of the period, after a classical and ordered start, the author seems to find himself with a great deal too much material to get through in the final acts. This sense of rush is reflected in the scenic rhythm. Instead of the clear gestures of the first acts, there is now a constant changing of location. In Act IV there is Pinchwife's lodgings, a bedroom, Horner's lodgings, then Pinchwife's house again; in the fifth Pinchwife's house, Horner's lodgings, the Piazza at Covent Garden, and Horner's lodgings. The reader becomes very conscious of the propriety of neo-classical tenets in a theatre that uses scenery to indicate place. The constant visual changes required in a scenic theatre seem clumsy and confused, and break up the logic of an act as a unit of action. In fact, however, it is another disproportion, that of feeling, that manages, in the theatre, to hold the unwieldy structure together. This depends, to a very great degree, on the development of the character of Pinchwife.

As has been pointed out, Pinchwife is a man of the same class as Horner and the gallants, and not of very much greater age – Alithea is after all his sister. He is not, therefore, a figure of grotesque comedy. Though his clothes are shabby, his outward manners are correct. This is very important, since the play traces the cracks in this social armour. In Act II we see that the trace of brusqueness in his behaviour in public comes close to cruelty in private. He is not a physically unpleasant person, and his wife could be fond of him. His behaviour to her is brutal:

MRS PINCHWIFE: O my dear, dear Bud, welcome home; why dost
                  thou look so fropish, who has nanger'd thee?

PINCHWIFE: You're a Fool.

              (*Mrs Pinchwife goes aside and cryes*) (II.i.33–5)

This is both nasty and very funny, and is also well observed. Her baby-talk is tiresome beyond words, but a neat stroke of character. His bluntness is both sympathetic and harsh, but there is a careless violence implicit that is definitely dangerous. Wycherley emphasises this in his directions. Pinchwife does not simply lock Margery in her room, for example, he *thrusts her in*. The brooding tone of this violence is quite alien to Molière's character, upon whom Pinchwife is based, as is the brutality of behaviour and its physical reality.

The direct consequence of this conception of Pinchwife's character is that the comic conventions by which it is contrived to display this character also serve to push him over the edge of comedy. When Pinchwife takes Mrs Pinchwife to the New Exchange in boy's clothes (Mrs Boutell liked boy's clothes, and even managed to get into them in *The Conquest of Granada*), Horner contrives to actually kiss Mrs Pinchwife in front of her husband. The scene is of course designed as the complement to that in which Sparkish invites Harcourt to kiss Alithea, given a new intensity since it is now in public (there are not only the actors present in the New Exchange, but also shopkeepers and customers painted on the set). He then carries her off into a shop. Pinchwife runs desperately in and out of the wings, searching for her, until eventually she reappears with a hatful of oranges and plums. Pinchwife's rising fury has as usual been communicated in asides; what is unusual is that these asides have an increasingly graphic and emotional tone – 'The Devil', 'I am upon a wrack', 'O Heavens! what do I suffer?' His language too, becomes extraordinarily physical, even within the conscious design of the scene:

PINCHWIFE: Come, I cannot, nor will, stay here any longer.

HORNER: Nay, they shall send your Lady a kiss too; here, *Harcourt*,

> *Dorilant*, will you not?
> (*They kiss her*)

PINCHWIFE: (*aside*): How do I suffer this? Was I not accusing another
just now for this rascally patience, in permitting his
Wife to be kiss'd before his face? Ten thousand ulcers
gnaw their lips. (III.ii.456–)

It is true that we tend to be rather over-squeamish these days about the
humiliations heaped so freely by the dramatic poets of the seventeenth
century upon their comic characters. Pinchwife is ridiculous, because his
exaggerated caution and distrust have brought him to precisely the pass
he was trying to avoid. He is hoist with his own petard. The last line,
too, is grossly melodramatic and therefore funny. But it is also important
to remember that Major Mohun was a great tragic actor, renowned for
those sudden outbursts of uncontained emotion Dryden exploited so
tellingly. Pinchwife's comments on his own behaviour are similar to
Abdelmelech's on his, but here, the strength of his suppressed feeling is
played out against the farcical manoeuvres of the wits and the greedy
complicity of his wife. This kind of aggressive comedy, the laughter at
pain while feeling it, gives backbone to Wycherley's work. It is the
laughter of Juvenal in his *Satires* (from the sixth of which the author took
a number of hints for this play), and has been called by Baudelaire, in a
fine essay, 'le rire de Satan'.[8] There is a very nasty note in it which has
nothing intellectual about it. It is a catharsis of personal hate. When Mrs
Pinchwife offers her husband one of her oranges, he strikes it out of her
hand.

The 'letter' scene in Act IV creates a fascinating tension from this
interaction of comedy and drama. In interrogating his wife, and in forcing
her to write to Horner, Pinchwife is violent in word and deed. While he
makes her write to her supposed lover of his 'nauseous, loath'd Kisses
and Embraces' (IV.ii.95–6), he threatens her with a penknife, which he
offers to stab into her eye unless she does as she is told. Pinchwife's
violence in this scene is obviously based on that of Corvino in *Volpone*,
whose threats to his wife not to get within three yards of the window,
Pinchwife adopts; but the aggression of Jonson's writing is here modified
by its being exercised on a far from passive victim. Pinchwife is both
comic and frightening: frightening because of the explicitness and intensity of the threats; comic, because Margery learns to manipulate them.
The audience finds itself in a position of constantly changing its side.
The balance between the two characters is finely maintained. Pinchwife's
violence makes us enjoy his discomfiture; yet Margery's innocent lust is
presented equally satirically in her graphic picture of the country girl's
heavy persistence at the card-table. Finally, the physical aggression of the
penknife is released in the farcical energy of the swapping and sealing of

the letters. Comedy and violence are perfectly matched, and Wycherley even manages to point up the psychological undercurrent of this terribly private scene by setting it in their bedroom.

The bedroom scene ends as Pinchwife, having locked Margery in, *holds up the letter* for the attention of the audience and promises to 'deal with the Foe without with false intelligence' (l. 204). The scene changes to Horner's Lodgings, and the china scene follows, reaching its climax as Pinchwife appears upstage framed by the proscenium arch. He is holding the letter in the very same attitude as that with which he ended the previous scene. His re-entrance binds the first three scenes of the act together, and his ferocity in the previous scene is revoltingly complemented by the smarmy self-satisfaction with which he demonstrates his supposed victory. The threat of his personality has not disappeared, however. Pinchwife himself is ever ready to join challenge with unction, and is constantly on the verge of calling Horner out. One of the most original aspects of Pinchwife's character, and one which must have been emphasised in Major Mohun's performance, is that there is no hint at all of the cowardice conventionally present in comic bluster of this type. Pinchwife becomes yet more aggressive, in the final scene of the act, when he catches Margery writing another letter and actually draws his sword on her. The weakness implicit in this violence against a woman is set off against his readiness for violence against his own sex. Pinchwife is clearly prepared to go through with both, and the absence of the physical impotence which is a cliché of characters of this sort gives the accumulating action a real sense of danger, as well as underlining the spiritual impotence that really lies at the root of Pinchwife's nature.

The emotional and violent presence of Pinchwife forms the unifying factor in the diverse scenes and images of the fourth act, and endows the farce with a kind of passionate seriousness. The fifth is held together by the spread of that violence to other supposedly comic characters. When Sparkish, for instance, learns, quite wrongly, that Alithea is unfaithful to him, he loses his complacency with a vengeance and pours scorn upon her, enabling Wycherley to contrast with the passionate violence of Pinchwife, the spiteful violence of the weak, as nasty as it is feeble: 'I wish you joy, Madam, joy, joy; and to him too, much joy; and to myself more joy for not marrying you' (V.iii.52–4). It is a waspish utterance, and Haines almost certainly made it even more unpleasant by that foppish lengthening of the vowels into an 'a' sound which Macaulay mentions as one of the verbal affectations of the upper classes at the time.[9]

Wycherley's satire conflates the moral and the social: he is interested in the way vice degrades its subject, and the growing sense of moral and physical squalor is brought to a striking climax at the beginning of the final scene, which returns at the last to Horner's lodgings. We have been prepared for this moment very cleverly in Act IV.

HORNER: I tell thee, I am now no more interruption to 'em when they sing, or talk bawdy, than a little squab French Page, who speaks no English.

QUACK: But do civil persons, and women of Honour drink, and sing bawdy Songs?

HORNER: O amongst Friends, amongst Friends; for your Bigots in Honour are just like those in Religion; they fear the eye of the world, more than the eye of Heaven, and think there is no virtue but railing at vice; and no sin, but giving scandal. (IV.iii.15–23)

Wycherley now stages a scene of 'good fellowship' for the ladies of quality. They assemble with 'a table, banquet and bottles',[10] and sit down with Horner in a kind of perverse parody of the male drinking-scene. This gets under way with a show-stopping drinking-song for Mrs Knepp as Lady Fidget:

Why should our damn'd Tyrants oblige us to live
On the pittance of pleasure which they only give?
We must not rejoyce
With Wine and with noise;
In vaine we must wake in a dull bed alone,
Whilst to our warm Rival, the Bottle, they're gone.
Then lay aside charms,
And take up these arms.* (*The Glasses) (V.iv.27–34)

The words are masculine in tone, and so are the actions. The image of the lady of quality, her foot on a chair, roaring her lungs out to the delight of her female colleagues is a telling one, heightened by the brilliant way the song itself inverts the usual male emphasis on drink and liberty. The ladies maintain the inversion in their conversation:

DAINTY: Dear Brimmer, well in token of our openness and plain dealing, let us throw our Masques over our heads.

HORNER: So 'twill come to the Glasses anon.

SQUEAMISH: Lovely Brimmer, let me enjoy him first.

LADY FIDGET: No, I never part with a Gallant, till I've try'd him.
(ll. 43–7)

The physical images of throwing off the masks in parody of the male custom of toasting and throwing the glass over the shoulder, and of elegant women huddling over their brimmers and cuddling them like lovers is magnificently perverse, and Wycherley develops the scene into a kind choral ode, similar to the choric style of earlier scenes, but here operating very differently:

LADY FIDGET: Dear Brimmer that mak'st our Husbands short sighted –
DAINTY: And our bashful gallants bold.
SQUEAMISH: And for want of a Gallant, the Butler lovely in our eyes, drink Eunuch.
LADY FIDGET: Drink thou representative of a Husband, damn a Husband.
DAINTY: And as it were a Husband, an old keeper.
SQUEAMISH: And an old Grandmother.
HORNER: And an English Bawd, and a French Chirurgeon.
(ll. 47–56)

The coarseness of the scene is far more shocking than the earlier *doubles-entendres*, as is the looseness of language and behaviour, characterised by little personal touches such as Mrs Squeamish's venomous 'and an old Grandmother'. The effect is both more naturalistic and more gestic. The table has been set up by the servants just inside the proscenium arch (the fore-stage needs to be clear for the complications of the dénouement). The ladies are seated about it, with Horner in the middle, crowned as it were with wine and roses. We again get a strong sense of a framed picture, of looking in on a private gathering, the squalor of which, both physical and moral, was doubtless brought out by the actresses in the way in which they sprawled about the table. It is like a Hogarth morality – at once intimate, observed and significant – as the eunuch joins the female chorus, adding his grievances to theirs:

HORNER: And an English Bawd, and a French Chirurgeon.
LADY FIDGET: Ay we have all reason to curse 'em.
HORNER: For my sake Ladies.
LADY FIDGET: No, for our own, for the first spoils all young gallants industry.
DAINTY: And the others art makes 'em bold only with common women.
SQUEAMISH: And rather run the hazard of the vile distemper amongst them, than of a denial amongst us. (ll. 56–64)

It is a long scene, and static in narrative terms; but it forms the climax to the play, arising compellingly out of the darkening emotional atmosphere of the last two acts. Emblematically, the ladies throw away their masks and we see their real personalities. The exposure is moving as well as unpleasant, because it comments not only upon the characters, but on the society that makes them what they are. Lady Fidget's song exposes the roots of hypocrisy in contemporary social and sexual relationships. It is shown to grow inevitably from the experiences of the individual life – the tradition of the loveless marriage and the search for alternative excitement, boredom, drunkenness, familiar things, the seeds of which we have seen being sown in the marital relationships of the play, in the essential selfishness of Horner, Sparkish, Pinchwife, Sir Jaspar Fidget. The private sore is literally exposed to the light, and the experience may well have been yet more painful then than now, since the audience could not conceal themselves in the dark comfort of a modern auditorium. As the ladies get drunk and accept Horner in common, the final touches are given to Wycherley's theme – the degradation of contemporary life, and the audience's complicity in it.

In spite of its gripping realism and its telling observation of detail, *The Country Wife* is a fantasy. It is intended as a carefully constructed fiction, playing with the real world to discover its inner truth. Though Wycherley's dramatic images are very physical, his method is abstract. Horner's trick of proclaiming himself a eunuch (borrowed, incidentally, from Terence) is used as a kind of proposition from which the rest of the action is then extrapolated. The play is not a mirror of life, despite its surface appearance; it is, like *The Conquest of Granada*, a commentary on the workings of the human animal, presented to the audience as a series of interlinked gestures. Its technique is in many ways strikingly modern. Wycherley works like Pinter in his handling of belief and imagination: I do not believe in Horner, as I do not believe in Ruth in *The Homecoming*; but I can imagine them both, and believe very easily in the behaviour they arouse in those around them. All I need to concede is the initial proposition – and it is worth conceding in both authors, since the fantasy becomes the means of clarifying a profoundly mysterious complex of human emotion. Where Dryden tries to reach the inscrutable areas of human action through paradox, Wycherley and Pinter do so through a logic of the imagination. They articulate an extremely subtle truth by the exploration of the consequences of their hypotheses, and by the imaginative light thus thrown on sexual hypocrisies, they enable us to see more deeply into the fear all men feel over the demonstrably tenuous connection between conscious choice and the urgency of unconscious impulses. As performed on the Restoration stage, *The Country Wife* sets the conventional artifices of comedy against the ready sympathies of the audience. A desire for the successful fulfilment of the basest wishes competes with an awareness of the essential absurdity of those wishes when fulfilled. This dialectic of response forms the moral and theatrical centre of the play. Wycherley gave the Epilogue to Knepp. In it, the actress of Lady Fidget challenges the audience with their erotic pretensions in public and their erotic failures in private. It is a fitting pendant to Hart's pimping Prologue and to the play itself. It gives the whole a neat frame, demonstrating the social and moral paradox that a man's honour is a woman's shame.[11]

Part Three

The market for feeling

Truth is relative, and always
behind it stands some interest,
furthering its own ends.

JOE ORTON

8 · Changing times

The Restoration theatre was a true product of the age which conceived it. It achieved a perilous harmony, the resolution of which undermined many of the values it held most dear. Physically, it was a hybrid: the passionate illusionism of baroque presentation on the stage was separated from the public by the fore-stage with its very different excitement derived from the actor's personal hold over the audience. This physical division reflected a similar intellectual dichotomy. In the minds of contemporaries, lower functions of the body seemed separate from the higher functions of the mind and spirit. It was only the detached curiosity of the Restoration gentleman that made a balance seem possible, for society itself was permeated with a similar dichotomy of value – that of the abstract right of hereditary nobility and that of the present right of financial prosperity. Like the society in which it lived, the Restoration theatre was Janus-faced, looking one way towards the glamorous patronage of the Court and another towards its own independent development as a commerical institution. The drama of the later seventeenth century is best understood as a playing out of the tensions implicit in such a position.

The actors' place as courtiers had always been ambiguous. The court attachment brought privilege. It gave the theatres glamour and attracted audiences. At least ten of the actors were liveried household servants, and as Grooms of the Chamber (the women were also sworn) could appeal direct to the king in personal difficulties. They were also immune from arrest except on the lord chamberlain's express warrant (when Lacy was arrested for speaking more than set down for him and satirising the Court in *The Change of Crownes*, Mohun went to the king and had him released). But there was little financial remuneration. The players were liveried 'without fee', though some of them occasionally received generous presents, and the fees for performance at Court were a mere £20 to the company, and for royal visits to the playhouse, only £10.[1]

There were other ties as well. The companies were subject to the Office of the Revels, which had been set up originally under Henry VIII to control actors and license plays for publication and performance. The duty of the Master of the Revels was to prevent the circulation of plays whose content might be deemed politically or religiously seditious. James I had brought all companies directly under royal patronage and so even closer to the Revels Office and Charles II perpetuated this. The Revels Office licensed plays at £2 a time for a new play, and £1 for a revival. It was a drain, therefore, on the managers' pockets as well as their patience. Detailed alterations of language and content could be required before a play could go to rehearsal. In times of crisis, whole plays could be banned or suddenly taken off. Such curtailments of theatrical freedom may well have been justified, but were rather frustrating in a period where topicality was so important – as was the Master's rather mean habit of sitting on doubtful scripts and forgetting to send them back for a while.[2]

Under such circumstances the playhouses needed a complementary commercial base for their operations. This was similar, but not identical, in the two companies, and the clearest picture of the nature of the business arrangements, which were to cause increasing conflict of interest as the century wore on, can be obtained from the copy of Davenant's agreement with his actors, found among the papers of Sir Henry Herbert, a termagant old gentleman who had become Master of the Revels under Charles I, and survived to lay claim to the office at the Restoration.[3] The agreement is in fact a double one, covering arrangements before and after Davenant had completed his new theatre in Lincoln's Inn Fields. The first part establishes a group of actors as a company under Davenant's management with liberty to act plays for profit. The takings for each performance are to go first to defraying the charges of that performance. Any residue is to be divided into fourteen 'proporcions or shares', four of which are to go to Davenant himself, and the rest are to be divided among the actors who sign the agreement. Davenant's larger share is presumably intended to defray the costs of the 'new theatre with scenes' which he covenants to provide. When the company moves into its new premises a different division of shares is to obtain. After the general charges, fifteen shares are to be made up. Of these, the manager takes ten – but these ten are allocated to specific purposes: two shares continue to defray his building costs, 'the house rent, buildinge, scaffoldinge, and making of frames for scenes'; one share is for the provision of 'Habbittes, properties and scenes for a Supplement of the said Theatre' – towards the cost of new productions in fact, and the replenishment of stock; seven shares go to the maintenance of actresses and for his own profit in consideration of his 'paines and expences' in creating the company and their theatre. The remaining five shares are divided among the parties to the agreement at the rate of half a share each. As their part of the bargain, these actors are contracted to work for Davenant, who retains control as manager and artistic director, on bonds of £500.

Davenant set up a collaborative management under the artistic director. Killigrew, on the other hand, set up a business speculation in which a set payment of £3.10s per acting day was allowed to all those who put up capital for the enterprise.[4] This payment appears to have taken no account of the production costs or variation of attendance and it seems hardly surprising that his company was the first to face financial disaster. The overheads of a Restoration playhouse were considerable. Because of demands on time and personnel, and the physical costs of presentation, theatre is an expensive art and notably so when taste demands a rich musical dimension. Cibber noted that a theatre manager in the eighteenth century was responsible for the conduct and well-being of over 140 people.[5]

In the first place there were the front of house staff – the theatre treasurer and his subordinates – the taking of money is a crucial operation and Davenant had a room by the theatre where this was done by three gentlemen of his appointment, supervised by two or three actor sharers. Presumably these came on duty just before noon on each playing day, when the doors of the playhouse were opened, since the practice of deciding the play for the day on the basis of the returns of the previous night meant that no advance booking was possible. The box-office shut soon after the start of the performance, and the duty of taking money for latecomers devolved on the door-keepers. There were about nine of these: one for each of the two doors of the pit, one for the left and right corridors leading to the boxes of the first and second tiers, and one each for the three gallery entrances. These may sometimes have been supplemented by ticket checkers at the bottom of the two main staircases, and at the two entrances to the pit corridors. Certainly there was a good deal of trouble over money. The door-keepers were inclined to keep what they could, and the aristocratic audience was inclined to think itself too important to pay.[6] Davenant provided his nephew Ralph as treasurer to oversee the matter. The job was no sinecure – Ralph Davenant was murdered by soldiers trying to steal the takings – and did not solve the problem. Farquhar wrote in the eighteenth century that one of the manager's main troubles was bribing the door-man sufficiently to make correct returns.

The number of back-stage personnel was even more considerable. Apart from the crucial book-keeper – Davenant had appointed Downes – there was the wardrobe-keeper and at least half a dozen 'tiring men and women' to dress the actors. There was also probably a chief scene-keeper, though he is not singled out in any document. The company had twelve registered scene-keepers in 1664, and Betterton's company at Lincoln's Inn Fields in 1695 had as many as twenty-four. This large number must have covered those who operated the machinery, as well as those who shifted scenes or set furniture on the stage. They may well have undertaken other tasks, too, such as trimming candles both on stage and in the auditorium, and occasionally doubling as extras – the Common People in Act I of *1 Granada*, for example. The Restoration theatre can be heavy on supernumeraries. Orrery's *Tragedy of Mustapha* notes proudly the presence of twenty-six on stage at the final curtain. A satirical poem on the Dorset Garden remarks that the stage prince is waited on by a guard of candle-snuffers,[7] and Pepys tells the story of how Killigrew, when a boy, used to see the play for nothing by volunteering to be a devil (30 October 1662).

The payment of staff and hireling actors was included by Davenant in the theatre's charges for an evening. An actor could be taken on only by consent of the company, and had to play about three months without salary. Cibber, when he began, played eight months, living at home, and then, when he at last began to get money, it was only 10s a week. The senior actors got about £4 a week, and the great Betterton, when he had given up his shares in the 1690s, a mere £5. The actresses got even less. Mrs Barry, at the height of her career, was getting 50s a week, supplemented by royal bounty and annual benefits. Dramatists were not paid directly at all. Dryden and Howard had shares in the King's Company, but a writer traditionally got the benefit of every third performance in a run. Further general charges would be the musicians, singers and dancers. Davenant hired his orchestra on these general charges at not more than 30s per acting day, and also kept a dancing-master, so his actors must have been consistently taught; but we find Killigrew hiring French dancers at 10s a day each in the 1670s, with a day rehearsal fee.[8] Killigrew may have had the general use of the Court musicians, but if so, he probably had to pay them extra. Charles was irregular in settling with his servants. In addition, though many of the actors sang – Hart, Knepp, and Ann Bracegirdle being obvious examples – they would need to be augmented for the elaborate musical pieces.

The scale of such enterprise is large and the average cost of performance – £25 at the beginning of the period, £35 at the end – may seem small. In the event, it was not. Cibber complained in the 1740s that London could not support more than one theatre, and this seems to have been the case by the later 1670s. The King's Company (originally the most experienced troupe, though Pepys never liked them) were growing old, and were divided by squabbles, both financial and artistic. After the Bridges Street fire, they seemed to have found the cost of rebuilding crippling. Davenant had found them so in the late 1660s, when he planned the new Dorset Garden. He had been forced to sell his shares to finance the enterprise and cover rising costs, bringing his finances in line with those of his rivals. The shares had gone well at £600–£800 each; but though the company had the asset of a spectacular new playhouse and a vibrant and skilful group of players, the demands of profit on such an investment, from people not practically involved with the theatre, put the management to considerable strain. Both houses were under a double burden – to recoup losses on buildings and effects, and to repay loans and meet demands of investors.

With increasing costs and dwindling audiences, the financial crisis became acute, and led, in 1681, to the union of the companies. This really amounted to the absorption of the King's Company into the Duke's Company under the new name of the United Company, for now Betterton's management ran both theatres, using the Theatre Royal for the straight drama and the Dorset Garden for spectacle or opera. The two theatres no longer played every day, and no longer competed with each other, and the companies' profits amounted to an average of £50 a playing night. When this is compared to the bonanza takings – Etherege's *Love in a Tub* took £1000 in the 1660s, and Shadwell had a record benefit of £130 for *The Squire of Alsatia* in the 1680s – it does not suggest many full houses.

It is hardly surprising, therefore, that the later part of the period is really dominated by a search for new audiences. Restoration drama emerged for the recreation of a particular society with a particular way of life. As the seventeenth century wore on, this lifestyle was gradually but implacably eroded. With the dangerous years of the Popish plot and the Exclusion Crisis, Charles and his immediate circle had less time and less inclination for the theatre and so did his brother James. After the Revolution of 1688, the situation that Killigrew had noted before the Civil War when 'the King never, and the Queen seldom come' (Pepys, 12 February 1667) was restored in London. Furthermore William did not like the damps of Whitehall, and removed first to Hampton Court and then to Kensington Palace. This physical distancing of royalty echoed a social fact. The Court of William and Mary was an austere place by comparison with that of Charles, and the interaction of the higher aristocracy and the gentry seemed to lessen; contrariwise, that of the gentry and the City seemed to increase. Puritanism, by its stress on the values of the individual conscience and its glorification of private industry, released a new energy which transformed the business world. The puritan of the seventeenth century has been called a 'spiritual aristocrat, who sacrificed fraternity to liberty'.[9] Secularised, this new energy and sense of individual rights helped to undermine the old order. The aristocracy of money confronted the aristocracy of blood, and won. By the end of the century, England had changed from a country whose wealth and interest lay in land, to a country whose wealth and interest lay in trade. As John Dennis pointed out in 1702: 'there are ten times more gentlemen now in business than there were in King Charles, his reign'.[10] The playhouses could not afford to address a leisured class that began to have both less leisure and less cash. Killigrew had lamented to Pepys (12 February 1667) that the citizens were coming less frequently to the theatre, and the positioning of the Dorset Garden in an area just beyond the walls may have been intended to redress the balance. Poets still mocked the City in acid prologues and epilogues, but they began to offer a citizens' diet in their plays.

Beaumont and Fletcher, along with some Jonson and altered Shakespeare, remain at the centre of the repertoire as the century wears on. It is the forms of original writing that are varied and weakened. Both heroic tragedy and comedy of manners lose their rigour while preserving a conventional intellectual base. It is a classic syndrome of decay, and Dryden, as usual, provides the classic example of the difficulty. In his famous prologue to *Aureng-Zebe*, the last and most brilliant of his rhymed tragedies, he gives what appears to be a renunciation of the bombastic epilogue to *Granada*. He confesses that:[11]

> Spite of all his pride a secret shame
> Invades his breast at Shakespear's sacred name;
> Aw'd when he hears his Godlike *Romans* rage,
> He, in a just despair, would quit the Stage.
> And to an age less polish'd, more unskill'd,
> Does, with disdain the foremost Honours yield.

This is nothing if not grudging. He does not renounce superiority of manners or language: he rather acknowledges superiority in feeling and form. At the centre is an abandonment of rhyme, which he sees as impeding the truth of the fiction. The rhyming author fails, Dryden suggests, because

> Passion's too strong to be in Fetters bound,
> And Nature flies him, like Enchanted Ground. (ll. 9–10)

He never again entrusted a full play to rhyming couplets, and tragic writers of the 1670s followed suit. Dryden wrote further, in his prefatory poem to Nathaniel Lee's famous blank-verse tragedy *The Rival Queens*:[12]

> Such praise is yours, while you the Passions move,
> That 'tis no longer feign'd, 'tis real Love;
> Where Nature Triumphs over wretched Art;
> We only warm the Head, but you the Heart.

The problem is this: that while we might agree with Dryden about rhyme, we are not very likely to concur in our judgment of Lee, or find his own attempts at blank-verse tragedy essentially more natural or convincing. Actually we might have taken a hint from that very Prologue to *Aureng-*

Zebe. The real point Dryden is making is that the audience has no longer a taste for true wit. He himself turns more and more to poetry.

The first blank-verse tragedy Dryden penned was *All for Love*, a neo-classical version of the story of Antony and Cleopatra. This focuses the period's love–hate relationship with the works of Shakespeare and the dilemma that this conceals. With blank verse comes sentiment and moral conventionalism. The intellectual structures of Restoration thought are symmetrical and pointed. They depend on their artificiality for their effect. The intrusion of feeling into structures that remain tied by their intellectual formulae does not make the plays more real. It rather blunts their edge, while the lack of rhyme similarly blunts their expression. The fetters that bind passion in the late seventeenth century are implicit in the thought of the time. To the age of reason it was possible to be right; but imaginative rightness unfortunately does not operate like scientific correctness. Clear ideas are static. Essentially, they bind feeling through the operations of plot, character or thought and it can be released, as Dryden found, only by a complex dialectic of ironies. Blank-verse and sentiment merely softens the effect. *All for Love* has many beauties. It is beautifully plotted, and beautifully written, with Dryden's usual precision of word and phrase. But it remains obstinately wooden. The attempt at feeling has banished all the wit. It is significant that when Dryden returned to the theatre in the late 1680s he favoured double-plot plays like *Marriage à la mode*. In *The Spanish Friar* and *Don Sebastian*, he restores wit to its throne through multiple ironies of plotting and an astringent comic action to counterpoint the melodrama.

The same erosion of wit is apparent in comedy. The central intelligence of the genre becomes diluted with farce, feeling and moralising. In the late 1660s and 1670s, Dryden, Wycherley and Etherege are at their peak, writing plays in which character, conversation and the analysis of human vagary dominate the design. In these plays the valued Fletcherian ease of utterance is polished with a new precision and intelligence. The authors are not, of course, of the same temperament – Wycherley is sharper, Etherege is freer, and Dryden more ritualistic; but the early plays of Shadwell, Aphra Behn, and triumphant farces like Ravenscroft's *The Cit turned Gentleman* signify change. Shadwell adds a heavy bout of Jonsonian humour to his comedies, and with it some often brilliant farce. Shadwell is not dull, but his prose is heavy, his moral implacable, and his most amusing scenes, though often wordy, depend for their effect on physical gimmickry of scene and performance, as in the playhouse scene in The True Widow, where the ladies' importunate lovers are carried away by devils, dropped through traps, or imprisoned in machines hanging above the stage at the blast of the prompter's whistle and the passing of a polite coin. This employment of the spectacular means available in the Dorset

Garden alters the balance of the comedy of manners. There are farcical moments in Dryden, Etherege or Wycherley, but there the exhilaration, the purely physical elation that is the particular property of the genre, is kept in proportion. In *The Cit turned Gentleman* on the other hand, Ravenscroft padded out his play by interweaving no less than three of Molière's plots, to give a vigorous, but muddled, farcical action that emerges as splendidly mindless entertainment.

The hard, intelligent comedy of the 1670s did not entirely die out. Crowne, throughout his career, writes consistently clear, elegant and well-observed comedies, which if they have not the verbal brilliance of the more famous authors are full of penetrating images. Southerne, too, is a fine writer of tragedy and comedy, but in his best plays, especially *The Wive's Excuse*, his technique is looser and glummer in tone. *The Wive's Excuse* is a bitter and moving play; but here, though the language is easy, it lacks edge, and this is replaced by a strong strain of morality softened by pathos. Southerne is a very honest writer, and seldom forces his moral, as became fashionable at the time – he is nearer to Vanbrugh, though not the penetrating brilliance of Congreve, than to the sentimentality of Cibber, Steele or even Farquhar; but even so the change of direction is clear: it is a move away from detachment and towards identification – away from description and towards involvement.

In 1698 the Reverend Jeremy Collier, a puritan divine with a nice gift for polemic, issued his *Short View of the Profaneness and Immorality of the Stage*. He attacked dramatic authors for, among other things, 'their smuttiness of expression, their swearing, profaneness and lewd application of scripture, their abuse of the clergy, their making of their top characters libertines, giving them successes in debauchery.'[13] Many of the greatest writers of the day, including Congreve, took it upon themselves to answer his charges, but where Collier is vivid and witty in his polemic, his antagonists seem pale and disingenuous. This was, in fact, inevitable. Given his assumptions Collier is clearly right, and the difficulty that faced the dramatists is symptomatic of a new problem that faced the theatre as a whole. It will not do to excuse blasphemy and ill-manners by saying that such things happen. That they undoubtedly do, is in itself no excuse for making them happen often, let alone in fun on stage. There is really only one answer: that many peoples have had many gods, and many societies many laws, and that under such circumstances, the idea of God or the laws of society are merely the constructs of men, and other men have a perfect right to criticise them, question them and demonstrate their ambiguities. The dramatists of the Restoration could not make such an answer. They could see the force of their empirical observation but were unprepared to abandon the hypothesis of classical morality and revealed religion in quite so cavalier a fashion. They were, therefore, left with an unbridgeable gap between their experience of life and their idea of it. The plays of Dryden, Etherege and Wycherley had explored this gap, but the theatre now lost its courage. The conventions of the last twenty years of the century cease to be the means for organising new observations, and become the means for reiterating old ideas and moral platitudes. Truth is no longer a subject for speculation; it is a matter of fact, and the audience needs to identify with it.

It is not unfair, I think, to consider this change of attitude as the function of the changing life-style of society, followed by the theatres' need to attract new audiences to their playhouses. The audience of Charles II's day was quick to take offence and to punish impertinence, but it clearly possessed a kind of aesthetic confidence born of right and blood. The elements of the Restoration style – curiosity, intellect, detachment and licence – are in this sense 'aristocratic'. The audience have a right to their place, and can afford intellectual speculation. The rising bourgeois audience, on the other hand, had no established position. They had to work to succeed in a competitive society, and lacked that confidence and that right. They wanted their entertainment to build it for them, and preferred a suitable moral to a clear idea. To attract such an audience the theatre needs to be 'respectable'. Comedy and tragedy, therefore, become 'exemplary', enabling their audiences to love the good and mock the foolish and so essentially confirm their own superiority.[14] Propriety became the hallmark of truth, and the softening of dramatic art into anodyne entertainment was excused as a form of good manners.

Significantly, these changes in the theatre are blamed upon the 'Ladies'. With the withdrawal of the Court interest, the fashionable world needed new leaders and they found them in the female element of society.[15] Ladies were not expected to be involved in the gravity of business, and, as opposed to that of women, their function was symbolic and decorative. As such they were fitting rulers for the lighter side of life, for drama had necessarily fallen victim to the basic puritan distinction between work and play.

There was one problem: such drama is confoundedly dull. Once plot and character are centred in conventional truths which cannot be questioned, another kind of excitement has to be found. This additional excitement, which could no longer be generated by the design of the play, was discovered in the elements of the presentation. Dryden had, of course, exploited sensational narrative and staging in an attempt to create a popular level to *Granada*, and he had come up against the dilemma of a rational theatre – that niceties are easily passed over by an audience hungry for entertainment. As the century draws to a close, sensational elements in writing, acting, and staging are given their head.

In his satirical description of the amusements of London, Tom Brown remarks that the playhouse is 'like an enchanted island, where nothing appears in reality what it is, or what it ought to be', and he notes of the actors or characters of the day:[16]

> The people are all somewhat whimsical and *giddy-brain'd*; when they *speak* they *sing*, when they *walk* they *dance*, and very often do both when they have a mind to it.

In spite of its clearly satirical intentions, this description strongly suggests the canting intonation and operatic gesture for which Quinn was known in the eighteenth century, and which is quite unlike the cool unenthusiastic style attributed to Betterton by Colley Cibber. It would, however, suit very well with the new kind of dramatic writing. When Calista, in Rowe's *The Fair Penitent*, is caught in the garden with her lover, Lothario, she hears Sciolto call within and exclaims:[17]

Is it the Voice of Thunder, or my Father?

It is a silly line. The categories of thunder and the human voice do not match well. But to the early eighteenth century a different association would have occurred – that of the voice of God's justice properly linked with that of the father she has wronged. It is a banal and conventional image of guilt, probably supported by the actor's thundering appropriately from the wings. Brown's satire seems to suggest a change in acting style that matches the change in the playwright's art. The actor no longer seeks new gestures to express his characters but is applauded for his execution of established and conventional attitudes and tones. In *The Female Wits*, such cant and gesticulation is parodied with merciless gusto:[18] (Plate 29)

> MARSILIA: Your pardon, Mrs., give me leave to instruct you in a
> moving Cry. Oh! there's a great deal of Art in Crying:
> Hold your Handkerchief thus; let it meet your Eyes, thus;
> now in a perfect whine, crying out these words,
> *By these Teares, which never cease to Flow.*

The author recreates the conventional claptraps with splendid effect, including Statira's stamp (see p. 18 above), the villain hugging herself in ecstasy, or the supporting actor's gesture of 'silent Surprize'. Mrs Betty, Marsilia tells us, 'doth a silent Surprize the best i'th'World; I must kiss her, I cannot help it, 'tis incomparable'. The danced heroics have become mechanical, as have the fluttering gesticulations of comedy of manners.

The reasons for such a decline are not far to seek. In the absence of new material to act, the actors are finding more sensational ways of acting it. In the last decade of the century, the managers of Drury Lane cut away the fore-stage, forcing the actors back into the scene. This manoeuvre, based on a desire to pack more people into the pit, broke the intimacy of the actor's relationship with his audience, and must have encouraged the development of a new style to bridge the gap.[19] It ceases to be accuracy or observation, novelty and rightness of gesture, that is important, but rather the generative energy of the performance itself. Late seventeenth-century dramatic language tends to be musical and conventional rather than rational and to sustain it before an audience the actors learn to thrill with the sound of the voice rather than grip with the sense of the line, just as their authors contrive to astound with wisdom rather than arrest with thought.

Perhaps the key figure in this change of style is the actress Elizabeth Barry. Mrs Barry's career began in the 1670s, and at first she was not a success. Apparently she had no ear, and could not learn the inflections of her part as instructed by the author or by previous actors in the role. She could not define character by vocal inflection being inclined 'to fall into a tone' and she was quite unable to dance 'even a country dance'.[20] Then she became Lord Rochester's mistress, and he, Pygmalion-like, seems to have taught her a new kind of art. On her return to the stage, she was a sensation. She seemed to live her part. What she lacked in character and deportment, she made up in passion, affecting the audience with a continuous flow of powerful emotion and even changing counten- ance during the speeches of others as their discourse 'affected her in the part she acted'.[21] This last should not be misinterpreted. It does not imply that actors usually fell out of their parts between speeches, though there is some evidence for this on off-days throughout the period, but simply that they sustained their attitude in relation to the speaker. It was 'his scene', and the listener was subordinated to him except at really excep- tional moments, as with Abenamar's conversion in Granada. Gildon regretted that the actors seldom achieved the illusion of concentrated attention in their varied portrayal of passion that Lebrun could achieve in a picture like 'The Tent of Darius' (Plate 34); but the illusion of emotional reaction was not a style suited to fore-stage acting. Mrs Barry began to change this with her feeling for immediate emotional response, and her new manner seems to have been particularly understood and exploited by her unhappy lover, Otway.

Otway contrives for her a new kind of dramatic situation in which passion is not to be defined but communicated. Such possibilities had been hinted at in Major Mohun's roles in Granada and The Country Wife, but Otway goes consistently further than Dryden or Wycherley. At a climactic moment of his tragedy The Orphan, Monimia discovers that she has been deceived by her husband's brother into lying with him under the belief he was her husband. It is their wedding-night, and he has taken her virginity. The situation is one of those contrived moral hypotheses of the period, but Otway handles it very differently. He does not explicate Monimia's passion in verse at that moment, so that it can be held up to the light. He gives the actress a half-line only. She thinks not of herself but of her husband and exclaims simply 'Ah, poor Castalio', as she leaves the stage. This was one of Mrs Siddons's great moments, and was also one of Mrs Barry's, who said she never spoke it without weeping. The point is that here the whole burden of the expression rests on the actress. It is she, and she alone, that is the instrument of emotion, and she is asked to make the audience share that emotion with her. Otway again and again writes scenes for her that have the same kind of climax – exclamatory phrases that can be meaningful only in the way they are uttered. He goes further, in fact, and even prints his texts so that different 'Oh's and 'Ah's are given varying intensity:[22]

JAFFEIR: How long is't since the miserable day
            We wedded first –
BELVIDERA: Oh h h.
JAFFEIR: Nay, keep in thy tears.

This is very new. Lee uses melodrama to affect the audience and excite them in a similar manner, and Dryden also takes a leaf out of Otway's book and imitates his limpid, musical blank-verse when it suits him; but neither dramatist understands so well the possibility of the actor's moment, and will let it alone.

Mrs Barry clearly had a dynamic presence, and it became an inevitable part of her style to elevate the feeling above the sense. Her tendency to 'tone' probably helped her, too. She was a great actress, and was often in demand in parts in the older style, demanding intelligence and grasp. She played Laetitia in *The Old Batchelour*, and Mrs Frail in *Love for Love*. Not only Otway, and Congreve but Dryden himself wrote some of his finest parts with her in mind. It is probable like all great actresses that she knew well enough not to drown a play in feeling, but reserved her emotions, and played for those climaxes where the poet himself gave her her head; but her technique, none the less, marks the beginning of an affective and sensational acting style intending to stir rather than penetrate human nature, and it would seem (if his comments on her, and his collaboration with her in such works as *Venice Preserv'd*, *The Wive's Excuse* are anything to go by) that she took Betterton and many of the other actors along with her. The Restoration experiment, the attempt to create a theatre of reason, an objective theatre that excited through description and demonstration, was over and done with.

Of course, one form of dramatic excitement, of physicalising the abstract conventions of the stage, remained, looking back to the very beginnings of Restoration theatre – the spectacle and music of semi-opera. Songs, masques and scenes of sacrifice had been, from the beginning a way of capturing the audience through its senses, and balancing the abstract rationalising of the plays themselves. Betterton had continually augmented and improved the machinery for such spectacles, though the designs themselves seem to have retained Torelli's symmetry, rather than following newer fashions for dynamic and angled perspectives. Dancing, too, had kept up with the Continent, importing the great figure-dances of Lully's opera-ballets to create climactic sequences of movement, particularly in the grand Chaconnes, theatrical versions of an old Spanish Dance, with their persistent ostinato, and exotic leaps and turns. It now so happened that as the need for splendour and excitement was at its height there was available to the theatre one of the great musical geniuses of the English stage, whom even Dryden admitted could warm the head as well as the heart.

Henry Purcell was born in 1659 into a musical family. In 1677, at the age of eighteen, he was appointed composer in ordinary for the royal violins, and organist of Westminster Abbey, where he had been organ-tuner for some years, in 1679. A year later he wrote his first music for the theatre – vocal and orchestral pieces for Nathaniel Lee's tragedy *Theodosius*. The scope of his art, as it was understood in those days, is neatly expressed in an ode Nicholas Brady wrote for the composer to set for St Cecilia's day in 1692:[23]

> 'Tis Nature's voice through all the moving wood,
> And creatures understood
> The universal tongue
> To none of all her numerous race unknown.
> From her it learnt the mighty art,
> To Court the ear, or strike the heart,
> At once the passions to express and move.
> We hear and straight
> We grieve or hate
> Rejoice or love.

It was the style of the Restoration to 'express' the passions, and the style of the turn of the century to 'move' them. It was Purcell's genius to do both.

Purcell wrote music of great range and power, from comical catches, through the stunning variety of the Birthday Odes for his beloved Queen Mary, to the stark sublimity of the music for her funeral, and in the theatre this range was given full scope in vigorous and haunting solo songs, sprightly Act-tunes, and imposing ensembles. He came particularly into his own in the masque-like episodes he composed for his semi-operas, *King Arthur*, *The Fairy Queen*, and *Dioclesian*. These are astonishing pieces, carefully contrived to allow musical scenes of increasing complexity to build a new dimension to the drama. These scenes are devised as shorter or longer sequences of musical numbers that, by a juxtaposition of precise images in sound, define the idea of the passions felt by the characters, while evoking those passions and so the nature of the moral predicament they cause, in the watching, listening audience. When Osmond attempts to seduce Emmeline, in *King Arthur* (Act III), Dryden provides a graphic episode in which the scene is magically transformed to 'a Prospect of Winter in cold countries'. Cupid descends, and summons Frost to rise from beneath 'those hills of snow'. The people enter, cold and shivering, and Cupid promises that they shall all be warmed by love, and changes the scene to spring. It is a charming fancy. The transformation of the frigid to the warm is meant to draw Emmeline from her allegiance, and Purcell brilliantly evokes the moods and ideas. Frost rises to shuddering, pulsing chords that seem to pull him back into the earth even as he is rising out of it. Cupid's sprightly declamation forms a sharp contrast, and humour is added by the musical wit of the orchestral tremolos that imitate the cold and shivering demon, and by his own and his people's vocal shivering to match it. Then the minor keys and the monotone melodies change to bright major keys and sprightly rhythms. As the stage grows green with spring the music becomes sunny and vigorous also.[24] The little scene is a musical and dramatic masterpiece, and we should not be deceived into finding it untheatrical simply because it seems tacked on in the light of modern theories of musical stagecraft. It is a visual and aural simile, which would have been both felt and understood by its original audience, who would have found such an expression of relevant feeling more interesting and more natural than a scene of seduction sung by the seducer and his prey. It has advantages too. Here the whole stage can be used to capture the tensions implicit in the action. The expression blossoms out of the dramatic situation. The lilting dance and charming chorus express the seduction in a different way, but in a way that is equally valid and equally exciting, given musical images of this quality.

Purcell's masterpiece is certainly *The Fairy Queen* which is a kind of summation of his genius and of the spectacular theatre that exploited it. The play is taken, probably by Elkanah Settle, from *A Midsummer Night's Dream*.[25] The original is very much shortened, to make way for musical interludes that are magnificent in scope and in themselves make up a full length opera. Settle concentrates the story of the Athenian lovers by severe cutting, and that of the mechanicals by combining rehearsal and performance, so that they are absent from the last scene. He also curtails the fairy scenes; but here it is simply to expand them into a series of lengthening and ever more splendid masques to Purcell's music. Roger Savage has suggested that this music puts back the magic that Settle had omitted.[26] This is only half-true. Shakespeare's magic is more ambiguous in its lyricism and more sinister in its undercurrents. *The Fairy Queen* is not really concerned with magic at all. Magic is replaced by an exercise of fancy that complements its human themes in an intense baroque celebration of the varieties of human feeling.

In the final masque we find the epitome of the composer's ability to both realise and define a dramatic idea in clear and evocative musical gestures. It also contains a problem that neatly characterises the taste of the day. Instead of Shakespeare's rustic entertainment, which Settle has moved to an earlier act, Theseus and the Athenian lovers are treated by Oberon and Titania to a triumphant spectacle. First, Juno descends in a chariot drawn by peacocks to sing an epithalamium. As she does so, the tails of the peacocks spread 'and fill the middle of the Theater'. After the song, the machine ascends, and Oberon says:

> Sing me the Plaint that did so nobly move,
> When *Laura* mourned for her departed Love.

There follows the superb 'O let me ever, ever weep', one of those intense utterances over a chromatic ground-bass that are so much the composer's own. Here, the effect is magical, with a solo violin sometimes echoing and sometimes decorating the soprano's lament. The two songs, so arbitrarily contrasted in mood, are profoundly moving, and form a prologue, a hint of the more expansive contrasts to come, oppose love and jealous despair in telling juxtaposition.

Now, appropriately, the scene is darkened, while the dancers hold the fore-stage for an elegant, formal entry dance, after which, to the radiant voice of the trumpet, the scene is illuminated to a fascinating spectacle. It is 'a transparent Prospect of a Chinese Garden, the Architecture, the Trees, the Plants, the Fruits, the Birds, the Beasts, quite different from what we have in this part of the world.' It is a split scene, with an arch, arbours and avenue below and a hanging garden above, which, with its pictures of exotic beasts and 'numbers of strange birds flying in the air', and its use of light behind painted gauze to give the effect of transparency must have been breathtaking, an effect that would have been enhanced by Purcell's ravishing trumpet tune, and the delicate sequence of songs and choruses that follow, culminating in a dance for six monkeys, transformed from china-orange-trees.

Another charming fancy, and if it here seems a trifle arbitrary, in fact it is so. What was originally intended, was, as indicated by the descent of Juno, a classical vision of the Golden Age. As the words go to the trumpet tune:

> Thus the gloomy World
> At first began to shine,
> And from the Power Divine
> A Glory round it hurl'd.

Innocence is being celebrated by the Classical deities for the hallowing of true love, and for proof the name of Daphne still appears in the score.[27]

But management had a better idea: to represent the freshness of their new world they hit upon the lyrical elegance of oriental silk and porcelain, now becoming known for the first time in England. The change was made without altering a word or note of the score, save to give the girl a new name, Xansi, and perhaps replace classical satyrs with Chinese monkeys. It may have been a success. It was certainly a novel and exciting idea. But it is impossible not to wonder if it did not spoil Purcell's carefully worked out climax.

As the soprano sings the thrilling 'Hark, the echoing Air' – with its vigorous rhythms, another yet more shining trumpet obbligato recalling the golden opening of the scene, and comical onomatopoeic reiterations as the Cupids (in China?) 'clap, clap, clap' their wings – a *coup de théâtre* is prepared. The marvellous music finishes, and suddenly there is silence. Hymen has not answered Juno's summons. The music takes on a lugubrious timbre and minor mode. The singers call again, and Hymen appears. But his torch has 'long been out'. He is like the spectre at the feast, and the sudden contrast wonderfully deepens the celebratory atmosphere of the whole. The upturned torch, the work of death and time, interrupts the marriage ceremony. This is a traditional and classical image. The setting of the Chinese garden must have spoiled its logic and weakened its effect. As the presence of the true lovers re-kindles the torch of the ancient world, the beautiful association of contemporary English society and its loved Classical inheritance is broken, though it remains in the delicacy of the music at this wonderful moment.

This final masque is strikingly conceived. A long span of music is sustained on four related sequences of images that gain richness from their contrasts: first, the stately Juno, then the freshness of the girls and boys of the golden age, then the desolation of Hymen, pointing the illusion of it all, and finally the renewal of hope in the promises of marriage and the harmony of a great Chaconne. The employment of music to give depth and feeling to such a logical sequence is typical of the Restoration theatre. The destruction of such a sequence for the sake of a novel scenic effect is as typical of the problems that theatre faced by the end of the century.

9 · Venice Preserv'd, or A Plot Discover'd

The mood of England in the 1680s was very different from the mood when Charles returned to London in 1660. The City's acclamation had turned to suspicion and resentment. In *Venice Preserv'd*, Otway reflects this disillusionment in a very personal way, exploring the sense of failure, inner searching and outward distrust in a strange mixture of formality and pathos. The play opens with Jacobean directness, the action in full spate.[1]

PRIULI: No more! I'le hear no more; begone and leave.
JAFFEIR: Not hear me! by my sufferings but you shall!

A young man confronts his father-in-law. He speaks passionately, and the verse does not limp as so often in Restoration tragedy when it lacks rhyme. It bends itself to the feeling.

> My Lord, my Lord; I'm not that abject wretch
> You think me: Patience! where's the distance throws
> Me back so far, but I may boldly speak
> In right, though proud oppression will not hear me!

PRIULI: Have you not wrong'd me?
JAFFEIR: Could my Nature e're
> Have brook'd Injustice or the doing wrongs,
> I need not now thus low have bent my self,
> To gain a Hearing from a Cruel father! (I. 3–10)

Jaffeir is hard pressed. He keeps beginning again. Once he stops in the middle of a line to control himself: 'Patience!' Exclamation marks litter the page, and the words fall over themselves and the metre. The older man is unrelenting, his sentences simple and absolute. The opposition is intimate and psychologically presented. It is possible to hear the feeling through the words, and believe in the language and the situation in a way that is never possible in Dryden. There is a sense of being present at the event which is not a part of Restoration style.

Yet this is all deceptive. The actors are performing in front of a pictorial scene which represents a street in Venice. The private encounter is set incongruously in a public frame. Further, Jaffeir, the chief source of emotion, employs formal gesture as well as frantic words. He kneels to his father, and is given a suspended, half-aside, out to the house, as he tries to regain his confidence in front of 'proud oppression'. The audience is as visibly present as in Dryden or Wycherley, and the intimacy of the dramatic confrontation is still in dialogue with the actor's intimacy with his public. Jaffeir and Priuli are 'characters': the rash young man who has stolen the daughter of the implacable minister. Youth and age are juxtaposed in an entirely classical way, and the tension of the scene is built in the words which explore and make explicit the antagonism inherent in the static 'attitudes' of the players. Otway dwells on the malice of the older man and contrasts it with the openness and simplicity of the younger. When Jaffeir mentions his child, the baroque juxtaposition of images becomes almost grotesque:

> JAFFEIR: May he live to prove more Gentle than his Grandsire,
> And happier than his Father!
> PRIULI: Rather live
> To bait thee for his bread, and din your ears
> With hungry Cries: Whilst his unhappy Mother
> Sits down and weeps in bitterness of want.
> JAFFEIR: You talk as if it would please you. (I.62–7)

The abstractions and the interaction with both audience and play are more flexible but they are still present, and the emotional quality of the language still gathers itself into characteristic gestures. 'Home and be humble, study to retrench,' Priuli brutally tells his bankrupt son-in-law. 'Get Brats, and Starve.' The audience are expected both to feel and understand the opposition.

The scene is a strange and surprising one for the period. Formal in arrangement and presentation, based on a conventional antagonism, it is graphic in its detail of the physical realities of a situation that is very far from heroism and rather close to life:

> I have now not 50 Ducats in the World,
> Yet still I am in love and pleas'd with Ruin.
> Oh *Belvidera*! oh she's my Wife –
> And we will bear our wayward Fate together,
> But ne're know Comfort more. (ll. 116–20)

As in an earlier tragedy, *The Orphan*, Otway studies in *Venice Preserv'd* what might be described as characters of 'middle life', not the heroic figures usually expected, and though size is added to them by their association with public revolution, it remains their private tragedy that is the centre of the interest. Otway himself was improvident and indigent, accepted by the great, and a participant in a good deal of cynical, aristo- cratic debauchery, but he was seldom supported by them, and so, in the memorable phrase quoted by Dr Johnson, 'languished in Poverty without the support of Innocence'.[2] The bitterness of such a position grows progressively through his work. He avoids poetic justice and heroic utterance, and in both comedy and tragedy alights on subjects that are inherently sordid, and explores them with striking realism and none of the glamour of language or of laughter so sought after by contemporaries.

The only luxury he allows himself is feeling, and in this he is both novel and excessive. His technique is singular. As the opening scene of *Venice Preserv'd* demonstrates, Dryden's objectifying of 'movements of the mind' in telling verbal and physical gestures is retained. The structure of the scene is formal and demonstrative. Yet the language is allowed to run over itself. One telling hint is the frequency with which Otway's text capitalises adjectives and verbs as well as nouns, an emotive, exclamatory technique, which comes to its climax in such actor's moments as Mrs Barry's 'Oh h h's' and 'Ah h h's', or Jaffeir's vocal gesture, presenting the sudden passion of joy that comes to him on mentioning his wife's name, 'Oh *Belvidera*! oh she's my Wife'. Otway seldom arouses emotion through images. Instead, he develops an emotional tension that is sometimes almost unbearable in the nakedness with which it dwells on the most private areas of human behaviour. Otway's world was neither virtuous nor decent, and he does not attempt to make it so. Neither does he attempt to offset it by examples of ideals he has not known. He provides an interplay between intimacy and objectivity which is almost voyeurish, and gives his style its characteristic quality.

It is difficult to decide if Otway's effective exploration of the theatrical techniques of his day arises from a real intention to challenge convention and create a new dramatic style, or is simply an unconscious compromise between the theatre he knew and his own need for personal expression. The play is seventeenth century in design. The plot to overthrow the tyrannous Venetian council echoes Jaffeir's attempts to cope with the tyranny of his father-in-law. Personal and political freedoms are intricately interwoven with related moral attitudes. In turn, the 'characters' of the drama reflect these attitudes, and explore their implications. Pierre, the revolutionary, has an implacable constancy in his aims which is contrasted with Jaffeir's havering, and their women form a related opposition, Belvidera melting and pathetic, Aquilina, fiery and waspish. *Venice Preserv'd* was one of the first plays of the newly United Company, and had the best actors in London. Smith and Mrs Currer as Pierre and Aquilina are in fact given clear characters in the true Restoration manner. Smith had taken over most of Hart's roles on his retirement, and Otway often used him in the more glamorous of his comic parts. Mrs Currer was new to the company, but Otway was to use her again as the married Sylvia in the acid second part of *The Soldier's Fortune*, his final work for the stage. Both roles suggest a woman who could combine venom with her beauty. Jaffeir and Belvidera, however, were played by Betterton and Mrs Barry, and here Otway gives his new, emotive style its head, using it to blur the clarity of his characters and present a telling kind of moral ambiguity. The comic scenes, too, fit with the English conventions of the time – forming calculated reflections of the main themes of the play, as in Jacobean tragedy or Dryden's double-plot plays. Yet here also, the style is coloured by an emotionalism, and a patina of realistic observation that clouds the meaning that would otherwise emerge from this careful patterning, and arouses responses of a different kind. Even Otway's handling of scenic rhythm combines the traditional Restoration juxtaposition of significant scene images with a contrasted dreamy dissolution of image from one scene to the next, which on occasions suggests the difference between a jump cut and a cross-fade in a modern film.[3] His feeling for the different rhythms is implicit in his stage-directions, phrased sometimes abruptly: 'SCENE The Ryalto', and sometimes with a greater sense of continuum: '*The* Scene *changes to* Aquilina's *house, the Greek Curtezan.*' While constructing separate scenic and dramatic gestures, Otway manages at crucial moments to create a dialectic between the representation of the flow of experience and the presentation of a pattern of ideas.

This is particularly important to the ambivalent structure of his dialogues. His characters appear really to encounter each other, as in the play's opening, yet at the same time the scenes are articulated to embody the design in strong visual gestures. Jaffeir and Pierre have both been wronged in their love, both by members of the Senate – Jaffeir by his wife's father, Pierre by the garrulous fool, Antonio, who has stolen his mistress, Aquilina. Their reactions are very different:

JAFFEIR: Ah *Pierre*! I have a Heart, that could have born
        The roughest Wrong my Fortune could have done me:
        But when I think what *Belvidera* feels,
        The bitterness her tender spirit tasts of,
        I own myself a Coward: Bear my weakness,
        If throwing thus my Arms about thy Neck,
        I play the Boy and Blubber in thy bosome.
        Oh! I shall drown thee with my Sorrows!

PIERRE: Burn!
        First burn, and Level *Venice* to thy Ruin! (I. 270–88)

Jaffeir dissolves in tears; Pierre readies himself to strike. They are fire and water – designed as opposites, while the embrace is to become a visual *leit motif* of the play. Otway has incarnated his basic ideas in both the social and the erotic characteristics of his two characters.

When reading Otway, it is more than ever important to remember the

staging conventions of his time, the lit auditorium, the applause, the
direct address, the acting that calculates the precise physical attitude that
is required to express both character and passion. For all his intimacy
and pathos, these conditions are accounted for, and are used to make his
characters' ruthless self-exposure more absolute and more public. They
are, in fact, the conditions of the nakedness of feeling the poet contrives.
Jaffeir's moral weakness is made more telling and more embarrassing by
its bleak physical exposure on the Restoration stage, while gestures of
ostentatious pathos gain a strength that perhaps they do not always
deserve from the underlying design and the audience's awareness of it.
Mrs Barry's first entrance is, to modern eyes, an absurdly calculated and
sentimental gesture, a sure pitfall for the unwary director who has not
captured the formal manner of the opening scenes. She enters attended.

JAFFEIR: Poor *Belvidera*!
BELVIDERA: Lead me, lead me my Virgins!
             To that kind Voice. My Lord, my Love, my Refuge!
             Happy my Eyes, when they behold thy Face. (I.316–18)

It is a ceremonious entrance for a lady just turned out by the bailiffs, and
the intrusive exclamation marks and rash of capital letters are indicative
of its emotional emphasis; but the entrance has been carefully prepared:

PIERRE: Hadst thou but seen, as I did, how at last
            Thy Beauteous *Belvidera*, like a Wretch
            That's doom'd to Banishment, came weeping forth,
            Shining through Tears, like *April* Sun's in showers
            That labour to orecome the Cloud that loads 'm,
            Whilst two young Virgins, on whose Arms she lean'd,
            Kindly lookt up, and at her Grief grew sad,
            As if they cach't the Sorrows that fell from her. (ll. 256–63)

It is one of those verbal presentations that raise the expectation of the
audience and assist their understanding, here used also to increase their
feeling. Mrs Barry enters droopingly, her arms spread forwards and back,
while the virgins, posed at either arm, look up at her with swimming
eyes. It seems rather of the eighteenth than the seventeenth century, a
moralised gesture by Greuze, calculated to catch all the pathos of poverty.
It is a claptrap; but here its sentimentality is given another dimension by
its place in the overall design. The audience is enabled to share Jaffeir's
feeling, but as they begin to comprehend the place of his feeling in the
pattern of the play, their own response is questioned.

The relationship between Jaffeir and his wife acts as catalyst in the
design of *Venice Preserv'd* in much the same way as Horner's trick does
in the design of *The Country Wife*. And there is a further important
similarity. Otway orchestrates his audiences' emotional responses towards
the same kind of complicity. On her first entrance, he plays for our tears

for Belvidera the paragon. She seems a conventional and 'ideal' creature, on whose behalf we are easily touched. Yet, time and again Otway pulls up a conventional image with a detail of precise physical observation which begins a complex dialectic of responses:

> BELVIDERA: Oh I will love thee, even in Madness love thee:
> Tho' my distracted Senses should forsake me,
> I'd find some intervals, when my poor heart
> Should swage itself and bee let loose to thine.
> Though the bare Earth be all our Resting-place,
> It's Root's our food, some Clift our Habitation,
> I'l make this Arm a Pillow for thy Head;
> As thou sighing ly'st, and swell'd with sorrow,
> Creep to thy Bosom, pour the balm of Love
> Into thy Soul, and kiss thee to thy Rest;
> Then praise our God, and watch thee 'till the Morning.
> (ll. 371–81)

The bare earth and meal of roots is reach-me-down stuff, prettily articulated; but the picture of the girl pressing close to him, his head on her arm, has the particularity of a different kind of poetry. In letting her heart 'loose', Belvidera gives another inflection to the concept of freedom. The idea of the soul and body dissolving or loosening in the act of love is constant in the organisation of the play, being shown in language, action, even in the flow of the scenes. This loosening of resolve in sensual indulgence is the centre of their relationship and of Jaffeir's 'character'. Where her father's harshness urges Jaffeir to stand up to tyranny, his wife's softness seduces him into compliance.

Otway constructs their scenes together as a series of gestures of this progression. When Jaffeir agrees to join the plot, he decides to leave Belvidera with the plotters for hostage and forswears her bed until the deed is done. He brings her in among them, and the closeness of their tie is illustrated in word and gesture:

> BELVIDERA: Oh! I have slept, and dreamt
> And dreamt again: Where hast thou been thou
> Loyterer?
> Tho my Eyes clos'd, my Arms have still been open'd;
> Strecht every way betwixt my broken slumbers,
> To search if thou wert come to crown my Rest;
> There's no repose without thee: Oh the day
> Too soon will break, and wake us to our sorrow;
> Come, come to bed, and bid thy Cares good Night.
> (II. 359–66)

But he takes her arms from about his neck, and gives her over to the men who watch them, and, with her, a dagger that is to be struck to her heart if he betrays them. It seems like Romantic melodrama; but the public presence, the embrace, and now the dagger develop the significance of previous episodes of which they are visual echoes, and present them to the judgment. The eroticism is strangely Oedipal. Warmth and closeness confuses mother and wife, and Jaffeir and Belvidera long constantly to fall back into this mutual comfort, as if to return to the protection of the womb. Jaffeir says:

> Every moment
> I am from thy sight, the Heart within my Bosom
> Moans like a tender Infant in its Cradle
> Whose Nurse had left it. (III.ii.17–20)

The speaker of such lines requires a sense of melody that would be impertinent in Dryden's pristine couplets, but it is a melody that must not lose itself in feeling and so miss the precision of inflection that conveys idea as well as mood. The melting tone is in fact the function of the melting will. It must be understood as well as experienced. Luxurious as it is, it is an emblem of moral sickness. Like Dryden, Otway is exploring in his personal way the concept of 'the lethargy of Love',[4] and adding a new dimension to it.

The music of love is continually contrasted with the harshness of violence and aggression. Belvidera imitates Brutus's and Shakespeare's Portia in demanding to know her husband's secrets. Jaffeir at last confesses, and the effect is like that of a blow:

> JAFFEIR: No: do not swear: I would not violate
> Thy tender Nature with so rude a Bond:
> But as thou hop'st to see me live my days,
> And love thee long, lock this within thy Breast;
> I've bound myself by all the strictest Sacraments,
> Divine and humane –
>
> BELVIDERA: Speak!
> JAFFEIR: To kill thy Father –
> BELVIDERA: My Father! (III.ii.134–40)

We are shown the sadistic product of their masochistic love-fantasies, a brutal over-compensation necessary to break the warmth of their together-ness. Jaffeir falters. She prompts him. He lashes out. The 'movement of the mind' is demonstrated in action, and then its tensions are made explicit in a speech from Jaffeir in which violence is explored as a prelude to love.

> JAFFEIR: Nay the Throats of the whole Senate
> Shall bleed, my *Belvidera*: He amongst us
> That spares his Father, Brother, or his Friend,
> Is damn'd: How rich and beauteous will the face
> Of Ruin look, when these wide streets run blood;

> I and the glorious Partner's of my Fortune
> Shouting, and striding ore the prostrate Dead;
> Still to new waste; whilst thou, far off in safety
> Smiling, shalt see the wonders of our daring;
> And when night comes, with Praise and Love receive me.
> (ll. 140–9)

Within the formal context of Restoration stage presentation the new emotionalism of tone does not disguise the firm pattern of moral idea: it rather gives it a new psychological dimension. Precision of gesture counters melodrama, while the warmth of tone adds another kind of dramatic excitement.

In the climactic scene between them, this interaction of thought and feeling is particularly striking. Jaffeir is seduced by his wife into betraying his friends. When they are condemned, he turns against her and blames her for the disaster. Here Otway brilliantly plays off an almost naturalistic presentation of Jaffeir's vacillations against the emblematic significance of set and gesture. The scene apparently takes place in the Chamber of the Council of Ten. In real terms, this is quite inappropriate, but it ensures that the 'idea' of judgment is present as the two judge each other:

> JAFFEIR: Murther – Oh! – hark thee, Traitress, thou hast done this
> Thanks to thy tears and false perswading love.
>
> (*Fumbling for his Dagger*)
>
> How her eyes speak! Oh thou bewitching creature!
> Madness cannot hurt thee: Come, thou little trembler,
> Creep, even into my heart, and there lie safe;
> 'Tis thy own Citadel – hah – yet stand off . . .
> (IV. 495–500)

The words clearly determine descriptive attitudes portraying the movements of his mind, but the rhythm is broken down by pauses and exclamations that enable the actor to effect truly felt transitions between the gestures. The episode lends itself to 'ham' in modern terms; but, at the time, it would have been saved from this by precisely such interplay between attitude and feeling. The undercurrents of the scene are felt, and flow on from one moment to the next, while the body selects the most significant pictures in the flow of action to dwell upon and articulate in speech. The audience is made to experience the hesitation, and perceive the precise elements of physical desire which produce it. They feel, recognise and understand. As a climax to the scene, the whole relationship is summed up in a *gestus* which brings together the physical emblems that have come to incarnate it:

> JAFFEIR: No, *Belvidera*, when we parted last
> I gave this dagger with thee as in trust
> To be thy portion, if I e'r prov'd false.

On such condition was my truth believ'd:
But now 'tis forfeited and must be paid for.
(*Offers to stab her again*)

BELVIDERA: Oh, mercy! (*Kneeling*)
JAFFEIR: Nay, no struggling.
BELVIDERA: Now then kill me.
(*Leaps upon his neck and kisses him*)
While thus I cling about thy cruel neck,
Kiss thy revengeful lips and die in joys
Greater than any I can guess hereafter.
JAFFEIR: I am, I am a Coward. (ll. 511–20)

This must be both designed and experienced by the actors to achieve its effect, as in the famous picture of Garrick and Mrs Cibber in the scene (Plate 36). The drawing back of the arm, her kneeling and placing her hand on his wrist are both formal gestures that need to be clearly articulated. The struggling is in the tension between the players, not in any imitative scuffling. Then comes the embrace, equally choreographic, echoing her greeting as she entered to the conspirators, and followed first by his drooping inability to act, and then by his throwing away the dagger and returning the embrace. His 'I am, I am a Coward', also echoes the previous scene, while Jaffeir's words as he sends her to plead with her father, objectify the scene before us:

Fall at his feet, cling round his reverend knees;
Speak to him with thy Eyes, and with thy tears
Melt the hard heart, and wake dead nature in him;
Crush him in th'Arms and torture him with thy softness.
(ll. 532–5)

Soft and hard grow together in paradoxical profusion, and the final line gives us an image their scenes together have enacted.

It may be felt that the sensual emotionalism of these scenes is bound to conquer the audience's awareness of the formal patterns upon which they are based; but there is another aspect of the original conception that must have done a great deal to keep the balance. *Venice Preserv'd* was first played in 1682, and given as its subtitle *A Plot Discover'd*. It was played, in fact, in the aftermath of the Popish Plot and the Exclusion crisis, when Shaftesbury, the Whig leader at that time, had finally been forced into exile, to die in Holland in 1683. Otway employs all the devices of incidental reference and indirect allusion found so entertaining by the period, to preserve the present in interaction with the fiction. The prologue, with its direct references to the Plot itself, the death of Sir Edmund Berry Godfrey that started the scare, and to Shaftesbury's supposed aspirations to the Polish crown, demonstrates that the relationships are not entirely casual, and from the outset that this is a Tory play. They stimulate the audience's attention to the development of the Venetian plot as the play proceeds. This is necessary because the relationship is complex. The Popish plot was, by 1682, already exploded and considered a product of Whig imagination. The plot in *Venice Preserv'd* undoubtedly exists. The Whig policy in proving the existence of the plot seems to have been intended to undermine the monarchy; but the plot that is discovered in *Venice Preserv'd* is against a republic, one of the Whig models of political propriety. It is not therefore possible to align the factions as they emerge in Otway's play with the political factions of the time. His references are incidental rather than structural. This is what produces the elaborate interplay of attitudes that keeps the action in a kind of dialectical relationship to contemporary events, which, with the contemporaneity of costume and domestic level of the action, encourages an objective approach to the story in the face of its personal expressiveness.

Some of these moments are remarkable examples of how such effects can actually be created from meanings that are really very different. Pierre tells Jaffeir:

> All that bear this are Villains; and I one,
> Not to rouse up at the great Call of Nature,
> And check the Growth of these Domestick Spoilers,
> That make us slaves and tell us 'tis our Charter. (I. 161–4)

The Tories would be happy to see through Pierre's lines to the king rousing himself against the 'Domestick Spoilers' of the City of London and taking away the Charter, the rights of which they were always quoting at him. They would probably give him a rousing cheer. It must be admitted, however, that the sentence really reverses the subject and the object – Pierre is talking about people who tell him what his rights are, not who claim a charter for their own. It is a remarkable thing about language in a theatrical context that these two meanings, really quite opposed, can be understood together. Otway's ambivalence is often not genuine ambiguity so much as a shameless coexistence of different meanings at different levels of interest and understanding.

Though we begin on the plotters' side, we soon learn of their intention to actually commit those very atrocities the prospect of which had so terrified Londoners during the crisis.

> Then fire the City round in several places,
> Or with our Canon (if it dare resist)
> Batter't to Ruin. But above all I charge you,
> Shed blood enough, spare neither Sex nor age,
> Name nor Condition; if there live a Senator
> After tomorrow, tho' the dullest Rogue
> That er'e said nothing, we have lost our ends;

> If possible let's kill the very name
> Of Senator, and bury it in blood. (II.ii.330–8)

Rumour had it that the Great Fire had been caused by a Catholic plot; and it was a mayor of London that called out the trained-bands during the crisis with the memorable phrase: 'Who knows but we may all rise tomorrow with our throats cut.' Even the sympathies of the town must be against such atrocities, although Charles had ordered the removal of part of the city walls so that they could no longer withstand the battery of cannon as they had in the Civil War. Otway masses different kinds of contemporary reference together to illustrate his fictional idea. Belvidera, pleading on the other side, gathers yet other references:

> Nay, be a Traitor too, and sell thy Country?
> Can thy great Heart descend so vilely low,
> Mix with hired Slaves, Bravoes, and Common stabbers,
> Nose-slitters, Ally-lurking Villains! joyn
> With such a Crew, and take a Ruffian's Wages,
> To cut the Throats of Wretches as they sleep?
> (III.ii.159–64)

Mrs Barry must have delivered this with fine scorn, but apart from the other reference to the Lord Mayor's remark, and the hint of the murder of Berry Godfrey, the hiring of ruffians here suggest rather aristocratic activities: it was Rochester who had Dryden beaten in Rose Alley, and possibly the king who had Sir William Coventry's nose slit for speaking ill of his mistresses in parliament.

Such dual awareness is at the very heart of the play in contemporary terms. It ensures a measure of distance towards the fictional emotions, and enables Otway to add to this objectivity by incorporating a political lampoon of outstanding dramatic effectiveness. Anthony Ashley Cooper, the Whig leader, is presented in the guise of two different characters – one on each side of the action, a senator and a leader of the conspirators.

Both lampoons are as cruel as they are brilliant. Renault is a blood-thirsty and treacherous old man who attempts to rape Belvidera, and threatens her life with the very dagger her husband left with him, and arouses the revolutionaries to their programme of atrocities. His other self is Antonio a 'fine speaker in the Senate' and the man who has bought Pierre's mistress, the Greek courtesan Aquilina. Both figures, in the manner of lampoons, profit from a false logic of feeling and arraign the subject's political beliefs by the presentation of nasty personal habits. In centring the most violent aspects of his plot and his comic underplot on two aspects of the same contemporary figure, Otway adds a new dimension to the play, for as Renault precipitates Jaffeir's betrayal, by his combination of violence and lechery, so Antonio, in his relations with

Aquilina, is made to reflect and parody the sado-masochistic stimulation of sexual response that underlies the relationships of Jaffeir and Belvidera.

The role of Antonio was designed for Antony Leigh, one of Otway's favourite actors. Cibber wrote:[5]

> *Leigh* was of the mercurial kind, and though not so strict an Observer of Nature, yet never so wanton in his Performance as to be wholly out of her Sight. In Humour he lov'd to take a full Career, but was careful enough to stop short when just upon the Precipice. He had great Variety, in his manner, and was famous in very different Characters.

This combination of extravagance and accuracy is perfect for Antonio, and it is possible to add to the picture, for it is clear from the roles that Leigh undertook that the extravagance of his humour derived from the talent of an extremely physical actor. Otway had employed him in the title role of his adaptation of Molière's *Scapin*, which requires a host of *commedia* tricks, while as Bartoline in Crowne's *City Politiques*, another anti-plot play, Cibber remarked that he presented to perfection 'the dotage and follies of extreme old age'. In Antonio, Otway exploits the actor's obvious talent for being hugely dynamic and excruciatingly embarrassing at one and the same time.

Antonio is first introduced in Act III. Pierre has given Aquilina an ultimatum that she is to get rid of him or else, but she has forgotten to tell her servants and so he breaks in upon her.

> ANTONIO: *Nacky*, *Nacky*, *Nacky* – how dost do *Nacky*? Hurry durry. I am come little *Nacky*; past eleven a Clock, a late hour; time in all conscience to go to bed *Nacky* – *Nacky* did I say? Ay *Nacky*; Aquilina, *lina*, *lina*, *quilina*, *quilina*, *quilina*, *Aquilina*, *Naquilina*, *Naquilina*, *Acky*, *Acky*, *Nacky*, *Nacky*, Queen *Nacky* – come let's to bed – you Fubbs, you Pugg you – you little Puss – Purree Tuzzey – I am a Senator.
>
> AQUILINA: You are a Fool, I am sure. (II.i.14–22)

His first speech is practically a *commedia lazzo* which runs through the various attitudes the scene is to expound. The nasty joke is based on a ridiculous presence that throws itself into different approaches to the woman, all of which are, by the nature of the man, parodies of themselves. He tries to get her to sit beside him. She won't. Suddenly he begins to bellow like a bull and chase her about. She sits down quickly. Now he snuggles up to her on the seat, calling her his little toad, and gazing up at her in a crooked fashion. Then:

> Ah, toad, toad, toad, toad! spit in my Face a little, *Nacky* – spit in my Face prithee, spit in my Face, never so little: spit a little bit – spit, spit, spit, spit when you are bid, I say, do, prithee spit . . . (ll. 90–3)

Both the comedy and the degradation of the scene lie in the tension between his perverse attempts to provoke a response, and her distasteful refusal to co-operate. His inventive games become more masochistic, and finally, provoked beyond endurance, she fetches a whip. The games become a reality and in spite of his protests she whips him out of the room, and he howls like a dog outside the door till her footmen take him away.

The various gestures of the scene catch brilliantly the ambivalence of provocative sex-play for the stimulation of a worn-out appetite and the attempt to get rid of an unwanted lover. The fantasy of the former prevents the reality of the latter. The technique is classical – the elements of the situation are incarnated in descriptive action; but the psychological content is horridly realistic, and catches up the similar vacillations of aggression and submission in the apparently fulfilled relationship of Jaffeir and Belvidera. The attaching of the degrading spectacle to a hated contemporary figure adds the audience's own sadistic delight to the complex of feelings aroused.

The second encounter of Aquilina and Antonio elaborates this parallel further. As Jaffeir threatens Belvidera with death, and then sends her to plead with her father for Pierre's life, so Aquilina comes to Antonio for the same purpose. Aquilina produces a dagger. He is terrified at first, but then thinks it is all part of the game. She flings him on the ground and threatens him. He shrieks 'Ah h h h.'

AQUILINA: Swear to recall his doom,
        Swear at my feet, and tremble at my fury.
ANTONIO: I do; now if she would but kick a little bit, one kick now
        Ah h h h. (V. 202–5)

Perverse as it is, it is also finely emblematic. Aquilina plays the man's part, the woman holds the dagger, and the man excitedly submits:

AQUILINA: Nay, then –
ANTONIO: Hold, hold, thy Love, thy Lord, thy Hero
        Shall be preserv'd and safe.
AQUILINA: Or may this Poniard
        Rust in thy heart.
ANTONIO: With all my soul.
AQUILINA: Farewell – (ll. 212–15)

As opposed to Aquilina's masculine behaviour, Jaffeir's vacillations throughout the play have been 'effeminate' – ruled by a woman, and this interplay of masculine and feminine in moral as well as sexual terms is vital in his relationships both with his wife and with his friend. Pierre leads Jaffeir into the plot as Belvidera leads him out of it. In both cases, in seeking vengeance or in saving the city, he is apparently taking an active role but is actually remaining passive to the energy of another. The reiteration of the motifs of the dagger and the embrace have made this psychological ambiguity manifest.

A dagger is destructive; but it is also glamorous. Its cut and thrust can be both villainous and heroic, and it is an emblem of masculine power for good or evil, pleasure or pain. Jaffeir brings it to the council of revolutionaries, delivering it, with Belvidera, into their hands. The flamboyance of the action arouses distrust. When Jaffeir has betrayed them, Pierre returns the dagger with scorn, but returns it as a pendant to a more degrading action. As Jaffeir tries to justify himself, his friend strikes him with his hand – a cold, real blow given to an inferior, a slave or a woman, and an echo of the verbal blows Jaffeir and Belvidera shower on each other. At it, Jaffeir cringes, and lies around at his friend's feet, as Antonio does at Aquilina's. The gestures are clear, significant, and observed; but their interrelationship carries an extraordinary emotional undertow. The final two scenes with wife and friend bring these gestures and feelings to their logical conclusion.

The scene with Belvidera restores Jaffeir to his dominant role. He has resolved to assist his friend at his death, and then take his own life. He speaks little and firmly against Belvidera's long, melodious utterances, while her words and thoughts return again and again so that orgasmic 'loosening' of the soul in love, the need for which has formerly undermined him. Her speech now associates the dissolution in love with the dissolution in death:

BELVIDERA: Yes, and when thy hands
       Charg'd with my fate, come trembling to the deed,
       As thou hast done a thousand thousand dear times,
       To this poor breast, when kinder rage has wrought thee,
       When our sting'd hearts have leap'd to meet each other,
       And melting kisses seal'd our lips together,
       When joyes have left me gasping in thy armes,
       So let my death come now, and I'll not shrink from't.
       (V. 243–50)

Never has the old pun on 'dying' been made more physically explicit than in her begging for death, and yet the words are subtextually ambiguous. Her speech is a trap. Throughout she is challenging him underneath it all to steal away to her bed again and reconvert death into love. When he refers to the miserable day of their wedding, the kind of verbal blow we have come to expect in their relationship, she cries 'Oh h h.' The sound sums up the pain she feels at his condemnation of their 'joyes'; but it is also an echo in a new key of Antonio's 'Ah h h h.' The comic and tragic actors' moments are juxtaposed with a cutting irony. So again at Jaffeir's moment of weakness:

BELVIDERA: Oh turn and hear me!
JAFFEIR: Now hold, heart, or never.
BELVIDERA: By all the tender days we have lived together,
                By all our charming nights, and joyes that crown'd 'em,
                Pity my sad condition, speak, but speak.
JAFFEIR: Oh h h.
BELVIDERA: By these armes that now cling round thy neck,
                By this dear kiss and by ten thousand more,
                By these poor streaming eyes – (ll. 317–24)

Otway leaves the moment to the actor, but engineers a striking visual irony in leaving him passive in her embrace at the point where his resolution is about to show itself. Now he draws the dagger on himself, and, as she prevents his using it, the passing-bell for the execution of the conspirators is heard. He puts away the dagger, and after a long, last embrace, he leaves her. It is a 'masculine' victory, but its consequence is that Belvidera's feelings 'dissolve' her mind at last into madness. It is the fulfilment of her earlier promise – 'Oh I will love thee, even in madness love thee' – and in this final dissolution, love, death, resolution and disintegration, harshness and softness merge emblematically in the action on the stage.

Priuli appears and orders his servants to lead his daughter home, but random images of pleasure crowd on her disordered brain:

BELVIDERA: Who's there?
PRIULI: Run, seize and bring her safely home.
                (*They seize her*)
                Guard her as you would life: alas poor creature!
BELVIDERA: What? to my husband then conduct me quickly,
                Are all things ready? shall we dye most gloriously?
                Say not a word of this to my old father,
                Murmuring streams, soft shades, and springing flowers,
                Lutes, Laurells, Seas of Milk, and Ships of Amber.
                (ll. 363–9)

Against these sensuous images, Otway directs that another sensual image, now of pain, glides into sight, in an almost dream-like manner.

Scene opening discovers a Scaffold and a Wheel prepar'd for the executing of Pierre, *then enter Officers,* Pierre *and Guards, a Friar, executioner and a great Rabble.*

The image is presented to our minds before the action, and then, in front of the emblematic wheel of torture the friends are reconciled, and Jaffeir performs one final act in which betrayal and redemption are strangely mixed. Again aroused by another to an active role, he takes his dagger

in hand once more and kills Pierre to save him from the agony of the
wheel. The heroic and the destructive aspects of the dagger image are
united, and Pierre dies laughing, in a vivid blend of pain and pleasure:

PIERRE: Now thou hast indeed been faithful.

               This was done Nobly – We have deceiv'd the Senate.

JAFFEIR: Bravely.

PIERRE: Ha ha ha – oh oh – (*Dies*) (ll. 467–9)

Again the melodramatic intensity of the scene should not distract us from
its formal structure. The two disjunctive gestures are indicated clearly by
the author and must not be blurred by the actor. The passing of Pierre's
spirit with a laugh and a groan is carefully arranged, as is the progression
of Jaffeir's final speech as he sends back to Belvidera the now bloodied
dagger she asked him to bequeath her, and dies at last in 'quiet'.

Since the scaffold is 'discovered', these final acts are played some way
behind the proscenium arch, giving them a calculated remoteness, and as
Jaffeir dies, the scene '*shuts upon them*' and Belvidera enters to '*Soft
Musick*'. The dream-like flexibility of the staging is made to reflect the
accomplishment of an erotic fantasy. Jaffeir and Pierre being dead, the
final scene as it were 'dissolves' the play by showing us Belvidera dying
in her madness; and again the method is essentially gestic, not histrionic
or melodramatic. It is really a kind of symbolic ballet, and is typically
accompanied by music from the gallery, as well as by the music of
Belvidera's melancholy cadences. Her words once more mix images of
pain and pleasure, and these are augmented by a series of careful stage
effects. Jaffeir's ghost rises, gently to the music. He looks as he did when
he was alive, and when the image of her husband vanishes, Belvidera
thinks he has finally rejected her and searches frantically about for him.
Then, the Officer enters with the now familiar dagger, and while he tells
Priuli of the scene on the scaffold, the ghost of Jaffeir rises again, Pierre
with him, 'both bloody'. There is a weird, slow-motion effect about the
rising and sinking figures and their silence. They seem to be in her mind.
No one has told her of their deaths. Otway is incarnating her morbid
awareness of the consequences of her love. These last moments have a
marvellous blend of convention, pathos, depth-psychology and real
tragedy. The actress's playing of the scene must flow formally, like the
music, only broken now and then by sudden, sharply felt dramatic
accents, which add unexpected emotional perspectives to the visual
emblems. Mrs Siddons's scream on seeing the ghosts used to freeze the
theatre, as did her enactment of Belvidera's death. For all its theatricality,
the climax is carried in strongly contrasted emotional gestures that focus
the basic tensions of the play in its conclusion. Belvidera runs to the
ghosts to catch them as they sink, and believes she has her husband once
more in her arms:

> I've got him, Father: Oh now how I'll smuggle him!
> My Love! My Dear! My Blessing!

Then she screams again:

> Help me, help me!
> They have hold on me, and drag me to the bottom.
> Nay – now they pull so hard – farewell – (*She dyes*)
> (ll. 506–9)

Even the fulsome emotion of a conventional mad-scene is made by Otway to reflect his personal perception of the 'character' of love, the need to possess another that is as cruel as it is kind.

The particular quality of Otway's work comes from his openness, his willingness to expose himself. Some will find this pathological, most – to some extent – embarrassing. The *double-entendre* in the phrase 'expose himself' is very near the mark; and yet he succeeds in making art out of indulgence because of a profound, uncalculated honesty. His theatrical effectiveness comes from teasing at his own feelings until he teases at ours; but this in itself would not be enough. As Dryden creates complex vibrations in the mind, Otway does in the senses. In no other poet, except perhaps Tennyson, are the two meanings of the word 'feeling' – as emotion and as sensation, touching (another ambivalent word) the subject, as it were, internally or externally – so closely united. Such a union was clearly achieved through an attempt to transmute deeply personal experience into the forms of art. Otway makes us voyeurs to his personal explorations, his self-castigation. The play is like a series of public confessions, and it is made tolerable only by his incorporation of this very idea into the dramatic structure, assisted by the demonstrative acting style of the day. The opening scene presented a series of private clashes in a public place, and the paradox is merely an explicit statement of something implicit in any theatrical experience – the exposure of personal existences to a public audience. This statement is made again and again in the play, and makes it not merely an enactment but also a criticism of the uncontrollable feeling it exhibits, a criticism which the rhythm of the acting, its formal gestures breaking out into passion or description could only enhance. Otway goes further himself in the exploration of passion, and demands that his actors go further in the exhibition of it than before; but these eruptions of feeling are contained in a style that still thrives on visual and verbal clarity.

In 1693 a division arose in the United Company. Charles Davenant had been bought out in the 1680s by his brother Alexander, who had an eye for rather shady business, and in consequence the theatres came under the control of two extremely determined gentlemen, Sir Thomas Skipwith and Christopher Rich. These two had in fact provided most of the money with which Alexander Davenant had bought into the business, and had left him to farm their shares. When he absconded to the Canary Islands, they stepped in to manage their assets. The company was in an unhealthy position financially, and Rich began to retrench. He bought out the actors' shares, and then proceeded to cut their salaries as the quickest way of reducing the charges of performances and getting more money for the shareholder. The actors were understandably annoyed, and in an attempt to discipline the company some of the most important parts of the leading players, Betterton and Mrs Barry, were re-allocated to younger actors. Such action struck at the very heart of their careers, and Betterton led a break away group back to the old Lincoln's Inn Fields theatre, taking with him most of the veterans of the stage, including the leading actresses, Mrs Barry and Ann Bracegirdle. The patentees objected. Betterton went to the king. This seems to be the last important intervention by a monarch in the affairs of the English stage. Under the patronage of the nobility, who gave generously to refurbish the old building which had reverted in the meantime to its original role as a tennis-court, the actors' company was able to open there in April 1695 with Congreve's comedy *Love for Love*, 'which ran on with such extraordinary success, that they had seldom occasion to act any other play till the end of the season.'[1]

Congreve was the most brilliant of the younger dramatists. His first play, *The Old Batchelour*, had opened in 1693 to a triumphant and legendary fourteen-night run. Congreve was twenty-three. His second play, *The Double-Dealer*, followed in October, and was also successful. Both plays had exploited the talents of Betterton, Mrs Barry, Mrs Bracegirdle, and the brilliant comedian Thomas Doggett. *Love for Love* was also designed for them, but after this second triumph, he wrote only two further plays: the tragedy, *The Mourning Bride* (1697), and *The Way of the World*.

Betterton's company presented *The Way of the World* at Lincoln's Inn Fields in March 1700. Although it stands on the threshold of a new century, it is to many people the archetype of Restoration comedy. In many ways, this is as it should be. Congreve can claim to be a 'Restoration' dramatist in the fineness of his observation, the neatness of his form, and the baroque resourcefulness of his comic design. But there is also a tension in his writing that is less susceptible of the forms of his day, and possibly explains his failure to continue writing for the stage.

In *The Way of The World* Congreve creates an archetypal gallery of fools and presents them to the audience in an arrangement that is designed to heighten its awareness of their characters through significant juxtaposition. He tells us himself, in the Epistle dedicatory, that he was moved 'to design some Characters which should appear ridiculous not so much thro' a natural Folly (which is incorrigible, and therefore not proper for the Stage) as thro' an affected Wit; a Wit which at the same time as it is affected, is also False.'[2] In a letter to John Dennis concerning the nature of humour in comedy, he makes this even more precise. He writes:[3]

Humour is from Nature, *Habit* from Custom; and *Affectation* from Industry.

Humour, shows us as we are.

Habit, shows us as we appear under a forcible Impression.

Affectation, shows us what we would be under a Voluntary Disguise.

This is an interesting gloss on the classical idea, and it is easy to see it in operation in the play. Witwoud and Petulant present two contrasted affectations: the loquacious and the laconic. Petulant wants to create an image of himself as a man of few words, Witwoud of himself as a man of genius. They are ridiculous because these affectations become habitual, and they are unable to adapt their behaviour to their situation. Such behaviour may well have originated in a melancholy or sanguine disposition or humour; but their own handling of themselves has aggravated this disposition. Witwoud's affability becomes an imposition, and Petulant's brevity petulance. They are both bad-mannered. Similarly with Sir Wilful and Lady Wishfor't: as Witwoud affects to be finer than he is, his brother affects to be coarser than he needs, while Lady Wishfor't at fifty puts on the airs of a sixteen-year-old and affects to rival Millamant.

The other characters complement this scheme. The protective affectations of Millamant, her thousand lovers and the disposition of a windmill turning with the wind, balance those of her aunt, but also form an inflection in a series of images of women in love, her hidden passion matching Marwood's, hidden for a different reason, and Mrs Fainall's, hidden for a different reason again, while Marwood and Mrs Fainall have characteristically different responses to the frustration of their love, and in this match Lady Wishfor't. The gentlemen are similarly related, both outwardly cool and rational, both men of the world, but in reality very differently in and out of control of their humour. Mirabell's uncertainty makes him pompous, and Fainall's calm is a cloak to violence. These characters are sharply etched, and even a minor figure like Mincing can take her place not only in the plot, where, in conformity with neo-classical rules, she is necessary as a witness to Mrs Fainall's deed of trust, but also as a 'character' in her own right, the maid with the airs of a lady, a complement to Waitwell, who in different circumstances puts on the airs of a gentleman.

Congreve displays these affectations in a series of actions that enable the players to present them to the audience for its judgment. Witwoud and Petulant are 'presented' for their scenes in Act I as were Sparkish and Pinchwife in *The Country Wife*, and, as Dryden recommended, we have their characters verbally first:

MIRABELL: He is a Fool with a good Memory, and some few Scraps of other Folks Wit. He is one whose Conversation can never be approv'd, yet it is now and then to be endur'd. He has indeed one good Quality, he is not Exceptious; for he so passionately affects the Reputation of understanding Raillery; that he will construe an Affront into a Jest; and call downright Rudeness and ill Language, Satyr and Fire.

FAINALL: If you have a mind to finish his Picture, you have an opportunity to do it at full length. Behold the Original. *Enter* Witwoud.

WITWOUD: Afford me your Compassion, my Dears; pity me, *Fainall*, *Mirabell*, pity me.

MIRABELL: I do from my Soul. (I.i.224–37)

Witwoud's first line gives the actor a splendid opportunity for creating an attitude that does indeed present a full-length portrait of a character in Lacy's manner (Plate 37), while Mirabell's studied ambiguity gives an immediate clue to the depths of the fop's self-absorption.

One of the most important aspects of Congreve's genius as a writer for the stage is his ability to create scenes in which the moral nature of his characters is precisely defined physically as well as intellectually. He devises action to capture the essence of each character. This is apparent from his earliest writing, and *The Way of the World* is no exception. The fourth act is, in fact, a magnificent series of such images in action, a brilliant sequence of contrasted cameos on the theme of wooing. First, Sir

Wilful attempts Millamant, marvellously shy and tongue-tied: Millamant prevents him proposing, which he daren't do, simply by pretending not to understand him. Then comes Mirabell, and the famous contract-scene. As he enters, she is mouthing Suckling to herself. He caps the quotation, and thus demonstrates the intimacy and equality between them. To Sir Wilful she had quoted Suckling, whose name he took as a slight on his maturity. Mirabell's wit creates understanding, Sir Wilful's humour, division, as the use of the verses neatly demonstrates. When the contract has been sealed the other gentlemen appear drunk. The ironical fact that they have got round to proposing at the precise moment that she is lost to them, adds to the humorous way their drunkenness summarises their natures. Petulant has been quarrelling with Sir Wilful over Millamant. In his cups he can rise to a laconic proposal which epitomises both his character and his affectation. Sir Wilful's drunkenness is brisker. Now he is primed by wine, he harps on the active nature of the family motto, '*Wilfull* will do't', but seems sanguine, if coarse, about the family honour:

> A Match or no Match, Cozen, with the hard Name, – *Aunt, Wilfull* will do't, If she has her Maidenhead let her look to't, – if she has not, let her keep her own Counsel in the mean time and cry out at the nine Months end. (IV.i.426–30)

Finally they tidy him away, and at last Lady Wishfor't can encounter Sir Rowland. Waitwell presents him as everything her fantasies have desired, and brings the sequence to a climax with wonderful extravagance, as he sweeps the old lady off her feet. The energy and invention are marvellous, the contrasted display of character as light as it is precise.

Much of Congreve's lightness of touch comes, of course, from his language, which marries so expertly with action and physical image. The magical phrases build superbly, each one as clear and as concrete as it is suggestive. Congreve has the verbal centre to be expected from a Restoration writer, and is finer than any of them in making absent things present in his words.

> MIRABELL: *Inprimis* then, I Covenant that your acquaintance be General; that you admit no sworn Confident, or Intimate of your own Sex; No she friend to screen her affairs under your Countenance and tempt you to make tryal of a Mutual Secresie. No Decoy – Duck to wheadle you a *fop* – *scrambling* to the play in a Mask – then bring you home in a pretended fright, when you think you shall be found out. – and rail at me for missing the Play, and disappointing the Frolick which you had to pick me up and prove my Constancy. (IV.i.234–43)

Mirabell brings a life-style before us, and the sharply pointed vocabulary and suggestive rhythm vividly conjure up the atmosphere of '*scrambling* to the play in a Mask', as well as defining a particular moral attitude, telling in the presence of the masked ladies in the audience. The beauty of this style is its ability, through precision and wit, to modulate between reality and fantasy without losing the core of truth. In combination with gesture, this provides great opportunity for describing the inner as well as the outer worlds of his characters, as when Lady Wishfor't contemplates her reception of Sir Rowland:

> Well, and how shall I receive him? in what Figure shall I give his
> Heart the first Impression? There is a great deal in the first
> Impression. Shall I sit? – No I won't sit – I'll walk – aye I'll walk
> from the door upon his entrance; and then turn full upon him – No,
> that will be too sudden. (IV.i.17–22)

Lady Wishfor't is talking to Foible, but Congreve gives the actress a typical opportunity to consult the audience, and take them into her confidence. Perhaps she walked away from them to illustrate her tactics, and it was the look on their faces when she turned that made her realise that it would indeed be too sudden. She tries again, and now attempts to make us share her dawning vision of herself as a young girl. The picture painted in her words is strongly opposed by the image of the raddled old bag herself:

> I'll lie – aye I'll lie down – I'll receive him in my little dressing room,
> there's a Couch – Yes, yes, I'll give the first Impression on a Couch
> – (IV.i.22–4)

There would have been no furniture on the Restoration stage. The speech is given standing. She conjures up her vision for the audience in mind and imagination, not in action. The action is in the evocative accuracy of the words themselves.

> I won't lie neither but loll and lean upon one Elbow; with one Foot
> a little dangling off, Jogging in a thoughtful way – Yes – and then
> as soon as he appears, start, ay, start and be surpriz'd, and rise to
> meet him in a pretty disorder – Yes – O nothing is more alluring than
> a Levee from a Couch in some Confusion. – It shows the Foot to
> advantage, and Furnishes with Blushes, and re-composing Airs
> beyond Comparison. (IV.i.24–32)

Congreve creates a double joke: the image itself is a brilliant evocation of the calculating vanity of a coquette and would be applauded as such, and the picture is given added edge by its presentation as an old lady's fantasy. It presents two kinds of truth for the audience to share with actress and author.

Congreve's comic techniques are very much of the Restoration. He talks to the audience, presents them with images, invites them to compare and distinguish, to exercise judgment. And yet, clearly as he does these things, their effectiveness only goes part of the way to describing the particular quality of his work. The nature of his characters is precise, but their moral categories are blurred. In Act I, it is Fainall who points out to Mirabell the unreasonableness of his behaviour, and his moderation makes Mirabell almost petulant. This is quite fair, and Millamant substantiates it, yet Fainall, by his name, is designated a villain, and Mirabell by his the hero. Fainall can behave like, and has some of the lines of, Molière's *honnête homme*, and yet is in reality both passionate and destructive. Witwoud is harmless and silly, and yet Mirabell has the leisure to be jealous of him. Sir Wilful Witwoud is introduced as an oaf, but proves to possess a rough honesty that enables him to hit it off with Mirabell who at first despises him, and even help his rival to obtain his end. Millamant, charming as she is, can be tiresome as well as naughty. As categories are blurred, so our reactions must reinterpret the object. This is difficult in the theatre. Audiences are inclined to settle to certain expectations, and such changes of direction can seem merely confusing.[4]

A similar confusion appears in the plotting. The trick to disguise Waitwell as Sir Rowland is in the great tradition of comedy. Disguise has always been grateful to comedy, not merely because it is fun in itself and a virtuoso challenge to the actor, but because the kind of disguise adopted by the trickster is a touchstone for the particular folly of the gull. Sir Rowland is conceived in just this way as a catalyst for Lady Wishfor't's vanity. Through the first act, the audience's appetite is constantly whetted by hints of the intrigue; in the second, it is brought out into the open and made to set off the general atmosphere of sexuality as Waitwell and Foible, newly married, bill and coo like a pair of turtles; it reaches a climax when Marwood's letter exposing the trick is delivered in Sir Rowland's actual presence, and we are amazed and delighted at the way the schemers manage to use the old lady's desperate need to believe in her admirer to get Waitwell safely out of the house. It is totally artificial, of course. It is simply a fiction designed to present certain kinds of folly for our judgment and enjoyment; but as such it fits excellently with the perspicuous presentation of its characters.

There are, however, constant hints throughout the play of a less abstract truth. Mirabell has ensured the servants' assistance by making good a lease for a small holding and stocking it in anticipation of their future wedded bliss – very precise commercial details unlike the generalised rewards such tricksters may usually expect, and a very real way of acquiring someone's loyalty. Similarly, Lady Wishfor't's anger when she discovers the deception put upon her is comically extravagant: she may cry out about how she took Foible from 'washing of old Gause and Weaving of dead Hair, with a bleak-blew Nose, over a Chafeing-dish of starv'd Embers, and Dining behind a Travers Rag, in a shop no Bigger than a Birdcage' (V.i.4–7), but it doesn't stop her sending for the police. This combination of the observed detail of English life and the excitement of intrigue links this conventional apparatus with a counter-plot that is both more lethal and more naturalistically motivated. Congreve's main action is not what we would now think of as a story; but it is not a formula either: it is an exploration of a social situation that is real and possible.

Congreve had enrolled for a time with the Middle Temple, and was obviously fascinated by what he learned and observed there, for he employs his knowledge of law in most of his plays, but particularly in *Love for Love* and *The Way of The World*.[5] Much of the excitement of his intrigue lies in this marriage of comic conventions and everyday realities. In *The Way of The World*, Fainall and Mrs Marwood are attempting to manipulate the law. Their situation, though it may seem tedious to a modern audience, would have been tantalisingly comprehensible to Congreve's contemporaries. As Fainall puts it to his mistress, 'wherefore did I marry, but to make lawful Prize of a rich Widow's Wealth and squander it on Love and you?' On his marriage, Mrs Fainall's money became his, a wife is her husband's property, and this money can be increased by half her cousin Millamant's fortune, which is in the control of Lady Wishfor't, Mrs Fainall's mother. Fainall and Marwood are therefore striving to enrage the old lady against her niece. She will disinherit her and naturally settle the money on her daughter instead. Fainall has attempted to accomplish this by encouraging the girl, Millamant, to elope with her lover Mirabell whom Lady Wishfor't detests. Though the problem of marriage against a guardian's consent is a convention of much comedy, a simple means by which a blocking figure can be provided to delay the happiness of the central characters, the situation here moves clearly beyond convention. Mrs Marwood has prevented the plot, and Fainall now accuses her of being in love with Mirabell herself. He is, of course, quite right: sex and money war in her for dominance. The procedures of the intrigue gain a psychological as well as a social dimension.

The alliance of Fainall and Mrs Marwood only just sustains the tension of this discovery, when new information reaches them and encourages them to develop their plans in a very different way. Marwood discovers the trick that is to be played on Lady Wishfor't and also Mrs Fainall's affair with Mirabell. She first encourages Lady Wishfor't to match Millamant with Sir Wilful, and then the lovers decide on a better plan: they will reveal the trick to Lady Wishfor't at the precise point that Fainall will accuse his wife of adultery. The double pressure will serve to make her ladyship disinherit Millamant, and at the same time frighten her into making a large financial settlement upon Fainall as a price for concealing the scandal of her daughter's behaviour. There is again an element of convention: Marwood learns of the plan when she is hidden in a closet waiting for Lady Wishfor't; but this cannot distract from the novel tone of the episodes. In the first place, Marwood's encouragement of the scheme is ambiguous; although the prevention of his marriage seems to be a fit revenge upon Mirabell, in fact it leaves him free for her without her giving up her association with Fainall. In the second place, the scheme to frighten the old lady by catching her between her own reputation and her love for her daughter has an emotional intensity that is very sinister, and a psychological realism that is assisted by the rather messy way in which the plotters are seen to have to continually improvise new ways and means. The status of the intrigue is being constantly changed by the psychological ambivalences of those involved.

Congreve's technique for handling these new dimensions of action can be observed from the magnificent scene with which he expounds the part in the action of Fainall and Mrs Marwood. The scene is of a lovers' quarrel, and is clearly comic in the accuracy with which it observes two people caught in their own traps, as well as the ambiguous excuses of lovers; but is extremely sinister in the currents of emotion their reactions imply. At first, it is a sequence of closely observed 'movements of the mind', cruelly pinning down the difference in their mutual need – his of her love, and hers of his assistance in obtaining another lover. But suddenly there is a change of key. Marwood's anger, comic in its hypocrisy, takes on a new dimension:

FAINALL: Your Guilt, not your Resentment, begets your Rage.
               If you lov'd you could forgive a Jealousy: But you
               are stung to find you are discover'd.
MRS MARWOOD: It shall all be discover'd. You too shall be discover'd;
               be sure you shall. I can but be expos'd – If I do it
               myself, I shall prevent your Baseness.
FAINALL: Why, what will you do?
MRS MARWOOD: Disclose it to your wife; own what has past between
               us. (II.i.184–92, p. 415)

The convention of the plotting mistress depends for its comic effect on her fear of exposure. By showing Marwood's ultimate determination Congreve reveals a desperation that is as shocking as it is surprising. It creates a singular problem for the actress, who must capture the desperation without losing the jokes. This demands a combination of truth of feeling with intellectual control in the delivery of the lines that is very taxing indeed.

Of course, Congreve had his actors in mind. The roles of Fainall and Mrs Marwood were conceived for Betterton and Mrs Barry. Like Wycherley in Pinchwife, Congreve has cast these comic roles for tragic actors of great power. But here he demands of them quite a new technique. Both folly and passion in the Restoration theatre are made explicit in the text. The writers and actors expect to describe them in word and gesture, and the audience expects to see them so described and applaud the description. But the actions and feelings of this couple are not explicit in the text, indeed they frequently contradict it. This is not simple deception either, for they are as often deceiving themselves as each other. Both characters need each other on two levels: because they can help each other's schemes, and because they are emotionally matched. Their tricks and deceits clash with the realities of feeling that underlie their relationship.

FAINALL: Will you yet be reconcil'd to Truth and me?

MRS MARWOOD: Impossible. Truth and you are inconsistent – I hate you, and shall forever.

FAINALL: For loving you?

MRS MARWOOD: I loath the name of Love after such usage; and next to the Guilt with which you would asperse me, I scorn you most. Farewell.

FAINALL: Nay, we must not part thus.

MRS MARWOOD: I care not – Let me go – Break my Hands, do – I'd leave 'em to get loose.

FAINALL: I would not hurt you for the world. (II.i.214–27)

Throughout this exchange, the silences, the gestures, the actions between the lines bear equal weight with the lines themselves. The physical violence with which Fainall seizes her and the gentleness with which he then lets her go witness an emotional unity the lines deny, a very real picture of such sexual ambivalence. Marwood's final manipulation of her lover comes not only from her head but from her heart. She manages so well because she is using real feelings which issue in real tears of rage, frustration and desire:

FAINALL: Have I no other hold to keep you here?

MRS MARWOOD: Well, I have deserv'd it all.

FAINALL: You know I love you.

MRS MARWOOD: Poor dissembling! – O that – Well, it is not yet –

FAINALL: What? What is it not? What is it not yet? It is not yet too late –

MRS MARWOOD: No, it is not yet too late – I have that Comfort.

FAINALL: It is to love another.

MRS MARWOOD: But not to loath, detest, abhor Mankind, myself and the whole treacherous World. (227–38)

Fainall is trapped by her outburst. He wants her as well as needs her and the combined foolishness and honesty with which he answers his own questions makes him at last wonderfully ridiculous. His speech is in reality a dialogue as the lady artificially prolongs a real outburst to seal her victory, and protracts the spontaneous with breathtaking art.

FAINALL: Nay, this is Extravagance – Come I ask your Pardon – No tears – I was to blame, I cou'd not love you and be easy in my Doubts – Pray forbear – I believe you; I'm convinced I've done you wrong; and any way, every way will make amends; – (239–43)

He is in the right; but she reduces him to fatuous subservience:

I'll hate my Wife yet more, Dam her, I'll part with her, rob her of all she's worth, and we'll retire somewhere, any where to another World. – I'll marry thee – Be pacify'd – (243–6)

Congreve brilliantly captures the inner action of the man, as he tries to soothe her, control her, calm her with helpful oaths, fantasies and promises of marriage. Then suddenly –

'Sdeath they come, hide your Face, your Tears – You have a mask, wear it a Moment. This way, this way, be persuaded. (247–9)

The real feeling that has burst through the polished surface of language and manners is suddenly concealed. The walking masks of the time covered the full face, and were held on by an amber bead gripped between the teeth. Sometimes they were black velvet, sometimes coloured like the face itself. Marwood claps on a painted face and is led away with a rigid smile. It is a striking image of the mask of manners covering the hidden feelings of society, and it focuses the new problem that Congreve has set the actor: how to convey those feelings and actions which shift and change unexpressed under conventional behaviour and conversation.

As Congreve conceives it, the mask of manners is a crucial and ambiguous element in that way of the world from which his play takes its name. The presentation of it requires the expression of a complex relationship between the text itself and the actions implicit in it (the subtext, to coin a modern phrase derived from Stanislavsky), that is evident from the very beginning of the play. *The Way of The World* opens in a chocolate-house, with Mirabell and Fainall rising from cards. This long scene can often seem difficult in performance, but it is in fact an expertly calculated counterpoint of language and inner action. The wit is rapid and enchanting and provides vivid images both of daily life and of the characters we are to expect upon the stage. The conversation is like that between two 'true-wits' discussing the nature of the town. But there are deeper currents flowing, and it is these currents that give the scene its special tension. Rising from cards, the two gentlemen play together a game of double-bluff. Fainall is probing the state of Mirabell's relationship with Millamant and sounding out Marwood's position in his favours. Mirabell is pursuing a necessary acquaintanceship while concealing from his friend both his plot against Lady Wishfor't and his relationship with that friend's wife. Both gentlemen are too knowledgeable in the way of the world to be explicit, but the tensions appear immediately.

MIRABELL: You are a fortuneate Man, Mr *Fainall*.

FAINALL: Have we done?

MIRABELL: What you please. I'll play on to entertain you.

FAINALL: No, I'll give you your Revenge another time, when you are not so indifferent; you are thinking of something else now, and play too negligently; the Coldness of a losing Gamester lessens the Pleasure of the Winner: I'd no more play with a Man that slighted his ill Fortune, than I'd make Love to a Woman who undervalu'd the Loss of her Reputation.

MIRABELL: You have a Taste extremely delicate, and are for refining on your Pleasures. (I.i.1–12)

Fainall's comment catches the relationship of excitement and calculation in the manipulation of life and society most expertly, but Mirabell's reply seems surprisingly barbed under the circumstances. His preoccupation is noted, its cause avoided; but the noting produces barely concealed malice. Fainall appears the more perfect gentleman; but his name, artfully inserted by Congreve into the opening sentence, might give the audience pause, and focus their attention on the ensuing dialogue.

Fainall probes further. Mirabell allows himself to be drawn on the subject of Millamant, but conceals any hint of the plot against Lady Wishfor't, although his preoccupation is really with that. Though this is a decoy, however, real feelings of a different nature wear through the veneer of manners:

FAINALL: You were to blame to resent what she spoke only in Compliance with her Aunt.

MIRABELL: She is more Mistress of herself, than to be under the necessity of such a Resignation.

FAINALL: What? Tho' half her Fortune depends on her marrying with my Lady's Approbation?

MIRABELL: I was then in such a Humour, that I shou'd have been better pleas'd if she had been less discreet. (I.i.41–8)

Fainall is pushing, Mirabell barely reining himself in; finally, as they come to the delicate subject of Mrs Marwood, the fire of their mutual interest flashes out.

FAINALL: You are a gallant Man, *Mirabell*; and tho' you may have Cruelty enough not to satisfy a Lady's longing; you have too much Generosity not to be tender of her Honour. Yet you speak with an Indifference which seems to be affected; and confesses you are conscious of a Negligence.

MIRABELL: You pursue the Argument with a distrust that seems to
be unaffected, and confesses you are conscious of a concern
for which the Lady is more indebted to you, than is your
Wife. (I.i.90–8)

Mirabell's interest in Mrs Fainall and Fainall's in Mrs Marwood are not
demonstrated until the second act; but the seeds of strife are implicit in
this opening dialogue, for all its Restoration wit, its 'characters', and its
verbal brilliance. They must be enacted; but great subtlety of inflection
is required if the audience is to be taken with the innuendo as well as the
wit. It is, after all, the innuendo that sustains the interest of the encounter.

This is equally true of the opening of the second act. Both scenes are
in public places. The chocolate-house is a man's world, and the shutters
may well have born reminders of this and been painted as in the coffee-
house, a water-colour in the British Museum (Plate 5). The second act,
at Rosamond's Pond (Plate 6), is an intermediate world, the park, where
men and women can freely meet, though the early eighteenth-century
engraving of the place demonstrates a difficulty in painting people to give
the 'idea' of a public place in contemporary plays: if the fashion changes
the scenery becomes out of date. Here Mrs Marwood and Mrs Fainall
are walking together in pretended friendship. Their conversation too is
elegant and witty, and again the wit conceals the tension between them
– Marwood is sleeping with Mrs Fainall's husband, but employing the
mask of confidence to pry into Mrs Fainall's secrets (precisely the trick
of which Mirabell warns Millamant), while Mrs Fainall in her turn is
guarding her liaison with Mirabell and testing Mrs Marwood's attitude
to him. Mirabell and Fainall enter and meet them. With an austere
politeness which marks the play out as from the reign of William III,
they greet each other and move away in pairs – not however husband and
wife, friend and gallant, but the other way round. It is the way of the
world incarnated. As Mrs Fainall acidly remarks:

He has a Humour more prevailing than his Curiosity, and will
willingly dispence with the hearing of one scandalous story, to avoid
giving an occasion to make another by being seen to walk with his
Wife. This way Mr. *Mirabell*, and I dare promise you will oblige us
both. (II.i.103–7)

The surprise re-grouping is a typical Restoration visual gesture, but its
emotional tone comes from a real feeling for the circumstances of the
characters.

This sense of the circumstances that feed into the comic situations even
informs Congreve's treatment of his lightest characters. Witwoud may be
able to construe an affront into a jest, but he does so with an ambivalence
that is tellingly natural:

MIRABELL: A Fool, and your Brother, *Witwoud*!

WITWOUD: Ay, ay, my half Brother. My half Brother he is, no nearer, upon Honour.

MIRABELL: Then 'tis possible he may be but half a Fool.

WITWOUD: Good, good *Mirabell*, *le Drole*! Good, good, hang him don't let's talk of him: – *Fainall*, how does your Lady?
(I.i.249–55)

He is plainly conscious of the affront, but does not wish to lose the company. His laughter and sudden change of subject is rather touching, and this is far from the only time it happens. Lady Wishfor't has such moments too. Congreve can create sympathy for his fools, and in doing so undermines the moral analysis of their folly. As her Ladyship completes her picture of herself rising from a couch in a pretty disorder, she stops suddenly:

LADY WISHFORT: Hark! There's a Coach.

FOIBLE: 'Tis he, *Madam*.

LADY WISHFORT: O dear . . . (IV.i.32–4)

For a moment, we see through the mask of the coquette that she forces on the world to her own fear and inadequacy. She becomes at once enchanting in her silliness and sad in herself, and this prepares us to watch with sympathy as her frailty is confronted in the last act by the demonic will of Marwood and the naked threats of Fainall, and particularly as she succumbs at last to the honeyed tones of Mirabell's 'false Insinuating Tongue'. Lady Wishfor't's love is ridiculous and ill-judged. But such things happen. It is real, and Congreve makes us take it seriously. He obviously realised that the absolutes of moral comedy can be strangely distasteful in real situations.

The interaction of surface brilliance and subtextual tension is especially marked in the central relationship of the play, and perhaps surprisingly so. The names of Millamant and Mirabell chime happily together and match them by their very sound; but their actual encounters do not produce the anticipated harmony. Congreve has obviously taken hints for his characters from Alceste and Célimène in Molière's *Le Misanthrope*. Mirabell is soured by the social *mores* of his age, and, with a certain contempt for his fellow men, finds himself in love with a girl whose conduct he cannot approve. Here Congreve departs from Molière: Mirabell's misanthropy is only an element in his character; it is a rational disapproval of artificiality and bad manners; as such it goes easily with Congreve's concept of comic affectation, but excessive personal integrity plays little part in it. While this loses the comic profundity of Molière's image of the folly and ambivalence of consistent plain-dealing, it gains another dimension in handling the same theme psychologically through the behaviour of a man of the world. Again Congreve chooses to play his ideas off the real situation in which the couple find themselves.

The marriage of an heiress like Millamant was likely to form part of a financial bargain between her guardians and the family of the chosen groom. Such bargains seldom consider the mutual interest of the couple except in financial terms, and Millamant is planning to marry outside this pattern. She risks losing half her fortune, and her situation is one of considerable insecurity with marriage laws as they were. Can she trust him? Can she risk becoming his property? Millamant is a coquette partly through a delightful variety of disposition, and partly in self-defence. When she makes up her mind it will be final, and she hides behind a dazzling screen of words and moods while she tests the ground about her. Millamant is in love, but she is also prudent. She wants to be her own woman as Mirabell wants to be his own man. As a result, he has to penetrate her mask of humour and she his mask of gravity. The situation between them is not an easy one, and their wit glitters across the surface of this inner action.

Their first encounter is not happy. She hardly looks at him, and he has to get Mrs Fainall to draw off the company. Once alone he is in to the attack at once:

MIRABELL: You had the Tyranny to deny me last Night; tho' you
            knew I came to impart a Secret to you that concerned
            my Love.

MILLAMANT: You saw I was engag'd.

MIRABELL: Unkind. You had the Leisure to entertain a Herd of
            Fools; Things who visit you from their excessive
            Idleness; bestowing on your easiness that time, which is
            the encumbrance of their lives. (II.i.429–36)

His wit is spiteful, she is off-hand with him. He lets himself be provoked.

MIRABELL: How can you find delight in such society? It is
            impossible they should admire you, they are not
            capable: Or if they were, it shou'd be to you as a
            Mortification; for sure to please a Fool is some degree
            of Folly.

MILLAMANT: I please myself – Besides sometimes to converse with
            Fools, is for my Health. (ll. 436–42)

She tries to banter him out of his mood, but he takes up the 'sickness' in her image, and the game goes rather sour.

MIRABELL: Your Health! Is there a worse Disease than the
            Conversation of Fools?

MILLAMANT: Yes, the Vapours; Fools are Physick for it, next to *Assa-
            foetida*.

MIRABELL: You are not in a Course of Fools? (ll. 443–7)

Their phrasing is vivid; but it is not an end in itself. It not only conveys the tension of the situation but the action beneath it, the struggle for mastery. Mirabell's malice in comparing her to an old lady at a watering-place is not well received.

MILLAMANT: *Mirabell*, if you persist in this offensive Freedom – You'll displease me – I think I must resolve after all, not to have you – We shan't agree.

MIRABELL: Not in our Physick it may be.

MILLAMANT: And yet our Distemper in all likelihood will be the same; for we shall be sick of one another. (ll. 447–52)

It certainly seems quite likely; but of course, underneath neither wants to let the other go. It is this level that comes out in the contract scene. From the moment he caps her couplets there, they play the game together, and, by building their verbal picture of the kind of marriage they fear, at last reach agreement. The contract scene is more conventional than the encounter in the park, but it still has the undercurrent of the test. Their very sharing out of the argument seems to encapsulate its centre:

MILLAMANT: But let us be very strange and well bred: let us be as strange as if we had been married a great while; and as well bred as if we were not married at all.
(IV.i.207–9)

Instead of being a mask, manners here preserve the individuality of the man and the woman, and perhaps, as the contract itself is sealed, suggest another and profounder difficulty.

MIRABELL: Then we're agreed. Shall I kiss your hand upon the Contract? and here comes one to be a witness to the Sealing of the Deed.
Enter Mrs Fainall

MILLAMANT: *Fainall*, what shall I do? Shall I have him? I think I must have him.

MRS FAINALL: Ay, ay, take him, take him, what shou'd you do?

MILLAMANT: Well then – I'll take my death I'm in a horrid fright – *Fainall*, I shall never say it – well – I think – I'll endure you.

MRS FAINALL: Fy, fy, have him, have him and tell him so in plain terms: For I'm sure you've a mind to him.

MILLAMANT: Are you? I think I have – and the horrid man looks as if he thought so too – Well, you ridiculous thing you, I'll have you – (ll. 281–95)

It is quite a triumph, that 'I'll have you.' The word is out before a witness. The contract is sealed at last without a qualification in the sentence. The hesitations are finally resolved, verbally; but not physically.

MILLAMANT: I won't be kiss'd, nor I won't be thank'd – here kiss my hand tho' – so hold your tongue now, and don't say a Word. (ll. 295–7)

It is a fascinating climax to the scene. The whole little episode is of course a wonderful 'gesture' of maidenly shyness and fright; but that shyness and fright have been elements in her behaviour with him throughout. In *The Way of The World*, Congreve adds the dimension of sexual fear to the girl's lightning shifts of mood, giving the character a psychological reality that is completely new. With her own sex, Millamant is far from frail, and Congreve used the only song in the play to point this out, contriving a chilling confrontation between Millamant and Mrs Marwood as the latter is forced to listen to an acid lyric which catches the essence of their relationship:

> Then I alone the Conquest prize
> When I insult a Rival's Eyes:
> If there's delight in Love, 'tis when I see
> The Heart which others bleed for, bleed for me.
> (III.i.386–90)

But when she is with men, this triumph is belied. Her coquetry is used to create distance between her and her admirers. She shrinks from any open sexual challenge, and prefers to protect herself with the company of fools. It is a startling and perceptive subtext to her variety of disposition.[6] Ann Bracegridle was, in fact, rather notorious as a professional virgin. It is easy to wonder about her relationship with the poet, and also about the effect of her performance of this part on the aware audiences of the period.

The final Act is a bravura interweaving of the different styles. Civilised wit, affectation and folly, passion and greed, all take their place in the complex pattern of responses. The arrangement of this dénouement has been much criticised. The sudden appearance of the deed of trust has been considered arbitrary, and the sudden outbreak of violence, when Fainall, at last dropping the mask of a gentleman, draws his sword on his wife, unsuited to the comedy. In fact, both have been carefully prepared. Fainall's violence at the last reflects his struggle with Marwood in the park, the quarrel and her tears, the intensity of their plotting, sealed with a kiss that is both erotic and mercenary in their great scene that ends Act III, and the presence in these roles of the two great tragedians. The deed is a beautifully planned and logical outcome of the legalistic and psychological undercurrent of the play. That these moments should still be difficult to accept pinpoints the theatrical problem the play presents.

Mrs Fainall's deed of trust is an idea that is ingenious, true to life and morally significant. It was common at the time for a widow to protect herself in this way from falling prey to a fortune-hunting husband who might seize her goods and cast her off, as Fainall is indeed contriving to do. It is precisely the step the audience would have expected her to take.

The trick is not that she has taken it, but that Congreve manages to cheat us into believing she has not. Apparantly Fainall himself has 'wheedled' a settlement out of her. The contemporary audience would take the problem. After all, who is there to make her trustee? Her mother is hopeless. Her cousins, the Witwouds are no better. Millamant's family are dead and were clearly forced to leave her in Lady Wishfor't's power. It is not surprising that Fainall thought Arabella Languish unprotected and an easy prey. The audience would agree with him. The *coup de théâtre*, and it is a good one, does not lie in the fact that the deed exists, but that its trustee is Arabella's ex-lover. For all Mirabell's absurd gravity and slightly selfish worldliness, Arabella Languish trusted him, and placed herself in his power – rightly as it proves. It says a great deal for Congreve's insight that he presents us with just the couple that can make this convincing.

Mrs Fainall is an unusual character. The cast-mistress of Restoration comedy is generally a figure of fun. Mrs Loveit in *The Man of Mode* by Etherege, and Mrs Termagant in Shadwell's *Bury Fair* are made ridiculous by their persistence in pursuing their lovers after the hour has passed. A woman who not only accepts the inevitable but assists her lover as far as it is in her power is a very different conception. In the relationships of Mrs Fainall to her husband, her husband's mistress, her cousin and her lover, Congreve creates a final skein to hold the fabric of his play together. Mrs Fainall provides a still centre in the whirlpool of intrigue. Unlike most characters of Restoration comedy, she remains entirely within the action and never takes the audience into her confidence. She plays entirely to the other characters, and requires a realism of performance that is highly original. The characters of comedy are usually making or unmaking themselves. Mrs Fainall is different. She incarnates Congreve's conception of the way of the world:

MRS FAINALL: Why did you make me marry this Man?

MIRABELL: Why do we daily commit disagreeable and dangerous Actions? To save that Idol Reputation. If the familiarities of our Loves had produc'd that Consequence of which you were apprehensive, where could you have fix'd a Father's Name with Credit, but on a Husband? (II.i.263–9)

It is frighteningly rational. They had obviously agreed that marriage was out of the question. He had his way to make and she was not rich enough. They have taken the proper precautions – as Mirabell remarks, 'When you are weary of him, you know your Remedy.' Mrs Fainall carries with her through the play the emotional consequences of her act, unspoken yet strongly present, even when she must witness the contract between her lover and his wife to be.

It is clear, in fact, that Mrs Fainall is not a comic character at all. She comes from a different sort of play. She would be more at home with the characters of *A Doll's House* than with those of *The Country Wife*. The same is true of the central issues in the characters of Fainall, Mirabell, and even Millamant, although with them different kinds of comic form are applied to the surface. But Congreve, even more than Ibsen later, had no model for the kind of social drama he had conceived. He knew either comedy or tragedy. In tragedy, vice is taken seriously: in comedy, folly is made ridiculous. The artist's business was to show the destruction ensuing on the one, and to describe the absurdity inherent in the other. But vice can be made ridiculous even if it is not so, and the tension implicit in this conception was obviously part of Congreve's own response to the world, as was the complementary fact that folly can be endearing. We would not change Lady Wishfor't, and the poverty-stricken future of Mrs Marwood is painfully real. When Fainall draws his sword on his wife the violence cuts across the dazzling surface of the comedy. Congreve instinctively knew that however outside comic decorum such an action may appear to be, it was right in the context of the play. It was comedy that had to yield.

At its first performance, the play does not seem to have achieved the success of Congreve's previous work. In fact, he professed himself satisfied, indeed surprised. In his dedication he wrote: 'That it succeeded on the Stage, was almost beyond my Expectation; for but little of it was prepar'd for that general Taste which seems now to be predominant in the Pallats of our Audience' (p. 390). The play is certainly both ambiguous and uncompromising. It eschews the moral certainties of exemplary comedy as much as the explicit clarity of the earlier style. Whether successful or not, Congreve did not try his hand at comedy again. It is perhaps worth speculating on his reasons. In Fainall and Marwood, Congreve creates characters whose surface behaviour is as controlled and dazzling as that of any Restoration hero, but whose reality is founded in precisely that moral obliquity such manners are supposed to prevent. That mask is shattered when Fainall draws his sword, and, as the bluff Sir Wilful throws the man about town's insult back in his face, a different and more sinister dimension of folly is revealed. Danger, viciousness, and absurdity are suddenly blended together. This blend has been achieved mainly by the continuous sense of inner action throughout the play. At this time, the art of the actor was still essentially demonstrative. It described emotion, as it described behaviour. But *The Way of The World* demanded continuous subtextual action. It is conceivable that even the greatest actors of the period could not have articulated the inner tensions of Congreve's play, so different from the purely emotional subtext of

Otway, and that if they could have done so, the audience could not have understood them.

In the spring of 1700, when *The Way of The World* was in rehearsal, Dryden was dying. He had been a tired and embittered man since his conversion to Roman Catholicism under James had led to the revocation of his laureateship on the accession of William and Mary. Now a mortification in his leg gave him much pain and prevented his getting about easily. It is unlikely that he was able to see Congreve's new play on the stage, but he must have seen it in manuscript. He had, after all, befriended Congreve on his arrival in London, helped him with his first play by giving it 'the cut of the town',[7] and acknowledged him as the true heir to his laurels. In an Epistle 'To my Dear Friend Mr. *Congreve* on his comedy *The Double Dealer*', he had praised both the grace and strength of the younger poet's work, giving him the palm over even Fletcher and Jonson, and equating him with Shakespeare. He recognised Congreve's wit, genius, observation and truth to nature; and it is impossible not to wonder if he did not also recognise the novelty of his latest piece, and if so what he thought of Congreve's attempt to link feeling and perspicuity through the intricate inner-actions of his characters – an original solution to a problem that had concerned Dryden so closely all his life in his pursuit of 'the geometric spirit'.

Notes

Chapter 1   Riding the audience

1 J. Evelyn, *Memoirs Illustrative of the Life and Writings of John Evelyn, Esq.*, vol. 1, pp. 321–2.

2 *The Diary of Samuel Pepys*, ed. Robert Latham and William Matthews, London, 1970–83. All Pepys quotations are from this edition and are further referred to simply by date of entry.

3 Samuel Chappuzeau, *L'Europe vivante, ou relation nouvelle, historique et politique, de tous ses estats, jusqu'à l'année presente*, 1666, pp. 214–15; S. Sorbière, *A voyage to England*, p. 69.

4 'Regents Restoration Drama Series', general editor J. Loftis. Goldsmith's *She Stoops to Conquer* was advertised as a 'rollicking Restoration Comedy' by the Birmingham Repertory Theatre in 1978.

5 E. A. Wrigley, 'A Simple Model of London's Importance in Changing English Society and Economy, 1650–1750', *Past and Present*, 37 (1967), pp. 44–70.

6 Sorbière, p. 143.

7 N. Brett-James, *The Growth of Stuart London*.

8 Sir Richard Steele, *Town-Talk, in a Letter to a Lady in the Country*, 1715–16, 1, p. 12, 5, p. 51.

9 Lorenzo di Magalotti, *Travels of Cosmo The Third, Grand Duke of Tuscany, through England during the Reign of Charles II (1669)*, p. 296; Sorbière, p. 14. The shops were mainly those of mercers and drapers, but there were also booksellers and purveyors of other fashionable wares; see *London Past and Present*, ed. H. B. Wheatley and P. Cunningham, 3 vols, London, 1891, vol, 2, pp. 581–3.

10 Glynne Wickham, *Early English Stages 1300–1600*, vol. Two, Part II, 'Regulating the Theatre'.

11 J. Freehafer, 'The Formation of the London Patent Companies in 1660', *TN*, 20 (1965–6), pp. 6–30.

12 'The Theatre Royal, Drury Lane, and the Royal Opera House, Covent Garden', *Survey of London*, vol. 35, London, 1970; Paul Sawyer, *The New Theatre in Lincoln's Inn Fields*, London, 1979; O. Brownstein, 'The Duke's Company in 1667', *TN*, 28 (1974), pp. 18–23.

13 'Epilogue Spoken at the Opening of the NEW HOUSE, March 26, 1674', *The Poems of John Dryden*, ed. James Kinsley, vol. 1, pp. 380, 33–4, hereafter referred to as *Poems*.

14 Christopher Hill, *The Century of Revolution, 1603–1714*, London, 1961; Lord Macaulay, *The History of England from the Accession of James II*, vol. 1, ch. III. Though strongly and entertainingly biased, Lord Macaulay's description of the lifestyle of Restoration London remains unsurpassed.

15 H. B. Wheatley, *Samuel Pepys and the World He Lived in*, London, 1880, and *London Past and Present*, vol. 3, pp. 168–9.

16 A. Everitt, 'Social Mobility in Early Modern England', *Past and Present*, 33 (1966), pp. 56–73; L. Stone, 'Social Mobility in England, 1500–1700', *Past and Present*, 33 (1966), pp. 16–55.

17 R. North, *Roger North on Music*, p. 303.

18 See Congreve's *Love for Love*, Act II. The World's End was a public house of entertainment with extensive gardens; T. Faulkner, *Chelsea*, London, 1821, p. 61.

19 Sorbière, p. 13.

20 François Brunet remarked that the Great Gallery in Whitehall appeared to contain nobody who was not in trade; Voyage d'Angleterre, 1676, British Library Add. MSS Fr. 35, 177, p. 48.

21 The *locus classicus* for this view is A. Nicoll, *A History of English Drama*, vol. 1, *Restoration Drama 1660–1700*, p. 8. His opinion is contested by Emmett Avery, 'The Restoration Audience', *PQ*, 45 (1966), pp. 54–61, and Harold Love, 'The Myth of the Restoration Audience', *Komos*, 1 (1967), pp. 49–56.

22 This kind of comparison is a bit dicey, since commodity prices fluctuate with the season, and references to them are scattered and arbitrary. See Thorold Rogers, *A History of Agriculture and Prices in England*, 7 vols, 1866–1902, vol. 5 (1583–1702), and Sir William Beveridge *et al.*, *Prices and Wages in England from the Twelfth to the Nineteenth Centuries*, vol. I, 1939.

23 Pepys has two notable references, 1 January 1663 and 1668. See also Peter Holland, *The Ornament of Action*, pp. 11 ff.

24 John Dennis, *Critical Works*, vol. 1, p. 294.

25 Mr Povey occurs in Sprat's list of members: *A History of the Royal Society of London for the Improving of Natural Knowledge*, 1667, p. 432. For Mr Proger see Avery, 'The Restoration Audience', p. 56. Pepys was especially impressed by Mr Povey's culture (31 December 1662). Significantly, the latter's nephew, William Blathwayt, also a civil servant, married Mary Wynter, heiress to the beautiful estate of Dyrham Park in Avon, which he much improved, employing the French architect Samuel Hauduroy to smarten up the dilapidated Tudor house.

26 'Epilogue to the King and Queen on the Union of the Companies', *Poems*, vol. 1, p. 324. Brunet notes that the servants were let into the upper gallery in 1676, but Dryden's reference is 1682.

27 Brunet, p. 79. Of course, it must have been more difficult for foreigners to follow the dialogue.

28 Otway, *Works*, Introduction, vol. 1, p. 25. See also Dryden's 'Epilogue . . . at the Opening of the NEW HOUSE', *Poems*, vol. 1, pp. 379–80; Otway's Epilogue to *Titus and Berenice* and *The Tricks of Scapin*, *Works*, vol. 1, p. 329; and Rochester's venomous Prologue, *Poems*, ed. V. de Sola Pinto, 2nd ed., London, 1964, pp. 54–5.

29 Hotson, *The Commonwealth and Restoration Stage*, pp. 303–6; Dryden, 'Another Epilogue' to *The Duke of Guise*, *Poems*, vol. 1, p. 328; and Davenant, Epilogue to *Man's the Master*, *The Dramatic Works of Sir William D'Avenant*, 4 vols, Edinburgh and London, 1872–4.

30 Nicoll, vol. 1, p. 360.

31 Nick Ward, *The London Spy*, 1706–4, p. 215.

32 Pepys, for example, saw *Macbeth* nine times and *The Tempest* ten times within the period of the diary. See also Lucyle Hook, 'James Brydges Drops in at the Theatre', *HLQ*, 8 (1945), pp. 306–11.

33 'PROLOGUE To a NEW PLAY, Call'd The Disappointment', *Poems*, vol. 1, p. 385.

34 John Genest, *Some Account of the English Stage from the Restoration in 1660 to 1830*, vol. 1, p. 118.

35 E. A. Langhans, 'Staging Practices in the Restoration Theatres, 1660–1682', p. 162.

36 *The Plays of William Wycherley*, ed. Arthur Friedman, Oxford, 1979, p. 128.

37 *The Female Wits* (1704), Augustan Reprint Society, no. 124, Los Angeles, 1967. Act II, p. 32.

38 *An Apology for the Life of Mr. Colley Cibber*, London, 1740, ch. V, p. 73.

39 Sorbière, p. 70.

40 Nahum Tate, *King Lear*, V. v. 113–14, in *Five Restoration Adaptations of Shakespeare*, ed. Christopher Spencer, p. 268.

41 *1 Granada*, V. i. 431–43, *The Works of John Dryden*, vol. 11, 1978, p. 190, hereafter referred to as *Works*.

42 Dryden, *Works*, vol. 10, p. 192.

43 Tom Brown (of Shifnal), *Works*, London, 1740, vol. 4, p. 312.

44 B. Brecht, *Brecht on Theatre*, p. 6.

Chapter 2 New forms

1 For the repertory patterns over the period see *The London Stage*, vol. 1; Marion Jones, 'Actors and Repertory', *The Revels History of Drama in English*, London, Methuen, vol. 5, pp. 119–57, and A. H. Scouten, 'Notes towards a History of Restoration Comedy', *PQ*, 45 (1966), pp. 62–70.

2 A. C. Sprague, *Beaumont and Fletcher on the Restoration Stage*, Gunnar Sorelius, *The Giant Race before the Flood: Pre-Restoration Drama on the Restoration Stage and in the Criticism of the Restoration Period*; G. C. Odell, *Shakespeare from Betterton to Irving*.

3 John Loftis, 'Exploration and Enlightenment: Dryden's *The Indian Emperor* and its Background', *Stud., Phil.*, 45 (1966), pp. 71–84.

4 S. Lamprecht, 'The Role of Descartes in Seventeenth Century England', *Studies in the History of Ideas*, Columbia University Department of Philosophy, New York, 1935. See also the important introduction to Sprat's *History of the Royal Society by* Cape and Whitcom Jones; Herbert Butterfield, *The Origins of Modern Science*.

5 Quoted by Margaret Whinney, *Wren*, London, Thames & Hudson, 1971, p. 9.

6 Hobbes, *Leviathan* (1661), Part I, ch. 5.

7 Sprat, p. 91.

8 Ibid., p. 113.

9 *Notes and Observations on 'The Empress of Morocco'* (1674), Dryden, Crowne and others, p. 406. The play and the critical writings that grew out of it have been edited and published together by M. E. Novak, *'The Empress of Morocco' and its Critics*, Los Angeles, 1968.

10 Basil Willey, *The Seventeenth Century Background*, London, 1934.

11 In C. Spencer (ed.), *Five Restoration Adaptations of Shakespeare*, Preface, p. 203.

12 *Macbeth*, V. ii. 28–32, *Five Restoration Adaptations*, p. 98.

13 Thomas Rymer, *The Tragedies of the Last Age Considr'd and Examin'd by the Practice of the Ancients and by the Common Sense of all Ages* (1678), pp. 110–11; the pedantic graphical arrangement is characteristic.

14 *The Miscellaneous Works in Prose and Verse of Sir Thomas Overbury*, ed. Edward F. Rimbault, London, 1890, p. 152.

15 La Bruyère, *Les Caractères*, ed. G. Garapon, Paris, 1962, p. 122. The translation is mine.

16 *Horace's 'Art of Poetry' Made English, by the Earl of Roscommon* (1684), p. 10.

17 *The Duke of Guise* (1683), p. 10.

18 The operations of the passions are discussed by both Locke and Hobbes. Descartes's *The Passions of the Soule* was printed in London in 1650. See also ch. 5 below.

19 'A Parallel betwixt Painting and Poetry', prefixed to *De Arte Graphica: the Art of Painting* by C. A. du Fresnoy, translated by Dryden in 1965. John Dryden, *'Of Dramatic Poesy' and other Critical Essays*, vol. 2, p. 201, hereafter referred to as *Critical Essays*.

20 B. Brecht, *Brecht on Theatre*, p. 104.

21 The Royal Society was interested in creating a form of universal language, such as G. Wilkins attempted in *An Essay towards a Real Character and a Philosophical Language* (1668). See Benjamin de Mott, 'Commenius and the Real Character in England', *PMLA*, 70 (1955), pp. 1068–81; W. H. Youngren, 'Generality, Science, and Poetic Language in the Restoration', *ELH*, 35 (1968), pp. 158–87.

22 *Leviathan*, Part I, ch. VIII.

23 *Letters upon Several Occasions* (1696), pp. 44–5.

24 Etherege, *She Wou'd if She Cou'd* (1668), Act I, pp. 1–2.
25 Dryden, *'Of Dramatic Poesy' and other Critical Essays*, vol. 1, p. 75.
26 *Marriage à la Mode*, Act I. i. 189–94, *Works*, Vol. 11, p. 234.
27 Dryden, *Notes and Observations*, p. 50.
28 Ibid., p. 28.
29 Harold Love, *Penguin Book of Restoration Verse*, Introduction, p. 25.
30 *1 Granada*, IV. i. 20–1, *Works*, 11, p. 63.
31 *2 Granada*, I. ii. 5–6, *Works*, 11, p. 110.
32 For this reason, the Restoration dramatists were very much interested in matters of scene and act division. Peter Holland, *The Ornament of Action*, pp. 133ff. examines the business in some detail.

Chapter 3 Music and spectacle

1 W. Davenant, *Dramatic Works*, vol. 3, p. 232.
2 The First Entry, p. 259. A number of Davenant's pieces are divided into Entries in this way, declaring their relationship to the Court masque.
3 The curtain was sometimes employed between acts if a very elaborate tableau had to be discovered, but this must have been a clumsy device in practice, and the better dramatists avoided it.
4 The problems of Drury Lane are considered in *The Survey of London*, vol. 25, and Richard Leacroft attempts a reconstruction in *The Development of the English Playhouse*, pp. 89–99. See also Edward Langhans's thesis 'Staging Practices', and his 'Wren's Restoration Playhouse', *TN*, 18 (1964), pp. 91–100; and D. Mullin and B. Koenig, 'Christopher Wren's Theatre Royal', *TN*, 21 (1967), pp. 180–7.
5 There are numerous problems in arriving at a satisfactory reconstruction of the Dorset Garden. See E. A. Langhans, 'A Conjectural Reconstruction of the Dorset Garden Theatre', *Theatre Survey*, 13 (1972), pp. 74–93; J. R. Spring, 'Platforms and Picture Frames: a Conjectural Reconstruction of the Duke of York's Theatre, Dorset Garden, 1669–1709', *TN*, 31 (1977), pp. 6–19; R. D. Hume, 'The Dorset Garden Theatre: a Review of Facts and Problems', *TN*, 33 (1979), pp. 4–17, and Spring's reply to Professor Hume, 'The Dorset Garden Theatre: Playhouse or Opera House?', *TN*, 34 (1980), pp. 60–9. The tone of these articles is entertainingly, if unnecessarily, acid. The fact is that not enough is known. See also E. A. Langhans, 'The Dorset Garden Theatre in Pictures', *Theatre Survey*, 6 (1965), pp. 134–46. In 'The Architect of the Dorset Garden Theatre', Diana de Marly considers whether Wren might have designed this playhouse also. *TN*, 29 (1975), pp 119–24. Professor Hume has summed up this matter in 'The Nature of the Dorset Garden Theatre', *TN*, 36 (1982), pp. 99–109.
6 II.i. The text of *The Empress of Morocco* can be found in *Five Heroic Plays*, ed. Bonamy Dobrée.
7 Per Bjürström, *Giacomo Torelli and Baroque Stage Design*.

8 S. Chappuzeau, *L'Europe Vivante*, pp. 214–15; S. Sorbière, *A Voyage to England*, p. 69.

9 R. E. Moore, *Henry Purcell and the Restoration Theatre*, p. 8.

10 The occasion of *Ariane* was the marriage of the Duke of York to Mary of Modena.

11 I quote from the English libretto which was printed separately but simultaneously with the French text in 1673.

12 Davenant, *Dramatic Works*, vol. 3, p. 234.

13 C. Gildon, *The Life of Mr. Thomas Betterton*, p. 163.

14 Dryden, *Poems*, I, pp. 19–22, p. 457.

15 Dryden, *Works*, vol. 11, I. i., pp. 228–9.

16 Cf. 'What shall I do to show how much I love her', in *Valentinian*, 'I attempt from love's sickness to fly', in *The Indian Queen*, and 'Love's but a fever of the mind', from *The Way of the World*.

17 The gallery appears to have been lit by windows on each side admitting daylight. A comparison of Plates 10–121 clarifies the curious perspective of the Dorset Garden engravings.

18 This is not easy to prove, since pieces of theatre-music when printed as suites are not necessarily in the order in which they were played. The music to *The Tempest*, which Locke published in 1675, does note, however, First Act Tune, Second Act Tune, unlike many Purcell collections which simply say Air, Minuet, etc. Sometimes vocal music was used instead; see Curtis A. Price, 'The Songs for Katharine Phillips' *Pompey* (1663)', *TN*, 23 (1980), pp. 61–6. Price suggests that nine pieces were usual, two each for the first and second music, the Overture, and four Act Tunes, but Purcell often prints only eight movements.

19 A. Scouten, *The London Stage*, I, p. cviii.

20 *The Empress of Morocco*, I. ii, in *Three Burlesques by Thomas Duffet*, p. 17.

21 I. K. Fletcher, S. J. Cohen and R. Lonsdale, *Fames for Dance: Essays on the Theory and Practice of Dancing in England*, New York Public Library, 1960; Marie-Françoise Christout, *Le Ballet de cour de Louis XIV, 1643–1672*; C. R. Baskerville, *The Elizabethan Jib and Related Song Drama*.

22 I. K. Fletcher, 'Italian Comedians in England in the Seventeenth Century', *TN*, 8 (1954), pp. 86–91; S. Rosenfeld, *Foreign Theatrical Companies in Great Britain in the Seventeenth and Eighteenth Centuries*.

23 'George Etherege and the Form of a Comedy', *Stratford-upon-Avon Studies*, 6: *Restoration Theatre*, London, 1965, pp. 43–69.

24 The dispute that led to this valuation is described by L. Hotson, *The Commonwealth and Restoration Stage*, pp. 250–3.

25 Dryden, Preface to 'Albion and Albanius', '*Of Dramatic Poesy*', vol. 2, p. 35.

26 C. Cibber, *An Apology for His Life*, ch. 2, pp. 240–1.

27 Shadwell, *The Virtuoso* (1976), p. 28.

28 R. Southern, *Changeable Scenery*; E. Langhans's thesis, 'Staging Practices in the Restoration Theatre', p. 84 ff.

29 Langhans, 'Staging Practices', p. 388 ff. see also note 5.

30 *The Empress of Morocco*, II. i. p. 114.

31 *Lucius Junius Brutus* (1681), Act IV, p. 47.

32 References to windows and balconies above the fore-stage doors also present a problem. It may be that some theatres had windows and others open balconies as suggested by Langhans ('Staging Practices in the Restoration Theatre'), but I cannot see that a real glass casement, or even an unglassed window-frame which could have been put in when required, are really necessary. It seems to me that playwrights use 'window' or 'balcony' simply according to the way they are thinking of the place in the particular action.

33 Wickham, *Early English Stages*, vol. Two, part I, p. 140; Southern, *Changeable Scenery*, pp. 100–6. Some of the curious effects of Restoration scenic conventions are examined by Colin Visser in 'The Anatomy of the Restoration Stage: *The Adventures of Five Hours* and John Dryden's Spanish Comedies', *TN*, 29 (1975), Part I, pp. 56–9, Part II, pp. 119–24.

34 Montague Summers (*Restoration Theatre*, p. 275) pointed out that footlights are shown in the frontispiece to Francis Kirkman's *The Wits* (1672), and their workings are described by Sabbattini, so it is certainly possible; but the frontispiece is rather a montage of theatrical images than a picture of a theatre, and I believe that had there been any, the row of burning lamps floating in oil would have been a sufficiently effective deterrent to those clambering onto the stage without the need for spikes or edicts.

35 N. Sabbattini in his *Pratica di Fabricar Scene e Machine ne' Teatri* suggests the use of *aqua vita* on the faces of flats to give real flames, but in his discussion of the subject ('Staging Practices', pp. 239–41) Langhans comes down on the side of painted scenery. Pepys saw *The Island Princess* on 7 January 1669 and noted 'a good scene of a town on fire'.

36 Rising and setting suns and moons do occur as special effects, but a spectacle of this kind needs to be played up by the text to be worth carrying out, and this is unusual except in scenes of operatic splendour or magic.

37 Cf. *She Wou'd if She Cou'd*, Act V, or *Sir Patient Fancy*, Act III. Aphra Behn seems particularly fond of the trick.

38 K. Burnim, *David Garrick, Director*, p. 66.

39 *Macbeth*, II. v. *Five Restoration Adaptations of Shakespeare*, ed. C. Spencer, p. 63.

40 A. Nicoll, *A History of English Drama 1660–1900*, vol. I, Appendix A, p. xi.

41 J. Genest, *Some Account of the English Stage from the Restoration in 1660 to 1830*, vol. 1, p. 184.

42 J. Downes, *Roscius Anglicanus*, p. 35.

Chapter 4 *The Tempest, or The Enchanted Island*

1 The text of *The Tempest, or The Enchanted Island* presents difficulties of provenance and authorship. The version by Dryden and Davenant was first printed in 1670, that of the so-called 'operatic' version in 1674. For some reason it was this version that became incorporated into later editions of Dryden's plays, though Montague Summers reprinted the original in his

Shakespeare Adaptations, and it is also in *The Works of John Dryden*, vol. 10, 1970. The operatic version is in Spencer's *Five Restoration Adaptations of Shakespeare*, and this is the text I quote.

2 It was Downes who attributed the operatic version to Shadwell, though Dryden and Betterton have also been suggested as authors. The question, which is a vexed one, is discussed at length by Spencer and Summers in their introductions. The song 'Arise, Ye Subterranean Winds' was printed as Shadwell's, and I think it likely that Betterton devised a slightly different scene-order to cater for the spectacular elements he was planning, and had Shadwell adjust the verbal detail where necessary. The words for music were printed separately as *The Songs and Masques in The Tempest* (1674), and have been edited by J. G. McManaway in *Theatre Miscellany*, Oxford, 1953, pp. 69–96, and see C. Haywood, '*The Songs and Masques in the New Tempest*: an Incident in the Battle of the Two Theatres, 1674', *HLQ*, 19 (1955), pp. 39–55. There are slight verbal variants in all versions including the words in the score itself.

3 Preface, *The Siege of Rhodes*, *Dramatic Works*, vol. 3, p. 235.

4 All the music for the operatic *Tempest* is extant except for Draghi's dances. Locke printed his incidental music in *The English Opera* (1675). Playford bound up Bannister's 'Ariel's Songs in the Play called *The Tempest*' with Hart's song for Dorinda 'Dear Pretty Youth', the words for which appear in no extant libretto, in a volume entitled *Choice Ayres, Songs and Dialogues* (1675). 'Arise, Ye Subterranean Winds' was printed in *Songs set by Signior Pietro Reggio* (1680). A manuscript of Pelham Humphrey's masques has been found in the library of the Paris Conservatoire. It has all been recorded on original instruments by Christopher Hogwood and the Academy of Ancient Music for L'Oiseau Lyre's Florilegium label, DSLO 507. See W. B. Squire, 'The Music of Shadwell's *Tempest*', *MQ*, 7 (1921), pp. 565–78. A later score was discovered towards the end of the eighteenth century and attributed to Purcell. The attribution is probably spurious (M. Laurie, 'Did Purcell set *The Tempest*?', *Proceedings of the Royal Musical Association*, 90 (163–4), pp. 43–56), though Purcell certainly contributed a new song for Dorinda, 'Adieu to the Pleasures', to a revival in the 1690s (*The Works of Henry Purcell*, vol. IX, 1912, pp. 147–9). The later score is clearly early eighteenth century in style and is quite different in effect from the earlier music. It is extremely charming, but it does not complement the seventeenth-century text anything like as well. It may have been by John Weldon, a pupil of Purcell, and has been recorded by the Monteverdi Choir and Orchestra under John Elliott Gardner on Erato, STU 71274. The dances of this version are very archaic and it has been suggested they may be survivals of Draghi's work. It was this score that was used in the only modern revival of the work at the Old Vic in the 1958–9 season. See 'The Shakespeare Season at the Old Vic, 1958–9, and at Stratford-upon-Avon 1959' by M. St Clare Byrne, *SQ*, 10 (1959), pp. 545–67, and John Russell Brown, 'Three Shakespeare Adaptations', *Shakespeare Survey*, 13 (1960).

5 The Order is printed by Nicoll, *A History of English Drama*, p. 356. See

Henry Cart de Lafontaine, *The King's Musick*, p. 271, and J. A. Westrup, *Purcell*, p. 44.

6 This Prologue is in The British Library, Egerton MSS. 2625, and quoted by Summers, *Shakespeare Adaptations*, pp. xliii–xlv. It is not certain it was used, but it seems characteristic, and very much in line with the company's attitude.

7 Since a whistle was used to cue the scene changes there was a possibility of confusion here. Perhaps the whistle was used to cue the flying-machinery. This would work quite well, and the scene-change would then be cued by the unusual lighting effect at the end of the storm.

8 I quote from T. Duffet, *Three Burlesques by Thomas Duffet*. It is also printed by Summers in *Shakespeare Adaptations*.

9 Edward Langhans notes that thunder effects are new in the Restoration theatre at about this time, and become popular ('Staging Practices', p. 222). Perhaps a proper thunder-run was installed as part of Betterton's new machinery and the other theatre followed suit. The old mustard-bowl method suggested by Summers (*Restoration Theatre*, p. 192) may not have suited the acoustics of the New Restoration theatres.

10 'This sudden clutter at our Appearance, so surpriz'd me, that I look'd as silly as a *Bumpkin* translated from the *Plough-Tail* to the *Play-House*, when it Rains Fire in the *Tempest*', Nick Ward, *The London Spy*, p. 3.

11 Sabbattini describes the process. His book is translated and edited in *The Renaissance Stage*, edited by B. Hewitt.

12 There is some interesting evidence here about the use of traps at the Dorset Garden. Only three are available at this point, though four are needed for the winds in Act V. The reason only two winds can rise, is apparently that a Devil is descending on the third trap. All three are available again by the end of the dance. Any traps on the fore-stage would have been unusable in *The Tempest* since the front of the stage was opened and the orchestra seated 'betwixt the Pit and the Stage', so perhaps the fourth trap was up-stage of the lower shutters. Alternatively, two of the Act V winds may have used the same trap if a central one of larger dimensions was provided.

13 Downes, *Roscius Anglicanus*, p. 34.

14 The fact that the scenes were left over the interval is suggested by the prompt-book for *The Change of Crownes* by Edward Howard. The prompter marks *ffirst whistle* before the opening of Acts IV and V. The dynamic effect is, of course, attractive.

15 Langhans suggests that shutters could change grooves during the performance so that a scene was sometimes deep and sometimes shallow. Scenes could certainly be taken from their positions, but I would have thought that the perspective would necessitate their always being used at the same point on the stage.

16 The use of painted theophanies is frequent and economical. There are too many figures in too few clothes, for example, in Inigo Jones's design for *Salmacida Spolia* (Plate 21), though quite elaborate glories for a number of

people could be arranged. Duffet's burlesque directions for the masque
suggest painted figures (Act V. ii, 107–9).

17 The Epilogue is also from the Egerton MSS., and quoted by M. Summers,
Shakespearean Adaptations, pp. xlv–xlvii.

Chapter 5 Building a character

1 C. Cibber, *An Apology for His Life*, chapter VIII, p. 158.
2 Ibid., chapter IV, p. 67.
3 This is Lebrun's analysis. *The Conference of M. Lebrun upon Expression* was
  printed in London in 1701. Lebrun is strongly influenced by Descartes's
  Les Passions de l'âme.
4 Dryden, 'A parallel betwixt Painting and Poetry', *Critical Essays*, vol. 2, p.
  201.
5 John Bulwer wrote three books on the significance of physical gesture, and
  they make up a kind of seventeenth-century *Manwatching: Chirologia, or
  the Naturall Language of the Hand*, and *Chironomia, or the Art of Manuall
  Rhetorique*, both 1644, and *Pathomyotomia*, on the nature of facial
  expression, in 1649. This is from *Pathomyotomia*, sig. A3.
6 The Restoration writers clearly derived the phrase 'movements or motions
  of the mind' from the word 'emotion', but their expansion of the word
  into a phrase is significant. It draws attention to the sequence of feelings
  and the impulses or movements that produce them. It conveys an analytical
  concept which is lost in more modern formulae such as 'expression of
  emotion'.
7 Bulwer, *Chironomia*, p. 23.
8 C. Gildon, *The Life of Mr. Thomas Betterton*, p. 43.
9 Ibid., p. 42.
10 *The Spectator*, no. 541, 8 vols, London, 1712–15, vol. 7, pp. 377–9.
11 Act I, 1. 305–7, *Works*, I, p. 449.
12 Cibber, chapter IV, p. 67.
13 George Taylor, ' "The Just Delineation of the Passions": Theories of Acting
  in the Age of Garrick', *Essays on the Eighteenth Century English Stage*, ed.
  Kenneth Richards and Peter Thomson, London, 1972.
14 A. C. Sprague, 'Did Betterton Chant?', *TN*, vol. 1 (1955–6), pp. 54–5.
15 *The Empress of Morocco*, V. 1.
16 E. Curll published a *History of The English Stage* under Betterton's name in
  1741. The passage is on p. 46.
17 Gildon, p. 106.
18 *The Spectator*, no. 40, vol. 1, pp. 223–5.
19 The rants are interpreted as passages for shouting by J. H. Wilson in 'Rant,
  Cant and Tone on the Restoration Stage', *Stud. Phil.*, 52 (1955), pp. 592–8,
  and to some extent by Philip Parsons in 'Restoration Melodrama and its
  Actors', *Komos*, vol. 2 (1969–70), pp. 81–8.
20 *Spectator*, no. 40, vol. 1, p. 223.
21 Cibber, chapter IV, p. 60.

22 It is perhaps worth noting that the more rapidly and lightly Restoration dialogue is spoken the easier it is to understand. If the actor takes it too slowly, the complex sentences break down into too many segments and become difficult for the ear to grasp as a whole. At a brisk pace, the wit falls naturally into place and provokes a continuous murmur of appreciation from the audience.

23 Bertram Joseph first used the gestural theories of the seventeenth-century rhetoricians as a clue to the art of the actor in *Elizabethan Acting*, London, 1951. His book aroused considerable controversy, and in a second edition (1964) he argued that such significant gesture was not necessarily 'unnatural', as I do here. He did not consider the theory of the attitude, or of facial expression.

24 Bulwer, *Chironomia*, sig. A5.

25 Gildon, p. 42.

26 Ibid., p. 70.

27 Dryden, 'A parallel betwixt Painting and Poetry', *Critical Essays*, vol. 2, p. 201.

28 Dryden, 'Of Dramatic Poesy', *Critical Essays*, vol. 1, p. 55.

29 Dryden et al., *Notes and Observations on 'The Empress of Morocco'* (1674), p. 71.

30 Gildon, p. 79.

31 Dryden, *Cleomenes, The Spartan Hero* (1692), Act IV, p. 41.

32 Cibber, chapter IV, p. 63.

33 Bulwer, *Pathomyotomia*, p. 176.

34 Bulwer, *Pathomyotomia*, p. 37.

35 Charles Lebrun, *The Conference of M. Lebrun upon Expression*, p. 8.

36 Bulwer, *Pathomyotomia*, p. 216.

37 Dryden, *Don Sebastian* (1690), Act II, p. 33.

38 A. Aston, *Supplement to Colley Cibber, Esq.*, p. 7.

39 Gildon, pp. 36–7. Cf. Pepys, 8 March, 1664

40 Cibber, chapter IV, p. 62.

41 Ibid., p. 61.

42 E. Langhans, 'New Restoration Theatre Accounts', *TN*, 17 (1963), pp. 118–34.

43 Techniques for operatic acting in the eighteenth century have been discussed by Dene Barnett in a series of articles in *Theatre Research International* under the general title 'The Performance Practice of Acting: The Eighteenth Century'. The subject matter is divided as follows: 'Part I: Ensemble Acting', 2 (1977), pp. 157–86, 'Part II: The Hands', 3 (1978), pp. 1–19, 'Part III: The Arms', 3 (1978), pp. 79–83, 'Part IV: The Eyes, the Face and the Head', 5 (1980), pp. 1–36.

44 Preface to Crown's *City Politiques* (1683), sig. A 2v.

45 *The Crisis and A Crisis in the Life of an Actress* (1848), trans. and introduced by Stephen Crites, London, 1967.

46 *She Wou'd if She Cou'd* (1668), Act I, pp. 3–4.

47 Cibber, chapter VII, p. 138.

48 Summers, *Restoration Theatre*, pp. 287–8.
49 Cf. Cibber's comments on Mrs Mountfort in similar roles.
50 B. Brecht, *Brecht on Theatre*, ed. John Willett, London, 1964, p. 92.
51 J. Downes, *Roscius Anglicanus, passim.*

Chapter 6   *Almanzor and Almahide, or The Conquest of Granada by the Spaniards*

1 The references are to Dryden, *Works*, vol. 11.
2 *The Dramatic Works of John Dryden with a Life of the Author by Sir Walter Scott*, ed. George Saintsbury, Edinburgh, 1882, vol. 4, p. 33.
3 The translation is that of Sir John Harrington in 1591.
4 For Hobbesian aspects of Dryden, see Anne T. Barbeau, *The Intellectual Design of John Dryden's Heroic Plays*; also Bruce King, *Dryden's Major Plays*, and D. W. Jefferson, 'The Significance of Dryden's Heroic Plays', *Proceedings of the Leeds Philosophic and Literary Societies*, 5 (1940), pp. 125–39.
5 Dryden, 'Grounds of Criticism in Tragedy', *Critical Essays*, vol. 1, p. 244.
6 Ibid., p. 248.
7 William Myers, *Dryden*, p. 34. Myers's whole account of the relationship of Dryden's thinking to his plays and his poetry is excellent.
8 *Horace's Art of Poetry, made English by the Right Honorable, The Earl of Roscommon* (1684), p. 13.
9 Thomas Rymer, *The Tragedies of the Last Age, Consider'd and Examin'd by the Practice of the Ancients, and by the Common sense of all Ages. In a Letter to Fleetwood Shepheard, Esq.* (1678), pp. 5–6.
10 Dryden, 'Cymon and Iphigenia', *Poems*, vol. 4, pp. 1744, 123–4, 133–4.
11 A number of portraits of Nell exist, notably by Godfrey Kneller. Judging by these the engraving in Plate 8 seems not unlike.
12 Pepys particularly objected to her Cydaria in *The Indian Emperour* (22 August 1667), but Dryden wrote this part for another actress. He composed a verbal description of her, *Secret Love*, II.ii.
13 *The Spectator*, 40, vol. 1, p. 224.
14 There is some dispute which of the two Mrs Marshalls was the actress here. For an appropriate encounter between Nell Gwyn and Rebecca Marshall see Pepys, *The Diary of Samuel Pepys*, 6 October 1667. J. H. Wilson, *All The King's Ladies*, discusses the careers of the major Restoration actresses.
15 *The Dramatic Works of John Dryden*, ed. Scott/Saintsbury, vol. 4, p. 5.
16 This clash of worlds is a continuous target in *The Rehearsal*, as when Prince Volscius sets out for Piccadilly and remarks that he has an army hidden in Knightsbridge. Like Genest's strictures (quoted above p. 60) and Duffet's frontispiece to *The Empress of Morocco*, Buckingham, perhaps deliberately, misses the point of the cool irony implicit in the mechanisms of Restoration stagecraft.
17 T. Betterton, *A History of the English Stage*, p. 21.

18 'Wintershall was a most excellent, Judicious Actor; and the best instructor of others.' The Key to *The Rehearsal* (1710).

19 The reference is to the execution of his own sons for treason by Lucius Junius Brutus, Livy, *Histories*, Book I. Lee made the tale into the finest of his tragedies in 1681.

20 Gildon, *The Life of Mr. Thomas Betterton*, p. 48.

21 *The Dramatic Works of John Dryden*, ed. Scott/Sainsbury, vol. 4, p. 5.

22 John Evelyn saw *Granada* on 9 February 1671 and refers to 'very glorious scenes and perspectives, the work of Mr. Streeter'. The play was performed two days running at Court, so both parts are probably referred to, explaining the use of 'scenes' in the plural.

23 Johnson *Lives of the English Poets*, vol. II, p. 192, p. 28.

24 The managers of the time particularly liked the effect of sudden bleeding created by squeezing 'bloody' sponges in the hands or beneath the garments. As Langhans points out ('Staging Practices', p. 29), there are only two precise references to the sponges; but it is significant that they occur in the plays of Killigrew (*The Princess* and *I, Tommaso*). The manager knew what he wanted, and doubtless described the method used to carry out the demands of his more literary colleagues.

Chapter 7 *The Country Wife*

1 The references are to the text in *The Plays of William Wycherley*, ed. Arthur Friedman.

2 From an MS. in the British Library, PS 3/3833 add. 27.407, see Kenneth Cameron, 'Jo Haynes *Infamis*', *TN*, 24 (1969–70), 56–67, p. 63.

3 It is not always clear on the Restoration stage if the actors are using the fore-stage doors or entering through the scene. The doors appear to have been more usual, but in the kind of sequence described here, where characters were presented, the centring of the incoming actor would be neater than his position at one side by the doors, and give his 'attitude' a stronger effect. His attitude would also gain from his not needing to fiddle with the door itself. There is another point, too. A sense of place is important in *The Country Wife*, and there is a danger here of confusion as actors enter and exit simultaneously on the same side.

4 *The Spectator*, no. 102, vol. 2, pp. 110–11.

5 Ibid., p. 111.

6 A favourite trick, cf. *The Orphan*, Act IV.

7 The sequence seems to require two fore-stage doors on each side. The two locked doors down left and right, with the door for Quack and the door to the 'back passage' upstage of them. The characters' entrances would again be on to the stage, making the 'picture-frame' effect already noted.

8 Baudelaire, *De l'Essence du rire et généralement du comique dans les arts plastiques* (1855).

9 T. B. Macaulay, *The History of England*, vol. 1, p. 369.

10 The combination of Horner's 'Pox, they are come too soon', with Lady

Fidget's, 'We have brought our Entertainment with us,' suggests the table may well have been set by footmen on the arrival of the ladies, the scene shutting on Covent Garden Piazza, which would have looked well as a deep scene.

11 For the serious side of Wycherley, see T. W. Craik, 'Some Aspects of Satire in Wycherley's plays', *English Studies*, 41 (1960), pp. 168–79; Ann Righter, 'William Wycherley', *Stratford-upon-Avon Studies* (1965), and Rose Zimbardo, *Wycherley's Drama*, 1965.

Chapter 8   Changing times

1 E. A. Langhans, 'New Restoration Theatre Accounts', *TN*, 17 (1962), pp. 118–34, and J. H. Wilson, 'Players' Lists in the Lord Chamberlain's Registers', *TN*, 18 (1964), pp. 25–30. For the Royal Household see *A Collection of Ordinances and Regulations for the Governance of the Royal Household, from King Edward III to William and Mary*, Society of Antiquaries, 1790, and J. M. Beattie, *The English Court in the Reign of George I*. The value of backstairs associations is demonstrated in David Allen, 'The Political Function of Charles II's Chiffinch', *HLQ*, 39 (1976), pp. 277–90.

2 Henry Herbert, *The Dramatic Records of Sir Henry Herbert*; A. F. White, 'The Office of the Revels and Dramatic Censorship during the Restoration Period', *Western Reserve Bulletin*, 34 (1931), pp. 5–45.

3 H. Herbert, *Dramatic Records*, pp. 96–100.

4 L. Hotson, *The Commonwealth and Restoration Stage*, p. 243 ff.

5 C. Cibber, *An Apology for His Life*, chapter VI, p. 312.

6 Thomas Shadwell, *A True Widow* (1678), Act IV.

7 E. L. Avery, 'A Poem on the Dorset Garden', *TN*, 17 (1963), pp. 121–4.

8 A. Nicoll, *A History of English Drama*, p. 324.

9 R. H. Tawney, *Religion and the Rise of Capitalism*, p. 229.

10 John Dennis, *Critical Works*, vol. 1, p. 294.

11 *Poems*, I, pp. 156, 11. 13–18.

12 'To Mr. Lee on his *Alexander*', *Poems*, I, p. 162, 11. 33–6.

13 p.l. For a discussion of the implications of the controversy see J. W. Crutch, *Comedy and Conscience after the Restoration*, New York, 1924 (rev. ed. 1949), and John Loftis, *Comedy and Society from Congreve to Fielding*.

14 Interestingly, the same kind of transformation was to be observed in the scientific thought of the period. The Royal Society counted among its original purposes the practical application of scientific investigation, especially to daily life and the expansion of trade; but the interest in applied science waned and its abstract and general principles were increasingly investigated. In the 1680s there was a reaction against induction and 'the method of doubt'. Even theories of language abandoned the search for colloquial directness and returned to the dominance of Latin style and syntax. M. Espinasse, 'The Decline and Fall of Restoration Science', *Past and Present* 14 (1958), pp. 71–89.

15 H. Misson, *M. Misson's Memoirs and his Observations in his Travels over England*, pp. 219–20. J. H. Smith, 'Shadwell, the Ladies, and the Change in Comedy', *Mod. Phil.*, 46 (1948), pp. 22–33.

16 Tom Brown, *Amusements, Serious and Comical: The Playhouse, Works*, III, p. 38.

17 Rowe, *The Fair Penitent* (1703), Act IV, p. 42.

18 *The Female Wits*, Act III, p. 50.

19 Cibber, chapter XII, pp. 240–1.

20 A. Aston, *Supplement to Colley Cibber, Esq.*, pp. 7–8.

21 C. Gildon, The Life of Mr. Thomas Betterton, pp. 40–1. J. Davies, *Dramatic Miscellanies*, 1784, vol. 3, p. 203.

22 Otway, *Venice Preserv'd*, Act V, ll. 256–8.

23 The ode has been recorded by the English Chamber Orchestra under Sir Charles Mackerras, on Deutsche Grammophon Gesellschaft Archiv 2533 042. The relevant movement is for counter-tenor and may have been originally sung by the composer. Gildon noted '*Purcel* penetrates the Heart, makes the Blood dance through your veins and thrill with the agreable Violence offered by his Heavenly Harmony', p. 168.

24 *The Works of Henry Purcell*, vol. XXVI, pp. 63–6; London, 1928, pp. 82–115.

25 F. C. Brown, *Elkanah Settle*, Chicago, 1910. *Works of Purcell*, vol. 12, ed. J. Shedlock, 1903, rev. Sir Antony Lewis, 1968.

26 R. Savage, 'The Shakespeare–Purcell *Fairy Queen*: a defence and a recommendation', *Early Music*, I (1973), pp. 201–21.

27 Ibid., p. 211.

Chapter 9 *Venice Preserv'd, or A Plot Discover'd*

1 The references are to Thomas Otway, *Works*, vol. 2.

2 Johnson, *Lives of the English Poets*, vol. 1, p. 142.

3 This may be compared with the similar technique in Lee's *Lucius Junius Brutus*, above p. 57.

4 Above p. 114.

5 C. Cibber, *An Apology for His Life*, chapter V, p. 87.

Chapter 10 *The Way of the World*

1 C. Cibber, *An Apology for His Life*, chapter VI, p. 114.

2 W. Congreve, *The Complete Plays*, p. 390. All references will be to this edition.

3 To Dennis, 'Concerning Houmour in Comedy,' *Letters upon several occasions . . .*, 1696, p. 86.

4 Collier was particularly sharp on this kind of ambiguity, as was L. C. Knights, in his famous article, 'Restoration Comedy: the Reality and the

Myth', *Scrutiny*, 6 (1937), pp. 122–63, reprinted in *Explorations*, London, 1946. Professor Knights's sometimes disingenuous arguments have been well analysed by Andrew Beare, 'Restoration Comedy and the Provok'd Critic', in *Restoration Literature*, ed. Harold Love, London, 1972, pp. 1–26. See also Jean Cagen, 'Congreve's Mirabell and the Ideal Gentleman', *PMLA*, 79 (1964), pp. 422–7.

5 G. Alleman, *Matrimonial Law and the Materials of Restoration Comedy*. See also Paul and Miriam Mueschke, *A New View of Congreve's 'The Way of the World'*.

6 Millamant would seem to be another of the sufferers from an 'inconstant Foot' if her name tells true (see p. 122 above), and it is interesting that Congreve arranges that from the moment Mirabell kisses her hand she hardly speaks or moves for the rest of the play. Consent and resolution have stilled her at last.

7 Southern's notes on Congreve, British Library Add. MSS. 4221, f. 341, printed in *William Congreve: Letters and Documents*, p. 151.

Select bibliography

Alleman, G. S., *Matrimonial Law and the Materials of Restoration Comedy*, University of Pennsylvania Press, 1942.

Aston, A., *Supplement to Colley Cibber, Esq*, London, 1747.

Avery, E. L., and Scouten, A. H., *The London Stage 1660–1700, A Critical Introduction*, Southern Illinois University Press, 1968.

Barbeau, A. T., *The Intellectual Design of John Dryden's Heroic Plays*, Yale University Press, 1970.

Baskerville, C. Reade, *The Elizabethan Jig and Related Song Drama*, University of Chicago Press, 1929.

Baur-Heinhold, M., *The Baroque Theatre*, trans. Mary Whittall, London, Thames & Hudson, 1967.

Beattie, J. M., *The English Court in the Reign of George I*, Cambridge University Press, 1967.

Betterton, T., *A History of the English Stage*, London, E. Curll, 1741.

Bjürström, Per, *Giacomo Torelli and Baroque Stage Design*, Nationalmusie Skriftsine, Stockholm, 1961.

Boswell, E., *The Restoration Court Stage (1660–1702), with a particular account of the production of 'Calisto'*, London, Allen & Unwin, 1966.

Brecht, B., *Brecht on Theatre: The Development of an Aesthetic*, ed. and trans. John Willett, London, Methuen, 1964.

Brett-James, N., *The Growth of Stuart London*, London and Middlesex Archaeological Society, London, 1935.

Bulwer, J., *Chirologia, or the Naturall Language of the Hand*, with *Chironomia, or the Art of Manuall Rhetorique*, London, 1644.

Bulwer, J., *Pathomyotomia, or a Dissection of the Significative Muscles of the Affections of the Minde*, London, 1649.

Burnim, K., *David Garrick, Director*, University of Pittsburgh Press, 1961.

Butterfield, H., *The Origins of Modern Science, 1300–1800*, London, G. Bell, 1949.

Campbell, L. B., 'A history of costuming on the english stage between 1600 and 1823', *University of Wisconsin Studies*, 2, 1918.

Cart de Lafontaine, H., *The King's Musick*, London, Novello, 1909.

Chappuzeau, S., *L'Europe vivante, ou relation nouvelle, historique et politique de tous ses estats, jusqu'à l'année presente, 1666*, Geneva, 1667.

Christout, Marie-Françoise, *Le Ballet de cour de Louis XIV, 1643–1672*, Paris, Picard, 1967.

Cibber, C., *An Apology for His Life, with an Account of the Rise and Progress of the English Stage*, London, 1740.

Collier, J., *A Short View of the Immorality and Profaneness of the Stage, together with the sense of Antiquity upon this argument*, London, 1698.

Collier, J., *A Short View of the Profaneness and Immorality of the Stage, &c., with the several Defenses of the same*, London, 1730.

Congreve, W., *The Complete Plays*, ed. H. Davis, University of Chicago Press, 1967.

Congreve, W., *William Congreve: Letters and Documents*, ed. J. Hodges, London, Macmillan, 1964.

Davenant, Sir William, *The Dramatic Works*, 4 vols, Edinburgh, William Patterson, 1872–4.

Dennis, J., *Critical Works*, ed. E. N. Hooker, 2 vols, Baltimore, John Hopkins Press, 1939–43.

Dent, E. J., *The Foundations of English Opera*, Cambridge University Press, 1928.

Dobrée, B. (ed.), *Five Heroic Plays*, Oxford University Press, 1960.

Downes, J., *Roscius Anglicanus, 1708*, ed. Montague Summers, London, Fortune Press, 1929.

Dryden, J., *The Letters of John Dryden*, ed. C. E. Ward, Duke University Press, 1942.

Dryden, J., *Works*, ed. H. T. Swedenborg *et al.*, University of California Press, 1956–.

Dryden, J., *The Poems of John Dryden*, ed. James Kinsley, 4 vols, Oxford, The Clarendon Press, 1958.

Dryden, J., *'Of Dramatic Poesy' and other Critical Essays*, ed. George Watson, 2 vols, London, Dent, 1962.

Duffet, T., *Three Burlesques by Thomas Duffet*, ed. R. E. di Lorenzo, University of Iowa Press, 1972.

Eliot, T. S., *Homage to John Dryden, Three essays on the poetry of the seventeenth century*, London, Hogarth Press, 1924.

Evelyn, J., *Memoirs Illustrative of the Life and Writings of John Evelyn, Esq.*, ed. William Bray, London, Henry Colburn, 2nd ed., 1819.

Fiske, R., *English Theatre Music in the Eighteenth Century*, Oxford University Press, 1973.

Genest, J., *Some Account of the English Stage from the Restoration in 1660 to 1830*, 10 vols, Bath, H. E. Carrington, 1832.

Gildon, C., *The Life of Mr. Thomas Betterton, the Late, Emminent Tragedian*, London, 1710.

Herbert, Sir Henry, *The Dramatic Records of Sir Henry Herbert*, ed. J. Q. Adams, Cornell Studies in English, 1917.

Holland, P., *The Ornament of Action*, Cambridge University Press, 1979.

Hotson, L., *The Commonwealth and Restoration Stage*, Harvard University Press, 1928.

Howard, E., *The Change of Crownes*, ed. F. S. Boas, Oxford University Press, London, 1949.

Hume, R. D., *The Development of English Drama in the Later Seventeenth Century*, Oxford, The Clarendon Press, 1976.

Jackson, A. S., 'Restoration Scenery, 1656–1680', in *Restoration and Eighteenth Century Theatre Research*, 3 (1964).

Johnson, S., *The Lives of the English Poets*, 2 vols, London, Dent, 1925.

Joseph, B., *Elizabethan Acting*, Oxford University Press, 1951, rev. ed., 1964.

King, B., *Dryden's Major Plays*, Edinburgh, Oliver and Boyd, 1966.

Knights, L. C., *Explorations: Essays in Criticism, mainly on the Literature of the Seventeenth Century*, London, Chatto & Windus, 1964.

Krutch, J. W., *Comedy and Conscience after the Restoration*, Columbia University Press, 1924.

Langbaine, G., *An Account of the English Dramatick Poets*, Oxford, 1691.

Langhans, E. A., 'Staging Practices in the Restoration Theatres', unpublished PhD dissertation, Yale University, 1955.

Leacroft, R., *The Development of the English Playhouse*, London, Methuen, 1973.

Lebrun, C., *The Conference of M. Lebrun upon Expression*, London, 1701.

Loftis, J., *Comedy and Society from Congreve to Fielding*, Stanford University Press, 1959.

Loftis, J., *The Politics of Drama in Augustan England*, Oxford, The Clarendon Press, 1963.

Love, H. (ed.), *The Penguin Book of Restoration Verse*, Harmondsworth, Penguin, 1968.

Lynch, K. M., *The Social Mode of Restoration Comedy*, University of Michigan, 1926.

Macaulay, Thomas Babington, Lord, *The History of England from the Accession of James II*, 2 vols, London, Longman & Co., 1849–61.

McAffee, Helen (ed.), *Samuel Pepys on the Restoration Stage*, Yale University Press, 1916.

Magalotti, Lorenzo di, *Travels of Cosmo The Third, Grand Duke of Tuscany, through England during the Reign of Charles II (1669)*, London, J. Mawman, 1821.

Milhous, J., *Thomas Betterton and the Management of Lincoln's Inn Fields, 1695–1708*, Southern Illinois University Press, 1979.

Misson, H., *M. Misson's Memoirs and his Observations in his Travels over England*, trans. D. Browne, etc., London, John Ozell, 1719.

Moore, R. E., *Henry Purcell and the Restoration Theatre*, London, Heinemann, 1961.

Morgan, F., *The Female Wits: Women Playwrights on the London Stage, 1660–1720*, London, Virago Press, 1981.

Mueschke, P. and M., *A New View of Congreve's 'The Way of The World'*, University of Michigan, 1958.

Myers, W., *Dryden*, London, Hutchinson, 1973.

Nicoll, A., *A History of English Drama 1660–1900*, vol. 1, *Restoration Drama, 1660–1700*, Cambridge University Press, 4th ed., 1952.

North, R., *Roger North on Music*, ed. John Wilson, London, Novello, 1959.

Odell, G. C., *Shakespeare from Betterton to Irving*, 2 vols, London, Constable, 1920.

Otway, T., *Works*, ed. J. C. Ghosh, 2 vols, Oxford, Clarendon Press, 1932.

Overbury, Sir Thomas, *The Miscellaneous Works in Prose and Verse of Sir Thomas Overbury*, ed. E. F. Rimbault, London, J. R. Smith, 1890.

Pepys, S., *The Diary of Samuel Pepys*, ed. Robert Latham and William Matthews, London, Bell, 1970–83.

Purcell, H., *The Works of Henry Purcell*, The Purcell Society Edition, London, Novello, Ewer & Co., 1878–.

Rameau, P., *Le Maitre à danser*, Paris, 1725, trans. Cyril Beaumont, *The Dancing Master*, London, 1931.

Rosenfeld, S., *Foreign Theatrical Companies in Great Britain in the Seventeenth and Eighteenth Centuries*, London, The Society for Theatre Research, 1955.

Sabbattini, N., *Pratica di Fabricar Scene e Machine ne' Teatri*, Ravenna, 1638, trans. J. H. McDowell, in *The Renaissance Stage*, ed. B. Hewitt, University of Miami Press, 1958.

Sorbière, S., *A voyage to England, containing many things relating to the state of learning, religion, and other curiosities of that kingdom*, London, 1709 (originally published as *Relation d'un voyage en Angleterre, ou sont touchées plusieurs choses, qui regardent l'estat des Sciences, de la Réligion, et autres matières curieuses*, Paris, 1664).

Sorelius, G., *The Giant Race before the Flood: Pre-Restoration Drama on the Restoration Stage and in the Criticism of the Restoration Period*, Studia anglistica upsaliensia, vol. 4, Uppsala, 1966.

Southern, R., *Changeable Scenery*, London, Faber and Faber, 1952.

Spencer, C. (ed.), *Davenant's Macbeth from the Yale Manuscript: An edition, with a discussion of the relationship of Davenant's text to Shakespeare's*, Yale Studies in English, 1961.

Spencer, C. (ed.), *Five Restoration Adaptations of Shakespeare*, University of Illinois Press, 1965.

Sprat, T., *History of the Royal Society*, ed. Jackson I. Cope and Harold Whitmore Jones, Washington University Studies, 1958.

Sprague, A. C., *Beaumont and Fletcher on the Restoration Stage*, Harvard University Press, 1926.

Summers, M. (ed.), *Shakespearean Adaptations*, London, Jonathan Cape, 1922.

Summers, M., *Essays in Petto*, London, Fortune Press, 1928.

Summers, M., *The Restoration Theatre*, London, Kegan Paul, 1934.

Summers, M., *The Playhouse of Pepys*, London, Kegan Paul, 1935.

Tawney, R. H., *Religion and the Rise of Capitalism*, London, 1926, and Harmondsworth, Penguin, 1969.

Vernon, P. F., 'The marriage of convenience and the moral code of Restoration comedy', *Essays in Criticism*, 12 (1962), pp. 370–87.

Wain, J., *Preliminary Essays*, London, Macmillan, 1957.

Waith, E. M., *The Herculean Hero in Marlowe, Chapman, Shakespeare and Dryden*, London, Chatto & Windus, 1962.

Westrup, J. A., *Purcell*, London, Dent, 1937, rev. ed., 1968.

Wickham, Glynne, *Early English Stages*, vol. Two: 1576 to 1660, Part I, London, Routledge & Kegan Paul, 1963, and Part II, London, Routledge & Kegan Paul, 1972.

Wildeblood, J., and Brinson, P., *The Polite World: A Guide to English Manners and Deportment from the Thirteenth to the Nineteenth Century*, Oxford University Press, 1965.

Wiley, A. N. (ed.), *Rare Prologues and Epilogues, 1642–1700*, London, Allen & Unwin, 1940.

Willey, B., *The Seventeenth Century Background, Studies of the poetry of the age in relation to thought and religion*, London, Chatto & Windus, 1934.

Williamson, G., *The Senecan Amble*, London, Faber & Faber, 1951.

Wilmot, J., Earl of Rochester, *Poems*, ed. V. de Sola Pinto, London, Routledge & Kegan Paul, 1953.

Wilson, J. H., *All the King's Ladies: Actresses of the Restoration*, University of Chicago Press, 1958.

Wilson, J. H., *A Preface to Restoration Drama*, Harvard University Press, 1968.

Wycherley, W., *The Plays of William Wycherley*, ed. Arthur Friedman, Oxford, The Clarendon Press, 1979.

Zimbardo, R., *Wycherley's Drama: A Link in the Development of English Satire*, Yale Studies in English, vol. 156, 1965.

Index

PR 691 .P68

Powell, Jocelyn, 1938-

Restoration theatre
  production

DEMCO